Judicial Discretion

Judicial Discretion

AHARON BARAK

Translated from the Hebrew by Yadin Kaufmann

Yale University Press

New Haven and London

Originally published as *Shikul Daat Shiputy,* © 1987

Published with assistance from the Louis Stern Memorial Fund.

Designed by Nancy Ovedovitz and set in Times Roman type by
Keystone Typesetting, Inc., Orwigsburg, Pennsylvania. Printed in
the United States of America by Vail-Ballou Press, Binghamton,
New York.

LIBRARY OF CONGRESS
Library of Congress Cataloging-in-Publication Data

Barak, Aharon.
    [Shikul da'at shiputi. English]
    Judicial discretion / Aharon Barak.
      p. cm.
    Translation of: Shikul da'at shiputi.
    Includes index.
    ISBN 0-300-04099-7
    1. Judicial discretion. 2. Judicial discretion—Israel.
I. Title.
K2205.4.B3713 1989
347'.014—dc19
[342.714]   88-20542
                             CIP

The paper in this book meets the guidelines for permanence and
durability of the Committee on Production Guidelines for Book
Longevity of the Council on Library Resources.

10   9   8   7   6   5   4   3   2   1

Contents

Preface   ix

Part One.
The Nature of Judicial Discretion

1 The Characteristics of Judicial Discretion   3
    Difficulties in Understanding Judicial Discretion, 3
    Judicial Discretion Defined, 7   The Object of Judicial
    Discretion, 12   The Scope of Judicial Discretion, 18
    The Problem—Does Judicial Discretion Exist? 27
    Judicial Discretion—In Every Case? 34

2 The Substantive Sources of Judicial Discretion   45
    Types of Sources, 45   Substantive Sources of Judicial
    Discretion in the Statutory Norm, 46   Discretion in the
    Statutory Norm: The Uncertainty of the Normative
    Scheme, 54   Discretion in the Statutory Norm:
    Uncertainty in the Rules of Interpretation, 55
    Uncertainty as to the Circumstances of Application of a
    Rule of Interpretation, 58   Uncertainty as to the Content
    of the Rule of Interpretation: "Legislative Purpose," 60
    Uncertainty as to the Content of the Rule of
    Interpretation: "General Principles," 64   Uncertainty
    about the Validity of the Rule of Interpretation, 72
    Substantive Sources of Discretion in the Case Law, 76
    Discretion in the Case Law: The Uncertainty of the
    Terms, 77   Discretion in the Case Law: Uncertainty in
    the Normative Order, 78   Substantive Sources of
    Discretion: The Lack of a Legal Norm ("Lacuna"), 83

3 The Formal Sources of Judicial Discretion   90
    Judicial Discretion and Judicial Law-Making, 90   The
    Formal Sources of Judicial Discretion and Judicial Law-
    Making, 95   The Scope of Judicial Law-Making—
    "The Zone of Formal Legitimacy," 101   Judicial
    Discretion—Creating Law or Declaring Law? 105

Part Two.
Limitations of Judicial Discretion—
The Zone of Judicial Reasonableness

4 The Zone of Reasonableness   113
    How Are the Hard Cases Solved? 113   The Zone
    of Reasonableness and Judicial Objectivity, 124
    Awareness of Judicial Discretion, 135   The Most
    Reasonable Possibility and the Distinction between
    Judicial Activism and Judicial Self-Restraint, 147

5 Fundamental Problems in the Normative System   152
    The Coherence of the System and Judicial
    Discretion, 152   The Fundamental Values of the
    System, 154   Organic Growth, 160   Judicial
    Discretion and the Problem of Retroactivity, 167

6 Fundamental Problems in the Institutional System   172
    Limited Judicial Discretion and Institutional
    Problems, 172   The Incidentality of Judicial
    Discretion, 173   Judicial Discretion and Judicial
    Partiality, 189

7 Interrelations among Institutional Systems   192
    Fundamental Problems in the Relations among
    Governmental Systems, 192   Judicial Discretion and
    the Democratic Problem, 192   Judicial Discretion and
    the Separation of Powers, 203   Judicial Discretion and
    the Society's Conception of the Judicial Function, 206
    Judicial Discretion and the Relations among the
    Branches of Government, 210   Judicial Discretion and
    the Public's Confidence in the Judicial Branch, 215

8 Judicial Policy and Models of Adjudication 222
  The Model of Adjudication, 229

9 The Use of Judicial Discretion: The Case of Overruling a
  Precedent 234
  The Question, 234   The Test of Reasonableness, 235
  Normative Considerations, 236   Institutional
  Considerations, 238   Interinstitutional
  Considerations, 239   Judicial Discretion in Weighing
  Conflicting Considerations, 240   The Problem of
  Reliance on the Prior Rule, 242   The Effect of the
  Nature of the Considerations Underlying the Existent
  Rule, 245   The Effect of the Passage of Time, 248
  The Effect of the Importance of the Question, 249
  Distinctions According to the Legal Field of the
  Rule, 250   Prospective Overruling? 254   Conclusion:
  Between Truth and Truth—Stability is Preferable, 259

Postscript: Judicial Discretion in a Democratic Society 261

Index 267

To Avner

Preface

This book is about the deliberation of the judge, who, within the framework of his judicial work, must choose among a number of ways of acting. I do not intend to cover this subject in all its aspects, for that mission would be too great. It would deal with the entire judicial function. My perspective is more limited. It does not include the entire intellectual process of thought and weighing that brings the judge to formulate his conclusion. It deals with the deliberation of the judge who, after thinking about and weighing the factors, finds himself facing a number of possibilities, all of them lawful. The question to which I want to respond is this: How should the judge exercise his discretion when he is faced with a legal problem that has more than one lawful solution?

Yet even this framework is too broad. The legal problem may refer to the facts (Did John drive his car at a speed of sixty miles per hour?). It may also refer to the application of a norm (Did John drive negligently in the specific situation?). Or, the legal problem may refer to the nature of the norm itself (What is negligence?). In this book I deal with the legal problem primarily from the last point of view, namely, How is the judge to exercise his discretion in the "hard cases," those in which he faces a number of lawful possibilities as to the legal norm itself? Which of the options should he choose?

Here are examples of this type of question: How should the judge interpret a statutory rule that has more than one linguistic meaning, when it is not possible to discover a specific legislative goal? Should the judge deviate from precedent? Should he recognize a new duty or right? How should he fill a lacuna in the system?

These difficult questions are important for the judicial process. Sometimes their answer determines the direction of the course and character of the entire system. The questions are located at the crossroads of the development of every system. They establish the balance between stability and change. The solution to these questions contains an inherent difficulty in the constant tension between the decision in the particular conflict (adjudication) and the establishment of the general norm (lawmaking). The judicial function requires focusing on the parties to the specific conflict and on the nature of the conflict between them. The legislative function requires focusing on the system as a whole—on the general normative order, on the institutional problems of the judicial branch, and on the reciprocal relations between the various governmental systems. I said the parties desire a solution to the specific conflict between them. But the judge who decides the hard cases not only must consider the specific case. He must also take into account the past and his integration into it and the future and the expectation for its development. This triangular goal is difficult to attain. Consequently, solving the hard cases is also difficult.

How is judicial discretion to be exercised in the hard cases? The thesis of this book is that judicial discretion is not absolute. Judicial discretion is limited. Its limitations flow primarily from the general normative system, from institutional problems of the judicial branch, and from the complex network of relations among the branches. Taking all these into account sifts out a number of possibilities of discretion. Sometimes only a single possibility remains. Yet sometimes the sifting is incomplete and leaves a number of possibilities. The judge must act objectively, yet he has no recourse but to decide on the basis of his personal experience and his worldview as a judge. Thus, the thesis of this book is that, in the final analysis, in the hard cases the judge's judicial philosophy, which is the product of his experience and his worldview, is what determines his choice. This book seeks to describe the various paths that lead to this judicial philosophy of the judge. The book attempts to show that before the judge has to use his philosophy, he must travel a long road. Sometimes he does not have any need for this philosophy, for objective standards lead to the solution of the problem facing him. Yet sometimes, and in the hard cases, the judge—alone with himself and his worldview—will take a stand and will decide the case according to them. This book seeks to explain this process.

I am not a philosopher. My field of specialization is not jurisprudence. I am a judge. My field is the doctrine of adjudication. Jurisprudence—

the doctrine of law—and the doctrine of adjudication are two different things. However, there are close ties between the two that are expressed in the hard cases. This book seeks to help the judge formulate his worldview as a judge. It does not contain a solution to specific problems. It is not a collection of legislation or case law. It is an effort to construct an appropriate model of a judicial worldview. It is a strictly personal attempt, laced with the difficulties that inhere in building a comprehensive thesis on the basis of limited personal experience. I have tried to cover the literature on the subject, insofar as I had access to it. A lack of philosophical training and an inadequate mastery of European languages made my task more difficult. From the outset, I did not set as a goal for myself the building of a philosophical model. My undertaking is situated on that delicate seam between rule and reality, between theory and practice, between the philosophy of adjudication and the act of judging. It is intended to enable judges, who are people of action, to grapple with the difficult problems that life places before them and that force them to weigh considerations that lie at the basis of their judicial labor.

This book is not about Israeli law. It is not about an Israeli judge. It is about the law and judging generally. The problems are universal. Judicial discretion exists in every legal system. Its use raises common questions. Therefore, I used legal materials from many countries and from different jurisdictions. Of course, though the problems are common the solutions may differ. Judges in different countries may use their discretion differently. I do try, thus, to bring out the different considerations the judge in any country should take into account. The considerations are common, but their balancing may differ from country to country. The use of judicial discretion should be integrated into the general culture of the country. Thus, my own approach to the use of judicial discretion in hard cases is closely connected with my personal experience as a judge in my own country—Israel.

My interest in judicial discretion in the hard cases dates from my days as a law student. More than once in reading a case, I found myself in agreement with both the majority opinion and the minority opinion. This was quite amazing to me. Does not every legal problem have only one lawful solution? How could both the majority and minority opinions provide solutions that appeared to me to be lawful? As a teacher of law I researched the problem further, drawing a distinction between a lawful solution and an appropriate solution. But not infrequently I was faced with the question, What is the appropriate solution and what considerations should be taken into account in formulating that solution? As attorney general of the state of Israel, I saw the governmental branches (legislative, executive, and judicial) in action. I realized that a solution that was appropriate if it came from the seminary of one of the branches was not necessarily appropriate if it came from the seminary of another branch. The institutional problems of each branch and the problems of the interrelations among the branches affect the wisdom of the solution. Now that I am a Supreme Court Justice, all of these have become practical problems. I must give each problem a solution and avoid turning a solution into a problem. Suddenly I find myself facing the hard cases, with my colleagues and myself bearing the personal responsibility of solving them properly. An inappropriate solution might hurt not only the parties in the case; it also could harm the entire judicial system. It might damage the public's faith in the judiciary. The sense of personal responsibility became oppressive. I began to reflect again on the fundamentals of things and to wonder about the nature of the judicial process. I was compelled to give myself a conscious accounting of what I am doing and why I do it. I formulated my experience.

Now that I feel I have reached a self-summation, I want to make public my ponderings and present them to the melting pot of intellectual struggle. My ideas are an invitation to further thought about the judicial function. The essentials are not new. They are a renovation of old ideas. Every generation, it seems, must reevaluate for itself the matter of the judicial function and its problems.

My words are directed first and foremost to my colleagues the judges who, like me, encounter the difficult legal problems to which judicial philosophy seeks to provide an answer. Only the judges can determine, in the final analysis, whether my approach is useful. The true test of a good theory is in its practical realization. Yet my words are aimed not only at judges. The judge does not work in a vacuum. He decides in a conflict that has parties, who themselves have attorneys. My words are directed to them also and through them to the general public and the lawyers. This book is aimed too at policymakers in the legislative branch and in the executive branch. My words are intended for the learned person who, although he may lack the tools of legal analysis, is sensitive to the fundamental societal problems that adjudication must confront. Yet above all, my words are directed to my good friends, teachers and students alike, in the law schools. From them I drew the desire to learn, the need to question, and the readiness to admit error. My hope is that renewed study of the nature of judicial discretion will lead to a better understanding of the judicial function, of the judicial decision, and of the judicial process. Even if my opinions are unacceptable, I hope that they, and the views raised in opposition to them, will advance thinking about the judicial process. Perhaps things that do not appear correct today will be seen in a different light tomorrow. Good ideas—like good wine—improve with age.

It seems to me that my experience in academia (as a law professor) and in practice (as attorney general) constitutes a necessary condition for this research. Yet the decisive reason for my writing it is my judicial work. From this perspective, the book is dedicated to all the judges in the various courts and especially to my colleagues in the Supreme Court of Israel, those with whom I sit in judgment as well as those who are no longer on the bench and whose learning emerges from books.

Judicial discretion is at the center of this book. I sketch lines of thought that guide a judge in solving difficult legal problems that have more than one lawful solution. My basic starting point is that there are situations in which the judge has discretion to choose among a number of lines of action, all of which are lawful. The first part of the book is devoted to an examination of this thesis. Without this examination, there is no point in continuing to investigate how judicial discretion should be exercised. This thesis is based on the assumption that judicial discretion exists, albeit limited, and albeit narrow, and albeit only in a few cases. The second part of the book operates from the assumption that limited judicial discretion exists as to the choice among various possibilities. In this part, I attempt to formulate the main considerations that the judge must weigh with respect to his exercise of that discretion. In the last part, I seek to apply my approach in practice, while examining its implications for the future of adjudication.

This book is a translation of my *Shikul Daat Shiputy*, which was published in Israel in 1987. The Hebrew text is larger; it contains three additional chapters dealing with constitutional interpretation, statutory interpretation, and the use of general legal concepts. The sources cited here have not been updated from the Hebrew edition, and hence this translation contains references only to works published through 1986.

None of the materials were previously published in English except chapter 9, though some were published in law reviews and festschrifts in Israel. Chapter 9 on overruling precedent was published in the *Israel Law Review* for 1987.

My thanks are given to all who helped in my writing of this book. Special thanks are due the dean of the faculty of law at the Hebrew University, Professor Izhak Englard, and to the deans of Harvard and Yale Law Schools, Professor James Vorenberg of Harvard and Professors Harry Wellington and Guido Calabresi of Yale. As in all my writings in the past, present, and future, my main debt, which is incapable of being repaid, is to my master and teacher, Professor Gad Tedeschi, who taught me to think law. My thanks to my father, who taught me the ways of life. And above all, my thanks to Elika, without whose perseverance and help this book would never have seen the light of day.

Part One
The Nature of
Judicial Discretion

Chapter 1
The Characteristics of Judicial Discretion

DIFFICULTIES IN UNDERSTANDING JUDICIAL DISCRETION

Judicial discretion is, for the most part, a mystery—to the general public, to the community of lawyers, to teachers of law, and to judges themselves.[1] Judge Edwards referred to this phenomenon in the following terms:

> One might expect that today, more than a half-century after the Legal Realist movement, the phenomenon of the exercise of "judicial discretion" would have been so exhaustively studied as to merit no more than a passing reference in preparation for the examination of more controversial matters. That turns out not to be true. Not only does the activity of judicial lawmaking remain mysterious, but a surprisingly large number of people, both within and without the legal community, question its legitimacy in any form.[2]

While administrative discretion has been the subject of extensive study,[3] little research and writing has been devoted to the discretion exercised by judges.[4] Judicial discretion remains mired in the realm of the unknown, enveloped by shrouds of mystery,[5] with even its philosophical foundations unclear.[6]

1. See A. Miller, *The Supreme Court: Myth and Reality* 11 (1978).
2. Edwards, "The Role of a Judge in Modern Society: Some Reflections on Current Practice in Federal Appellate Adjudication," 32 *Clev. St. L. Rev.* 385, 388 (1984).
3. See K. Davis, *Discretionary Justice* (1969).
4. But see A. Paterson, *The Law Lords* (1982).
5. See Mason, "Myth and Reality in Supreme Court Decisions," 48 *Va. L. Rev.* 1385 (1962).
6. See B. Cardozo, *The Growth of the Law* 144 (1924).

There appear to be several reasons for this lack of knowledge about judicial discretion. First, most judges do not explain how they exercise discretion, and non-judges frequently lack information about the way judges exercise discretion. In the words of Justice Felix Frankfurter,

> The power of searching analysis of what it is that they are doing seems rarely to be possessed by judges, either because they are lacking in the art of critical exposition or because they are inhibited from practicing it. The fact is that pitifully little of significance has been contributed by judges regarding the nature of their endeavor, and, I might add that which is written by those who are not judges is too often a confident caricature rather than a seer's vision of the judicial process of the Supreme Court.[7]

Second, several philosophical doctrines concerning law do not deal with the court. Those philosophical theories neglect judicial discretion and attach no importance to it in the field of law.[8] Third, other philosophical doctrines that do recognize the centrality of the judicial process discuss it in a way that does not permit of any normative approach and that prevents the formulation of a doctrine of judicial discretion. Thus, for example, the declaratory theory that is accepted in British common law, according to which the judge declares the law without creating it, does not focus on judicial discretion, for the doctrine does not acknowledge judicial creation. The American Realists[9] and neo-Realists,[10] on the other hand, recognize both the centrality of the judicial process and the centrality of judicial discretion to that process, yet for these schools, discretion is largely a subjective affair. This view of the world precludes a scientific approach to judicial discretion.

These factors, though they help explain the relative dearth of knowledge about our subject, do not justify it. Indeed, many writers now acknowledge the centrality both of the act of judging in law[11] and of

7. F. Frankfurter, *Of Law and Men* 32 (1956).

8. Such as Kelsen's doctrine. See H. Kelsen, *The Pure Theory of Law* 194 (trans. W. Ebenstein, 1945).

9. See J. Frank, *Law and the Modern Mind* 357 (Anchor Book ed., 1963); White, "From Sociological Jurisprudence to Realism: Jurisprudence and Social Change in Early Twentieth-Century America." 58 *Va. L. Rev.* 993 (1972).

10. Singer, "The Player and the Cards: Nihilism and Legal Theory," 94 *Yale L.J.* 1 (1984); Unger, "The Critical Legal Studies Movement," 96 *Harv. L. Rev.* 561 (1983).

11. See G. Calabresi, *A Common Law for the Age of Statutes* (1982); R. Keeton, *Venturing to Do Justice* (1969).

judicial discretion in the act of judging.[12] Montesquieu's approach, according to which the judge is simply the mouth that repeats the language of the law,[13] is no longer accepted, and the days of the "mechanical" approach to judging are gone.[14] Justice Yoel Sussman referred to this when he said,

> The image of the judge, in the eyes of Montesquieu, is the image of a man skilled in finding his way in the hidden paths of the forest of legislation. But his opinion is flawed with the accepted error, that these paths always exist and all their talent lies only in uncovering them. Montesquieu did not consider that the paths are sometimes not marked by the legislature at all, and the judge himself must mark them.[15]

Against this background, the importance of the question of judicial discretion increases. What characterizes this discretion? What are its appropriate limits? How can it be accommodated with the doctrine of separation of powers and the democratic nature of the regime? Is judicial discretion consistent with judicial objectivity and with the rule of law, which is based on the preexistence of the norm before someone is brought to justice for having violated it? These questions are particularly important in legal systems that have a rigid, formal constitution, where the interpretation that the court gives to the constitution enjoys the formal character of the constitution itself. What discretion is appropriate in the interpretation of a constitution? How is it possible to ensure—in the context of a democratic system—stability with flexibility, while protecting the legitimacy of judging? How is it possible to ensure that the judges' personal views will not dictate the interpretation they give to constitutional norms? Similar questions arise in the framework of the interpretation of a regular statute. Therefore, as interest in statutory interpretation has increased, so too has interest in judicial discretion. This heightened interest is also the result of recent philosophical approaches that negate "strong" judicial discretion.[16] Thus, for example,

---

12. H. L. A. Hart, *The Concept of Law* 121 (1961); J. Raz, *The Authority of Law* 180 (1979).

13. C. Montesquieu, *The Spirit of the Laws* ch. 6, 226 (trans. Nugent, 2d ed., 1752).

14. See Pound, "Mechanical Jurisprudence," 8 *Colum. L. Rev.* 605 (1908).

15. Sussman, "Some Observations on Interpretation," *Rosen Book* 154 (1962).

16. See Dworkin, "Judicial Discretion," 6 *J. of Phil.* 624 (1963); R. Dworkin, *Taking Rights Seriously* 81 (1977); Sartorius, "The Justification of the Judicial Decision," 78 *Ethics* 171 (1968).

Professor Ronald Dworkin argues that for each legal problem there is one right answer, and only one. This approach leaves no room for judicial discretion. Is this view acceptable?

I noted that judicial discretion has been the subject of little research and writing. Yet the few studies that we have concerning judicial discretion include a number of most important works.[17] The cornerstone for any understanding of judicial discretion is Justice Benjamin Cardozo's trilogy—*The Nature of Judicial Process* (1921); *Growth of the Law* (1924); *Paradoxes of Legal Science* (1928). Cardozo's writing still serves as the "Urim VeTummim"—Lux et Veritas—of any approach to the nature of the judicial process.[18] One must note the important contribution of Professors H. L. A. Hart and Dworkin[19] to the better understanding of judicial discretion in hard cases. Their writings, and the literature that sprung as a response to their theories[20]—mainly that of Professor Joseph Raz[21]—paved the way for my own understanding of the way I use my judicial discretion in hard cases. One must also mention the important work of H. Hart and A. Sacks, *The Legal Process: Basic Problems in the Making and Application of Law* (Tentative Edition, 1958) to the understanding of the role of judicial discretion in the legal process.

In sum, therefore, the subject is not one in which we must create something out of nothing. Rather, it is necessary, at most, to reorganize the "something" that already exists. The words of Justice Moshe Landau bear on our subject:

---

17. See Holmes, "The Path of the Law," 10 *Harv. L. Rev.* 457 (1897); Pound, "The Theory of Judicial Decision," 36 *Harv. L. Rev.* 641, 802, 940 (1923); Friedmann, "Legal Philosophy and Judicial Lawmaking," 61 *Colum. L. Rev.* 821 (1961); Weiler, "Two Models of Judicial Decision-Making," 46 *Can. Bar. Rev.* 406 (1968); Landau, "Rule and Discretion in Law-Making," 1 *Mishpatim* 292 (1968); Witkon, "Some Reflections on Judicial Law Making," 2 *Isr L. Rev.* 475 (1967).

18. See *supra* note 12; Hart, "Positivism and the Separation of Law and Morals," 71 *Harv. L. Rev.* 593 (1958).

19. See *supra* note 16, and *infra* notes 84, 86, 87, 91.

20. See Greenawalt, "Discretion and Judicial Decision: The Elusive Quest for the Fetters that Bind Judges," 75 *Colum. L. Rev.* 359 (1975); Greenawalt, "Policy, Rights and Judicial Decision," 11 *Ga. L. Rev.* 991 (1977); Wellington, "Common Law Rules and Constitutional Double Standards: Some Notes on Adjudication," 83 *Yale L.J.* 221 (1973); N. MacCormick, *Legal Reasoning and Legal Theory* 195 (1978).

21. Raz, "Legal Principles and the Limits of Law," 81 *Yale L.J.* 823 (1972); Raz, *supra* note 12.

It appears that all that our generation—like all generations—can do is to reorganize our few building blocks—the fundamental legal concepts that have been well-known in legal thought since the beginning of time—and to adapt the entire structure to the social and economic development occurring outside the field of law. And if some progress is made in this process, it lies at most in a review of the very same phenomena in a more sophisticated, or perhaps more complex manner, in keeping with the complexities of our social and economic life.[22]

Let us turn, then, to the task of reorganizing the building blocks.

JUDICIAL DISCRETION DEFINED

The study of the nature of judicial discretion must begin with its definition. This is by no means an easy task, for the term *discretion* has more than one meaning, and indeed means different things in different contexts.[23] Some authors have despaired of analyzing it and recommended against using the term.[24] Yet we must reject this advice because the concept of discretion is central to an understanding of the judicial process.

To me, discretion is the power given to a person with authority to choose between two or more alternatives, when each of the alternatives is lawful. Justice Sussman referred to this definition, saying, "Discretion means the freedom to choose among different possible solutions."[25] Hart and Sacks offered a similar definition: "Discretion means the power to choose between two or more courses of action each of which is thought of as permissible."[26] Judicial discretion, then, means the power the law gives the judge to choose among several alternatives, each of them being lawful. This definition assumes, of course, that the judge will not act mechanically, but will weigh, reflect, gain impressions, test, and study.[27]

22. Landau, *supra* note 17, at 292.
23. See Isaacs, "The Limits of Judicial Discretion," 32 *Yale L.J.* 339 (1922); R. Pattenden, *The Judge, Discretion, and the Criminal Trial* 3 (1982).
24. See Isaacs, *supra* note 23, at 340.
25. F.H. 16/61 *Registrar of Companies v. Kardosh,* 16 P.D. 1209, 1215.
26. See H. Hart and A. Sacks, *The Legal Process: Basic Problems in the Making and Application of Law* 162 (Tentative Edition, 1958). See also C. Radcliffe, *Not in Feather Beds* 271 (1968).
27. See Tedeschi, *Legal Essays* 1 (1978): "Interpretation is not a mechanical nor even a psychological process. It is a reconstruction of another's thought—normative thought, if

Yet this conscious use of the power of thought does not define judicial discretion. It only suggests how the judge must act within the framework of his discretion. Indeed, judicial discretion, by definition, is neither an emotional nor a mental state. It is, rather, a legal condition in which the judge has the freedom to choose among a number of options. Where judicial discretion exists, it is as though the law were saying, "I have determined the contents of the legal norm up to this point. From here on, it is for you, the judge, to determine the contents of the legal norm, for I, the legal system, am not able to tell you which solution to choose." It is as though the path of the law came to a junction, and the judge must decide—with no clear and precise standard to guide him—which road to take.

Freedom of Choice: Narrow and Broad Discretion

Discretion assumes the freedom to choose among several lawful alternatives.[28] Therefore, discretion does not exist when there is but one lawful option. In this situation, the judge is required to select that option and has no freedom of choice. No discretion is involved in the choice between a lawful act and an unlawful act. The judge must choose the lawful act, and he is precluded from choosing the unlawful act. Discretion, on the other hand, assumes the lack of an obligation to choose one particular possibility among several. Discretion assumes the existence of several options, of which the judge is entitled to choose the one that most appeals to him. In the words of Justice Cardozo,

> Other cases present a genuine opportunity for choice—not a choice between two decisions, one of which may be said to be almost certainly right and the

we are dealing with legal interpretation—and it cannot be compared at all to the emptying of a substance from one vessel to another, nor to the reflection of an image in a mirror or to a photograph. Interpretation is the copying of another's thought into the range of our spiritual life, and it can be done only by our thought process." See also Levy, "The Nature of Judicial Reasoning," 32 *U. Chi. L. Rev.* 395, 396 (1965). The image offered by Professor Radin, according to which the judge is merely a machine that gives a result after the coin has been deposited, does not reflect the judicial process, not even in the most self-evident cases. See Radin, "The Theory of Judicial Decision: or How Judges Think?" 11 *A.B.A.J.* 357 (1925).

28. See Rosenberg, "Judicial Discretion of the Trial Court Viewed from Above," 22 *Syracuse L. Rev.* 635, 636 (1971): "If the word *discretion* conveys to legal minds any solid core of meaning, one central idea above all others, it is the idea of choice." This is what Llewellyn termed the Law of Leeways: K. Llewellyn, *The Common Law Tradition: Deciding Appeals* 219 (1960).

other almost certainly wrong, but a choice so nicely balanced that when once it is announced, a new right and a new wrong will emerge in the announcement.[29]

Thus, discretion assumes a zone of possibilities rather than just one point. It is founded on the existence of a number of options that are open to the judge. It is built on the existence of a real fork in the road. There the judge stands, forced to choose, without being required to select one path or the other. Justice Cardozo described this process in his image-rich style:

> There have been two paths, each open, though leading to different goals. The fork in the road has not been neutralized for the traveler by a barrier across one of the prongs with the label of "no thoroughfare." He must gather his wits, pluck up his courage, go forward one way or the other, and pray that he may be walking, not into ambush, morass, and darkness, but into safety, the open spaces, and the light.[30]

The zone of lawful options may be narrow, as when the judge is free to choose between only two lawful alternatives. Or the range of lawful options may be considerable, as when the judge stands before many lawful alternatives and combinations of alternatives. In this sense one may distinguish between narrow and broad discretion. This distinction, of course, is only relative.

Judicial Discretion and the Legal Community

I noted that discretion does not exist when the choice is between a lawful possibility and an unlawful possibility. The significance of this requirement is that whether the judge chooses one option or the other, each of the choices will be lawful in the framework of the system. Thus, the options are determined not by physical criteria of the feasibility of carrying out the choice, but by legal criteria of the legality of the execution. The existence of the alternative is determined not by its effectiveness but by its lawfulness.[31] It is not the choice that makes the

---

29. Cardozo, *supra* note 6, at 58.
30. Cardozo, *supra* note 6, at 59.
31. On the other hand, Professor Davis defines discretion in the following manner: "A public officer has discretion whenever the effective limits on his power leave him free to make a choice among possible courses of action or inaction." In explaining this definition, the author notes that "discretion is not limited to what is authorized or what is legal but includes all that is within 'the *effective* limits' on the officer's power. This phraseology is

chosen option lawful; rather, the choice is based on the fact that the option in question is lawful.[32] Thus, the judge has no discretion to choose an alternative that is unlawful, even if his choice may not be challenged, and even if the decision—if it is that of the Supreme Court— will stand and obligate others. One must distinguish between the power to achieve a particular result, and the authority to do so.[33] The judge enjoys freedom of choice only when each of the options open to him is permissible from the perspective of the system. According to this approach, discretion exists only when each of the alternatives is lawful. The legal question to which discretion is applied does not have one lawful solution, but rather several lawful solutions. As Professor S. A. de Smith wrote, "To say that somebody has a discretion presupposes that there is no uniquely right answer to his problem."[34]

As we shall see,[35] Professor Dworkin believes that the judge has no discretion in the meaning in which we are using this term, because in his view, each problem—even the most difficult—has only one legal solution. For our purposes, the term *discretion* assumes the existence of a legal problem for which there is more than one lawful solution. As we shall see, these are the difficult problems, and discretion exists, therefore, only in hard cases.[36]

An important question arises: How is the lawfulness of the options before the judge to be determined? Surely, it is not sufficient for the judge subjectively to believe that the alternative in question is a lawful one. What, then, is the test for the lawfulness of the option? This is not an easy matter. We are not possessed of a legal litmus paper that can calculate the lawfulness of a legal possibility. The law has not developed precise instruments or advanced laboratory tools for deciding what is permitted and what forbidden, what is lawful and what unlawful. Nonetheless, there exist possibilities that every knowledgeable lawyer can

---

necessary because a good deal of discretion is illegal or of questionable legality." Davis, *supra* note 3, at 4. I do not accept this approach. When one of the alternatives is not lawful, there is no discretion to choose it, even though it may be chosen in practice.

32. See G. Gottlieb, *The Logic of Choice* 117 (1968).

33. See Sartorius, *Individual Conduct and Social Norm* 283 (1975).

34. S. de Smith, *Judicial Review of Administrative Action* 278 (4th ed., 1980).

35. *Infra* notes 93–102 and accompanying text.

36. The expression *hard cases* I take from Professor Dworkin, who has a "copyright" on it: see R. Dworkin, *supra* note 16, at 81.

readily identify as lawful, and there are other possible solutions that any lawyer would immediately understand to be unlawful. Between these two poles exist possibilities as to which knowledgeable lawyers might disagree about the degree of their lawfulness. I suggest relying on this standard of knowledgeable lawyers or the legal community[37] as the standard for determining the lawfulness of a possibility. The legal community is the professional outlook of the collectivity of lawyers in a particular state.[38] An option is lawful if the legal community views it as such and if the legal community's reaction to the choice of this option is not one of shock and mistrust. An option is unlawful if the legal community sees it as unlawful and considers it impossible that a knowledgeable lawyer would choose this option. A lawyer who chooses this option would thereby be "uprooting the written word, in effect calling the day night and the night day."[39]

Of course, this standard is not precise. Between the two poles are a number of situations about which the legal community is itself divided. These scenarios should not be called unlawful, just as one cannot say about them that they are lawful. Indeed, it is the judicial decision itself that will determine the lawfulness of these possibilities. To be sure, the term *legal community* is also imprecise, and, as we have seen, many borderline cases are left without clear resolution. Still, this should not prevent us from using this terminology. The term *reasonable person* is not sufficiently precise, and yet it constitutes the cornerstone of many of our laws. In truth, one cannot avoid operating in broad realms of uncertainty. With time, it will be possible to improve on this terminology, which itself changes with the passage of time. In any event, for the purpose of testing judicial discretion, this test appears to me to be appropriate. Thus, we can say that judicial discretion exists where the legal community believes a legal problem has more than one lawful solution. Judicial discretion does not exist where the legal community believes that for a certain legal problem there is only one lawful solution. Where the views of the legal community are divided, the judge has discretion to determine whether or not judicial discretion exists.

37. As to the "legal community" or the "interpretive community," see Fiss, "Objectivity and Interpretation," 34 *Stan. L. Rev.* 739 (1982).

38. See Greenawalt, "Discretion and Judicial Decision," *supra* note 20, at 386; J. Bell, *Policy Arguments in Judicial Decisions* 24 (1983).

39. Cheshin J. in H.C. 1/50 *Grosman v. The Military Prosecutor,* 4 P.D. 63, 70.

This legal community test is intended to make the judge aware of the need to distinguish between his subjective views and the legal conception of the society in which he lives and operates. At the same time, however, the judge need not conduct a public opinion survey to ascertain the views of the legal community. Each judge must make this decision for himself. In doing so, however, the judge must not give expression to that which is unique and exceptional in himself. He must, rather, give expression to what appears to him to be the basic conception of the society (the community) in which he lives and acts. He must observe himself from a distance. Thus, the legal community test is simply another aspect of the basic premise of this book, according to which judicial discretion must be exercised objectively. The legal community is one way to portray this objective conception.

Summary: The Zone of Formal Legitimacy

Judicial discretion presupposes a zone of lawful possibilities, each of which is lawful in the context of the system. Any option that is outside the zone is, by definition, unlawful, and the judge has no discretion about whether or not to choose it. He is required not to select this possibility. Discretion, then, defines a formal zone of legitimacy, the zone of formal legitimacy. This zone marks the border, imprecise as it may be, between the possibilities as to which there is discretion and the possibilities as to which there is no discretion at all. The exercise of judicial discretion is possible only within the boundaries of the zone. A similar zone exists for each authority that exercises discretion, be it the legislative branch (which acts in the framework of a constitution) or the executive branch (which acts in the framework of a constitution, in the framework of statutes, and in the framework of regulations). Still, the judicial branch has a special sensitivity to the question of the formal legitimacy of its actions, since it has the authority and the responsibility to establish the legitimacy of the actions of the other authorities. It is only natural for the judicial branch to exhibit heightened caution and to be especially demanding of itself in this matter. Whoever criticizes the acts of others must apply exacting self-criticism to his own acts.

THE OBJECT OF JUDICIAL DISCRETION

Fact, the Application of a Norm, and the Norm Itself

We defined judicial discretion as the power given to a judge to choose among a number of lawful options. What are these options? In principle, they may refer to three matters.[40] The first is the facts. Judicial discretion chooses from among the set of facts those that it deems necessary for making a decision in the conflict. The second area is the application of a given norm. Judicial discretion selects from among the different methods of application that the norm provides the one that it finds appropriate. The third area of discretion lies in the establishment of the norm itself. Judicial discretion chooses from among the normative possibilities the option that it deems appropriate.

Judicial Discretion and Facts

The first area of judicial discretion deals with deciding the facts. This type of discretion refers, for example, to the question whether X was present at location Y at time Z, or not. This discretion is arguably the most important in the judicial process, since most disputes that are brought before the courts concern only facts. Indeed, the classic role of the judge is to determine the facts on the basis of a given rule. Thus, the crux of the service that the court system provides to society is in the authorized determination of facts. In the large majority of controversies the parties do not dispute the law or its application, and the only disagreement between them is over what actually took place. In this, they fail to agree, and the only way to solve the conflict is to hand it over to a third party, objective and independent, which will decide the facts and the conclusions that follow from them. This service is performed primarily by the courts of first instance, whose main function lies in the determination of facts.

Does the judge enjoy discretion in the determination of facts? This question may surprise the reader, for in the layman's eyes, the *only* discretion the judge has—like a referee in a sporting event[41]—is in the determination of facts. According to this approach, the judge has discretion, even broad discretion, in deciding the facts. Here the term *discretion* has a mental connotation: the judge is supposed to study and weigh, while wielding the power either to believe or to doubt.[42] But does the judge have discretion in the sense in which we are using this term, that is, can he choose between two or more lawful results? This is a difficult question, tied as it is to philosophical and psychological debates about

40. See J. Stone, *Social Dimensions of Law and Justice* 674 (1966).
41. See Hughes, "Rules, Policy and Decision Making," 77 *Yale L.J.* 411, 414 (1968).
42. See W. Greene, *The Judicial Office* 10 (Holdsworth Club, Presidential Addresses, 1938).

the nature of reality. Is there a reality that the judge simply "finds" and "uncovers," or is there rather no objective reality at all, and does the judge "invent" and determine the facts?[43] If only one "real" and "true" reality exists, does the judge have any discretion, or is he instead obligated to choose that reality and to find it as fact for the purpose of deciding the conflict? These questions are crucial, yet consideration of them is outside the scope of this essay, since our subject is judicial discretion in the normative plane, not in the factual plane.

Judicial Discretion and the Application of a Norm

The second type of discretion concerns the choice among a number of alternative ways of applying a norm to a given set of facts. Frequently, a legal norm gives the judge the power to choose among different courses of action that are fixed in its framework. This grant of authority may be explicit, as when the norm is actually phrased in terms of discretion. The grant may also be implicit, such as when the norm refers to a standard (for example, negligence or reasonableness) or to a goal (such as the defense of the state, public order, the best interests of the child) or to a value (for example, justice, morals). In these situations the parties might agree among themselves about the facts, for example, that the trip in question was made at speed X, at time Y, and at place Z. They may also agree about the content of the norm. Thus, the parties all accept that the test for deciding the reasonableness of the behavior is the reasonable person standard. The conflict between them concerns the application of this norm to the facts. In this example, the disagreement is about whether or not the driver, in the circumstances, was acting unreasonably or negligently.

In this type of situation, the judge's activity is one of concretization. He "translates" the normative decree to the specific case before him. Justice Sussman discussed this in the following terms:

> The law is an abstract norm and only the judgment of the court translates the rule of the legislature into an obligatory act that is enforced on the public. The judge gives the law its real and concrete form. Therefore one can say that the statute ultimately crystallizes in the shape the judge gives it.[44]

These situations, involving the need to decide how to apply a norm to a given set of facts, are by no means rare. Not infrequently, statutes are

43. See J. Frank, *Courts on Trial* (1949).
44. Sussman, "The Courts and the Legislative Branch," 3 *Mishpatim* 213 (1971).

worded so as to give the courts discretion expressly.[45] The justification for this lies in the need for individualization. One cannot know in advance what the future holds, and the legislature seeks to grant the court "discretion" to accomplish the aims of the statute. Debate has swirled about the desirability of this type of legislation and about whether the "price" we pay for the individualization is not too high. The words of Lord Camden, who sharply criticized this type of discretion, are famous:

> The discretion of a Judge is the law of Tyrants; it is always unknown, it is different from different men; it is casual and depends upon constitution and passion. In the best it is often, at times, capricious; in the worst it is every vice, folly and madness to which human nature is liable.[46]

Even if one does not share this dark view, there is no doubt that giving the court discretion to carry out the concretization of the law has, along with its advantages, a number of drawbacks.[47] These stem primarily from the impossibility of foretelling the outcome of the exercise of discretion, and, as a result, judicial certainty and the ability to plan for the long term suffer.

Does the judge have discretion in this second type of case? The reader may be taken aback by this question. Can anyone doubt that the judge has discretion when the statute explicitly states that he has "discretion"? But at times the discretion provided for in the statute is simply discretion in the mental sense of the term and does not constitute discretion as we have defined it. Indeed, the question arises whether the judge has the freedom to choose among several possible ways of concretizing a given norm. I will deal with this question in due course.

Judicial Discretion and the Norm Itself

The third type of discretion concerns the choice among different alternatives regarding the norm itself. This state of affairs is found in a number of typical situations.

First, there occasionally is a given legal norm, and the question concerns its reach. The given norm may be a statutory norm, and the

45. See Dugdale, "The Statutory Conferment of Judicial Discretion." (1972) *N.Z.L.J.* 556; Wexler, "Discretion: The Unacknowledged Side of Law," 25 *U. Toronto L.J.* 120 (1975); Finlay, "Judicial Discretion in Family and Other Litigation," 2 *Monash U.L. Rev.* 221 (1976); Burrows, "Statutes and Judicial Discretion," 7 *N.Z.U.L. Rev.* 1 (1976).

46. This quote appears in Isaacs, *supra* note 23, at 343.

47. See Atiyah, "From Principles to Pragmatism: Changes in the Function of the Judicial Process and the Law," 65 *Iowa L. Rev.* 1249 (1980).

question is a matter of interpreting the scope of that norm. For example, the Israeli Civil Wrongs Ordinance states[48] that a duty of care exists toward all persons whenever "a reasonable person ought in the circumstances to have contemplated as likely in the usual course of things to be affected." What is the scope of application of this rule?[49] Does it place a duty on an individual to rescue another person from danger? Does it obligate a state body not to be negligent in its governmental powers? Does it place a duty on a physician not to be negligent with respect to a person who, without that same negligence, would never have been born?[50] The given norm may be a common law rule, in which case the question concerns the scope of the *ratio decidendi*. Does the common law obligation to act reasonably include a duty to act efficiently? In all these cases, there is a given legal norm, and the question concerns the interpretation of the scope of application of the norm. Second, at times one finds norms that are mutually inconsistent. The judge must determine the existence of the inconsistency and give preference to one of the norms. Third, sometimes there is a common law norm with which the court disagrees, and the question arises whether or not the court should deviate from the norm and overrule it. On other occasions there is a legal vacuum or lacuna that the court must fill by choosing one normative option.

The question—and this is the hardest question of them all—is whether, in this third type of case, the judge has discretion. Is there a situation in which the judge stands before two normative possibilities, each of which is lawful in the context of the system? As we have already said, there are those who maintain that no such discretion exists, not even in the hard cases, since each legal problem, they claim, has only one correct solution. As I noted, I do not share this view. I will discuss this issue further.

The Distinction among the Various Objects of Judicial Discretion

I spoke of three objects of judicial discretion: fact, application of a norm, and the norm itself. The first type of discretion concerns facts vis-à-vis a

48. Sec. 36 of the Civil Wrongs Ordinance (New Version).

49. See J. Fleming, *The Law of Torts* (6th ed., 1983); J. Smith, *Liability in Negligence* (1984).

50. The "wrongful life" question. The Israeli supreme court imposed liability on doctors toward the child and his parents: C.A. 518/82 *Zeitzoff v. Katz*.

norm; the second type deals with a norm vis-à-vis facts; the third involves the norm vis-à-vis itself and the rest of the normative system. The distinction among the three objects of judicial discretion is blurred. The difficulty is inherent in the fact that we do not have accurate instruments for determining what constitutes a fact and what a norm, and where the border between them lies. Moreover, the judge cannot decide the facts before he formulates for himself, if only at first glance, a view of the law, since the number of facts is infinite and he must focus only on those that are relevant, which is determined by the law. Yet the judge cannot determine the law before he takes, again if only as a first impression, a stand regarding the facts, since the number of laws is great and he must concentrate on the law that applies, which is determined by the nature of the facts. There exists, then, an intimate link between norm and fact.[51] The two are subject to judicial determination, through internal and mutual dependence. The norm sifts through the facts and focuses only on those that are relevant. The facts sort through the norms and concentrate only on those that apply. Thus, the image of the judge who deals only with facts is a myth. The judge must concern himself with norms as well as with facts, at one and the same time.

At times the three objects of judicial discretion collapse into one judicial decision. Take the question whether to allow parents to revoke their consent to put their child up for adoption. The Israeli Child Adoption Law (1981) stipulates that the revocation is subject to the court's discretion,[52] which is guided by the principle of the best interests of the adoptee.[53] In this situation, the judge must establish the facts that concern the child's welfare (discretion of the first type). He cannot do so without establishing the meaning of the term "the best interests of the adoptee": are these the interests of the child in the short run only, or must the judge take into account also long-term considerations, and how should he balance these two in the event of a conflict between them (discretion of the third type). The judge must determine what the best interests of the adoptee require in the circumstances before him (discretion of the second type). As we noted, all this is done in a single judicial ruling, with the different stages intertwined. Still, sometimes there is no

51. See J. Cueto-Rua, *Judicial Methods of Interpretation of the Law* 25 (1981).
52. Sec. 10 of the Child Adoption Law (1981).
53. Sec. 1(b) of the Child Adoption Law (1981).

avoiding a sharp distinction among the stages. Thus, a court may use one set of criteria for reviewing decisions of the executive branch on questions of fact or application of the laws, and another set of criteria for the reviewing of questions of law.[54]

THE SCOPE OF JUDICIAL DISCRETION

Limited Discretion and Absolute Discretion

I distinguished between narrow discretion and broad discretion. This distinction refers to the number of lawful options open to the judge: when discretion is narrow, the number of options is small, although it never drops below two; when discretion is broad, the number of options is large. A different distinction considers the degree of direction and restriction that the law imparts to the person exercising the discretion, in choosing among the various alternatives (be they narrow or broad). This distinction concerns not the number of options but rather the degree of liberty that the authorized party has—with respect to form as well as content—in choosing among the options that exist. This distinction focuses on the procedural and substantive tests that must be considered in the choice among the various options. The definition of the term *discretion* as freedom of choice among a number of lawful alternatives requires that there exist an area in which the authorized party is free to choose among the various options; if no such area existed, the discretion would evaporate. Yet the extent of this area of choice may vary. When there are but few limitations on the scope of considerations and the decision-making process, then the number of matters that the authorized person may take into account when he chooses among the options is great. When the method of decision and the number and character of the factors is left to the subjective determination of the exerciser of discretion, who may decide in whatever way appears best to him, according to any consideration he likes, we say that the holder of authority wields absolute discretion.

On the other hand, when the number and nature of considerations is not left to the subjective decision of the person with discretion, and he is not permitted to decide however he sees fit, but rather is restricted in terms of both the form of the decision and the scope of the factors he may

---

54. See L. Jaffe, *Judicial Control of Administrative Action* 572 (1965).

take into account, we say the authorized person has only a limited discretion.[55]

Judicial Discretion Is Never Absolute

A judge does not have absolute discretion. Every exercise of discretion in the context of the law—whether by the legislative, executive, or judicial branch—is subject to limitations placed on it by the law. Discretion exercised by virtue of law is never absolute. Even if a statutory pronouncement states explicitly that the discretion it grants is absolute, this discretion is interpreted[56] as requiring the holder of authority to act according to certain procedures (such as granting a hearing and acting impartially) and in such a way as to achieve the goals of the legislation from which his authority is derived. The words of Deputy Chief Justice Shimon Agranat in H.C. 241/60, *Kardosh v. The Registrar of Companies,*[57] which dealt with administrative discretion, apply with equal force to judicial discretion:

> The general principle is that every administrative body must act within the four corners of the purpose for which the law vested in it the authority at issue; and this rule applies also to an authority that it may exercise with "absolute discretion." It follows that where the court finds that the use of this type of authority—as broad as the discretion vested in the administrative body may be—is made for a purpose that is foreign to the statutory intent, the court will intervene, unless it is prevented from doing so by the explicit language of the statute.[58]

The same principle follows from the Supreme Court's opinion in the rehearing of the *Kardosh* case. Justice Sussman wrote,

> But the discretion that is given to an administrative body—even if it is absolute—is always tied to the duty that the body must fulfill, namely the tasks of administration for which the body was authorized to act according to

55. See MacCormick, *supra* note 20, at 251.

56. Thus, in principle it is possible to create absolute discretion. My determination that discretion that is exercised by virtue of law is never absolute is an interpretive determination. When all the legislature says is that the discretion is absolute, this is interpreted as limited discretion. But the legislature can go beyond this and explicitly establish that the absolute discretion is not limited. This, too, requires interpretation, yet the faithful interpreter would give it the full meaning that flows from the legislative purpose.

57. 15 P.D. 1151.

58. At 1162.

its discretion; great as the freedom to choose may be, it will never be unlimited.[59]

The Court stressed the very same principle in H.C. 742/84, *Kahane v. The Chairman of the Knesset et al.*, where I said,

> Indeed, statutory discretion may be broad or narrow, but it is always limited. The number of possibilities open to the decision-maker may be great or meager, but the freedom to choose among them is never unlimited. Thus the law ensures the freedom of the individual. . . . These principles apply to every discretion that derives its force from a statutory pronouncement. They apply to the discretion of every office-holder in the executive branch. These principles apply to every office-holder in the judicial branch. These principles apply to every office-holder in the legislative branch.[60]

Therefore, judicial discretion, which always derives its force from the law—whether it be a constitution or statute passed by the legislature or the common law—is never absolute. Indeed, just as we fear absolute discretion in the administrative sphere, we fear it in the judicial sphere. The law's shining hour comes when it simultaneously places restrictions on administrative, legislative, and judicial discretion. In the oft-repeated words of Justice William Douglas, "Absolute discretion, like corruption, marks the beginning of the end of liberty."[61] He elaborated further on this idea in another case:

> Law has reached its finest moments when it has freed man from the unlimited discretion of some ruler, some civil or military official, some bureaucrat. Where discretion is absolute, man has always suffered. . . . Absolute discretion is a ruthless master. It is more destructive of freedom than any of man's other inventions.[62]

Even the most absolute of discretions must restrict itself to the framework of the statute that created it. No judicial authority of any judicial instance is ever absolute. Every judicial authority of every court—especially of the Supreme Court—is always limited.

Judicial Discretion as Limited Discretion

As I have demonstrated, judicial discretion is not absolute. The manner of choice among the possibilities and the factors that may be taken into

59. F.H. 16/61, *supra* note 25, at 1216.
60. 39 P.D.(4) 85, 92.
61. *State of New York v. United States*, 342 U.S. 882, 884 (1951).
62. *United States v. Wunderlich*, 342 U.S. 98, 101 (1951).

account in the selection are not left to the subjective decision of the judge, and he is not entitled to decide them as he sees fit.[63]

In other words, there are limitations that bind the judge with respect to the manner in which he chooses among the possibilities (procedural limitations) and with respect to the considerations he takes into account in the choice (substantive limitations). As Lord Mansfield wrote, "Discretion when applied to a court of justice, means sound discretion guided by law. It must be governed by rule not by humour; it must not be arbitrary, vague and fanciful, but legal and regular."[64] Chief Justice John Marshall took a similar position concerning the discretion enjoyed by judges:

> When they are said to exercise a discretion, it is a mere legal discretion, a discretion to be exercised in discovering the course prescribed by law; and when that is discovered, it is the duty of the Court to follow it. Judicial power is never exercised for the purpose of giving effect to the will of the judge; always for the purpose of giving effect to the will of the legislature; or, in other words, to the will of the law.[65]

These are general statements requiring concretization. A more concrete approach may be found in the words of Justice Cardozo:

> Given freedom of choice, how shall the choice be guided? Complete freedom—unfettered and undirected—there never is. A thousand limitations—the product some of statute, some of precedent, some of vague tradition or of an immemorial technique—encompass and hedge us even when we think of ourselves as ranging freely and at large. The inscrutable force of professional opinion presses upon us like the atmosphere, though we are heedless of its weight. Narrow at best is any freedom that is allotted to us.[66]

Elsewhere he added,

> The judge, even when he is free, is still not wholly free. He is not to innovate at pleasure. He is not a knight-errant, roaming at will in pursuit of his own ideal of beauty or of goodness. He is to draw his inspiration from consecrated

63. See Lord Scarman in *Duport Steels Ltd.* v. *Sirs* [1980] 1 All. E.R. 529, 551: "Legal systems differ in the width of the discretionary power granted to judges; but in developed societies limits are invariably set, beyond which the judges may not go. Justice in such societies is not left to the unguided, even if experienced, sage sitting under the spreading oak tree."

64. *R v. Wilkes* (1779) 4 Burr. Rep. 2527, 2539.

65. *Osborn v. The Bank of the United States,* 22 U.S. 738, 866 (1824).

66. Cardozo, *supra* note 6, at 60–61.

principles. He is not to yield to spasmodic sentiment, to vague and unregulated benevolence. He is to exercise a discretion informed by tradition,
methodized by analogy, disciplined by system, and subordinated to "the
primordial necessity of order in the social life." Wide enough in all conscience is the field of discretion that remains.[67]

Professor Hart also addressed the limitations on judicial discretion:

> At this point judges may again make a choice which is neither arbitrary nor
> mechanical, and have often displayed characteristic judicial virtues, the
> special opportunities to which the legal decision explains why some feel
> reluctant to call such judicial activity "legislative." The virtues are: impar-
> tiality and neutrality in surveying the alternatives; consideration for the
> interest of who will be affected, and a concern to deploy some acceptable
> general principle as a reasoned basis for decision.[68]

Thus, there are two main types of limitations: procedural and substantive.

Limited Judicial Discretion: Procedural Limitations

The way in which a judge chooses among the options open to him is not
left to his unbridled discretion. There are limitations on the procedure he
must follow and on the traits he must exhibit during this process.[69] These
limitations may be grouped under the general heading "fairness." The
fundamental characteristic of the process is impartiality.[70] The judge
must treat the parties equally, giving them an equal opportunity during
the trial. He must not have any personal interest, however remote, in the
outcome of the case. He must give the parties an opportunity to air their
arguments. The discretion must be based on the evidence that comes
before the judge. His decision must be reasoned. This requirement that
the judge explain his decision is especially important. Anyone who has
had experience in writing opinions knows this. An idea that takes over a

---

67. B. Cardozo, *The Nature of the Judicial Process* 141 (1921).

68. Hart, *supra* note 12, at 200.

69. This issue is not unique to judicial discretion. It exists in every discretion: see
Summers, "Evaluating and Improving Legal Processes—A Plea for 'Process Values,'"
60 *Cornell L.R.* 1 (1974).

70. See Eckhof, "Impartiality, Separation of Powers and Judicial Independence," 9
Scandinavian Studies in Law 11 (1965); Lucke, "The Common Law: Judicial Impartiality
and Judge-Made Law," 98 *Law Q. Rev.* 29 (1982); Hoeflich and Deutch, "Judicial
Legitimacy and the Disinterested Judge," 6 *Hofstra L. Rev.* 749 (1978).

person's thinking is one thing. Quite another thing altogether is putting it into words. Many are the ideas whose downfall was brought about by the need to explain them, since they contained only external force for which it proved impossible to find a foundation. The duty of giving reasons is among the most important challenges facing a judge who seeks to exercise discretion. Justice Landau described this in the following words:

> Judging through the use of discretion must not become arbitrary judging. There is no better tested way of avoiding this danger than the full explanation of the judgment. This kind of explanation trains the judge to think clearly and to raise his reasons—including his intuitive thoughts, to which Pound referred—above his subconscious, to the light of day, in order that they should stand the test of criticism by the appeals court, by professionals, and by the general public.[71]

These procedural limitations place restrictions on the judge's behavior inside as well as outside the courthouse. He must act with propriety in the courtroom. He must also act with propriety outside the courtroom. Judging is not a profession. It is a way of life. Thus, the judge must distance himself from the parties and their lawyers during the conduct of the trial. He must lead his life in a way that is consistent with his judicial office. In the words of Judge Robinson,

> One given the power to render decisions in formal adjudicatory proceedings is accorded the highest of honors and gravest of responsibilities; those who take on this judicial role may no longer participate in the daily intercourse of life as freely as do others. They have a duty to the judicial system in which they have accepted membership fastidiously to safeguard their integrity—at the expense if need be of "neighbours, friends and acquaintances, business and social relations." This is their "part" in their "day and generation" and one who is unwilling to make the sacrifices is unsuited to the office.[72]

From this flow the rules of ethics—the written and the unwritten—that guide the judge in the execution of his judicial function. These rules must strike a balance between the limitations placed on a person in his capacity as a judge and the freedom that must be given the judge as a person. Care must be taken not to exaggerate either side in this balance. Too much freedom might affect the fairness of the judicial process. It is

---

71. Landau, *supra* note 17, at 303.
72. *Professional Air Traffic Controllers Org. v. F.L.R.A.*, 685 F.2d 547, 599 (1982).

not enough that justice be done; justice must also appear to have been done. Judges work and live in a glass tower. The public follows their behavior in the courthouse as well as outside it. Whoever does not act appropriately outside the court will lose the public's confidence that he will act appropriately within the four walls of the courthouse. Yet one should also not exaggerate in the other direction, isolating him from the society in which he lives. A judge must know the moods of the society in which he serves as a judge. He must know the nation and the variety of its problems. He must, therefore, come into contact with the general public. I discussed this issue in a case:

> One should not go from one extreme to the other. One must not erect a wall between the judge and the society in which he operates. The judge is a part of his people. At times he is in an ivory tower, but this tower is in the hills of Jerusalem and not in the Greek Olympus. A judge is a citizen, and a good judge must be a good citizen. He must do his share in the building of his society.[72a]

It follows that it is appropriate for the judge to assume nonlegal functions, although he must limit himself to those activities—which are many and varied—that do not affect the public's confidence in the judicial system.

Limited Judicial Discretion: Substantive Limitations (Reasonableness)

Are there substantive limitations on judicial discretion? Of course, the judge must act on the basis of the accepted rules of interpretation and on the basis of the rules of the system related to the common law and to filling gaps in the system. When he does so, however, and within the framework of these parameters, are substantive limitations imposed upon the exercise of judicial discretion? Thus, for example, the judge examines the linguistic options of the statutory rule. He faces a number of possibilities as to the legislative goal. Do the rules of the system place limitations on the use of judicial discretion from this stage on?

The question is far from easy. The answer depends on one's philosophical conception of law and on one's views concerning legal reasoning and the role of the judge in society.[73] There are different approaches

---

72a. H.C. 547/84 *Caban v. Minister for Religious Affairs*, 40 P.D.(4) 141.
73. See Hart, *supra* note 12; J. Raz, *supra* note 12; MacCormick, *supra* note 20.

to these issues. The Naturalists disagree with the Realists, and both of these groups disagree with the Positivists. All agree that the judge may not simply flip a coin and decide, based on the result, among the various possibilities. Yet there is no common approach to the types of factors that the judge may weigh. Some insist that a judge apply objective criteria in making decisions. Others leave it to the subjective feeling of the judge. For my part, I do not have adequate training to take a philosophical stand in the argument among the different philosophical schools. I can simply express my own view, my personal judicial philosophy, which is based, on the one hand, on a study of the various philosophical approaches, and, on the other hand, on my experience as a judge.

It appears to me that the substantive limitations may be summarized by the conclusion that the judge has a duty to exercise his discretion reasonably.[74] He must act as a reasonable judge would act in the circumstances of the case.[75]

The test for this is an objective one. It includes in its duty, of course, a prohibition against arbitrariness, yet it consists of more than this. At the center of this determination lies the requirement that the judicial discretion be rational[76] and that it consciously take into account the structure and development of the normative system, of the judicial institutions that create and apply these norms, and of the interrelationships among the judicial and legislative and executive branches of government.

Sometimes the requirement of reasonableness will indicate a single solution. In these cases, no discretion will exist, in the final analysis. Often, however, the requirement of reasonableness will only point to a zone of reasonableness. The considerations of reasonableness will yield a wide zone, within which more than one possibility exists.[77] Reasonableness is essentially a process, not merely a result. Tossing a coin may lead to an appropriate outcome, yet the process cannot be called reasonable. Reasonableness is a conscious intellectual struggle among several

---

74. As I said in H.C. 547/84 *Off Haemak v. Ramat Yishai*, 40 P.D. (1), 113, 141: "The judge is not entitled to flip a coin. He is not entitled to consider any factor he likes. He must deliberate reasonably."

75. See Pollock, "Judicial Caution and Valour," 45 *Law Q. Rev.* 293, 294 (1929).

76. See Freund, "Rationality in Judicial Decisions," in 7 *Nomos, Rational Decisions* 107 (C. Friedrich, ed., 1964); H. Slesser, *The Art of Judgment And Other Studies* 36 (1962).

77. See H.C. 547/84, *supra* note 74, at 141.

lawful possibilities, with the judge applying objective standards. At times, these standards will point to more than one possibility. Then, the judge's solitary obligation is to choose from among the possibilities arrayed before him the one that seems best to him.[78] As Professor Raz said,

> Within the admitted boundaries of their law-making powers courts act and should act just as legislators do, namely, they should adopt those rules which they judge best. This is their only remaining legal duty. That it is a legal duty follows directly from the fact that by law the courts are not allowed to act arbitrarily; not even when making new law. They must exercise their judgment in order to reach the best solution.[79]

So, the use by judges of discretion in the choice of the possibility ''which they judge best'' is accomplished ''within the admitted boundaries of their law-making powers.'' Therefore, the choice of the best alternative is made within, not outside, the framework of the zone of reasonableness.[80]

Does this duty to act reasonably—including the duty to choose the best solution within the confines of the zone of reasonableness—negate the existence of judicial discretion? The answer is no. The zone of reasonableness often yields a number of possibilities, and the obligation to choose among the various possibilities in a reasonable manner does not force the judge to choose one particular option; rather, it places before him a number of possibilities. Thus, the reasonableness standard applied to two similar cases does not necessarily lead to identical solutions. Two reasonable judges might disagree, and yet act reasonably. A third judge, acting according to the reasonableness standard, might find himself in a veritable dilemma. There are many possible reasons for this. Even though the principle of reasonableness requires the judge to con-

78. See Clark, ''The Limits of Judicial Objectivity,'' 12 *Am. U. L. Rev.* 1, 10 (1963).

79. Raz, *supra* note 12, at 197.

80. In the quoted section, Professor Raz notes that the judge must act like the legislator. Nonetheless, he himself emphasizes that the limitations imposed on judicial discretion may cause the result the judge reaches to differ from the one the legislator reaches. Professor Raz (*supra* note 12 at 193): ''The limitation on the law-making power of the courts and the existence of legal duties which they are bound to observe in exercising such power may prevent the courts from adopting the best rule and may force them on occasion to settle for the second best.'' This phrasing does not seem to me to be successful, and the referral to the legislature may mislead. Both the judge and the legislator may want to achieve the ''best,'' but each one's ''best'' is different. The legislature's ''second best'' is the judge's ''best.''

sider various systemic factors, it does not establish exactly what weight must be given to these factors. As a result, different judges may arrive at different reasonable results. Here one recognizes the presence of judicial discretion.[81] Professor Kent Greenawalt emphasized this, saying,

> I believe . . . that when a judge is left to decide among controversial and complex theories of moral and social philosophy, each of which can find some support in our structure of government, all the legal profession demands and all the framers of states and constitutional provisions could reasonably expect is that a judge act reasonably and conscientiously choose the theories he thinks soundest. If these two requisites are met, we do not think the judge's actions merit blame, a typical consequence of a perceived failure to perform a duty, even though we would have acted differently. It is in this sense at least that we can say that a judge has discretion when faced with very difficult cases.[82]

And elsewhere he says, "The presence of a duty to decide conscientiously and an external standard of correct decision are not sufficient by themselves to signal the absence of discretion."[83]

Thus, procedural limitations (fairness) and substantive limitations (reasonableness) constrict the judge's freedom of choice, both with respect to the manner of choosing and with respect to the nature of factors that he may take into account. Yet even after all these have been resorted to, there will still be cases—surely not many—in which the judge will be free to choose among a number of possibilities, without having his choice directed by the legal system.

THE PROBLEM—DOES JUDICIAL DISCRETION EXIST?

Though limited, judicial discretion does exist. Yet this conclusion is contested by an entire stream in modern thought that holds that for each

81. See MacCormick, *supra* note 20, at 125: "The discretion is then indeed limited discretion: it is a discretion to give the decision which is best justified within those requirements, and that is the only discretion there is whether or not it is or can be often abused or transgressed (Quis custodiet ipsos custodes?) But although it is only such a limited discretion, it is not what Dworkin means by discretion in the 'weak' sense, with all that is implied in that. The requirement and the sustaining theory tell us by what modes of argument to justify a decision, they do not settle what decision is in the end *completely* justified. Within them/these may arise many issues of speculative disagreement which can in principle be resolved, but there is an inexhaustibly residual area of pure practical disagreement."

82. See Greenawalt, *supra* note 20, at 377.

83. Ibid., at 368.

legal problem—even the most difficult—there is one, and only one, lawful solution, which the judge is required to adopt. According to this approach, judicial discretion does not exist. Those who hold this view agree, of course, that judicial discretion is never absolute, yet they further maintain that by the same measure it is also not limited. In their opinion, there is no judicial discretion at all (in the meaning that we have given it), and all that remains is discretion in its mental sense, that is to say, the act of thinking. Indeed, they accept that the act of adjudication is not a mechanical activity, but rather an activity that requires weighing and balancing, yet they insist that at the end of this process, each legal problem—complex as it may be—has a single lawful solution that the judge must select.

Each Legal Problem Has One Lawful Solution

Professor Dworkin[84] and those who share his view[85] believe that each legal problem has one lawful solution. In their opinion, even in the hard cases, the judge is never free to choose among alternatives that are all inside the bounds of the law. According to this approach, even in the hard cases, the legal norm directs the judge, forcing him to choose one of the possibilities, and only that one. The hard cases, consequently, are not hard, and the judicial discretion in them is not discretion in the sense in which we are using the term. The hard cases are complicated, and they require study and weighing, but at the end of this study and on the basis of the existing normative guidelines, they have only one lawful solution. This approach stems from the general philosophical position that trumpets liberalism and natural rights.[86] This approach attempts to "take rights seriously."[87] These rights do not follow from judicial discretion, but rather they direct judicial discretion. Our rights, in the hard cases, are not in the hands of judges; rather, the judges must, in the hard cases, recognize our rights. According to this approach, law is a closed system that contains a solution to every difficult problem and that leaves no room for judicial discretion.[88] From this one gets the similarity between this

84. See *supra* note 16, and Dworkin, "No Right Answer?" 53 *N.Y.U.L. Rev.* 1 (1978).

85. See Sartorius, *supra* note 16.

86. Dworkin, "Liberalism," in *Public and Private Morality* (S. Hampshire, ed., 1978); Dworkin, "Natural Law Revisited," 34 *U. Fla. L. Rev.* 165, 168 (1982).

87. R. Dworkin, *supra* note 16.

88. See Dworkin, "Law's Ambitions for Itself," 71 *Va. L. Rev.* 173 (1985).

approach and the declaratory theory of law, according to which the judge does not "invent" or "create" new legal norms but instead "uncovers" and "reveals" legal norms already recognized by the existing law.

The Legal Rules That Guide the Judge

Professor Dworkin's approach is an interpretive approach.[89] Its starting point is a text—statutory or judicial—that has to be interpreted. He agrees, to be sure, both that there are difficult texts that raise problems of interpretation and that on occasion the interpreter will have several possibilities. But he claims that the interpreter must not give up, must not turn to his own discretion. Even in these hard cases, the law directs the interpreter in the choice among the different possibilities, while requiring him to choose one particular alternative, and it compels him to reject all the others. What is this guidance that the law gives the interpreter? Here Dworkin distinguishes between the normative direction in the matter of interpreting a statute and the normative direction concerning the interpretation of a precedent.

In the field of statutory law, the rule Dworkin champions is that the judge must give each statute the interpretation that best achieves the principles and policies that will justify it maximally as a political creation at the time of its enactment. He writes,

> The impact of the statute on the law is determined by asking which interpretation, of the different interpretations admitted by the abstract meaning of the term, best advances the set of principles and policies that provides the best political justification for the statute at the time it was passed.[90]

As for precedent, the legal rule that the judge must follow is that he must establish the ruling that will best realize the principles established in the system as a whole.[91]

According to this approach, there is a difference between the legal

89. See Dworkin, "Law as Interpretation," 60 *Tex. L. Rev.* 527 (1982).

90. Dworkin, *supra* note 84, at 68.

91. R. Dworkin, *supra* note 16, at 116: "But if the gravitational force of precedent rests on the idea that fairness requires the consistent enforcement of rights, then Hercules must discover principles that fit, not only the particular precedent to which some litigant directs his attention, but all other judicial decisions within his general jurisdiction and, indeed, statutes as well, so far as these must be seen to be generated by principle rather than policy."

norms that a judge must follow in interpreting a statute and those he must follow in interpreting a precedent. Dworkin says,

> His "interpretation" of judicial enactment will be different from his interpretation of statutes in one important respect. When he interprets statutes he fixes to some statutory language . . . argument of principle or policy that provide the best justification of that language in light of the legislature's responsibilities. His argument remains an argument of principle; he uses policy to determine what rights the legislature has already created. But when he "interprets" judicial enactments he will fix to the relevant language only arguments of principle, because the rights thesis argues that only such arguments acquire the responsibility of the enacting court."[92]

The difference between the legal norms that decide the interpretation of a statute and the legal norms that decide the interpretation of a judicial precedent is twofold: first, in the matter of a statute, the judge must give effect to the principles and policies that justify that statute to the greatest extent. He need not take into account the entirety of legislative enactments. As far as precedent is concerned, on the other hand, the judge must give effect to the entire system. Second, for a statute, both the principles and the policies that underlie it must be given effect, while for precedent, only the principles, and not the policies, need be considered. The reason for this distinction stems from Dworkin's approach, according to which a precedent radiates from within it principles that may be relied upon by analogy, whereas statutes are limited to their context alone.

A Critique of Dworkin's Approach: Judicial Discretion Exists

Much has been written about Dworkin's approach.[93] His position regarding judicial discretion stems from his position on the law and from his general philosophical conception, which I cannot examine because I do not have the necessary tools. Yet it appears to me that a general examination is not essential for critiquing Dworkin's attitude toward the narrow issue before us, whose subject is judicial discretion. For a number of reasons, I do not accept his approach.

First, Dworkin assumes the existence of two legal norms that bind the

---

92. Ibid., at 111.
93. See *Ronald Dworkin and Contemporary Jurisprudence* (M. Cohen, ed., 1984).

judge and that solve the hard cases. He has not proven this assumption.[94] For myself, I am not aware of any legal system in which Dworkin's two rules are accepted. Thus, for example, it does not seem to me that everyone would agree that there is a rule of interpretation according to which the statute must be given the interpretation that accords it maximum political justification at the time of its enactment. One has trouble finding support in the legal literature for this view. I prefer to say—and even this may be debatable—that one must give the statute the interpretation that best integrates it into the complex of values (the principles, policies, and standards) of the society, such as they exist at the time of the decision, while preserving the system's coherence and its organic growth and taking into account the institutional and interinstitutional problems of adjudication. As for Dworkin's "interpretive" rule regarding precedent, I know of no rule according to which the judge must consider and give effect to the body of principles, yet not to the policies of the system. Here, too, I would argue that the rule of interpretation is identical to that which exists with respect to legislation, that is, giving the precedent the interpretation that best integrates it with the array of the society's values (principles, policies, and standards), as they exist when the decision is given, while protecting the system's coherence and organic development and considering the institutional and interinstitutional problems of adjudication.

Second, even if we accept that Dworkin's proposed rules exist in some legal system, that would not negate the existence of judicial discretion in the hard cases. His rules are themselves legal rules. Like every legal rule, they too require interpretation. Whoever studies them learns quickly that there is uncertainty in these rules themselves and that there is more than one way of applying them. Thus, for example, much has been written about the question What are principles? and about how they are to be distinguished from policies.[95] Anyone who examines this literature is struck by the many problems involved in the very existence of such a distinction. A key expression in Dworkin's writings is "best justification." How is one to define the term "best"?

94. See Parent, "Interpretation and Justification in Hard Cases," 15 *Ga. L. Rev.* 99, 115 (1980).

95. See Raz, *supra* note 21; MacCormick, *supra* note 20; Hughes, *supra* note 41; Wellington, *supra* note 20.

Third, even if this terminology became clear, by what standard would the lawful solution be determined? One often finds several conflicting principles that apply to a given problem. Principles tend to come in pairs of opposites. How is the judge to decide among the opposing principles? Doesn't he have discretion in this situation? Moreover, at times it is possible to derive from the same principle rulings that are maximally consistent with it, but that contradict each other. How is this contradiction to be resolved, and why does the judge have no discretion in this resolution? Indeed, it appears that Dworkin himself and his supporters are aware of this possibility. Their response is that these situations are statistically insignificant.[96] Yet they offer no proof for this contention. In my view, these situations—which imply judicial discretion—are not rare at all.

Fourth, life experience teaches us (and Dworkin recognizes as much) that different judges, applying the same principle or policy, may reach different conclusions because of differences in their personal makeup. Yet Dworkin notes that the individual judge must decide for himself, and that from each judge's own point of view there is only one correct solution. But this is not the true state of affairs. If two reasonable judges, acting on the basis of the same principle, may legitimately arrive at different results, then a third judge, whose personality composition is complex, combining the personality traits of both his colleagues, may find himself in a real dilemma, with either choice he makes being lawful. Empirical studies bear this out. Thus, for example, Professor Alan Paterson, who researched the views of judges who served in the House of Lords in 1972 as well as those who had quit the bench yet who had served in the House of Lords between 1957 and 1973, concluded that the vast majority of them believe that in certain cases they faced a real dilemma of having to choose among several options, all of them lawful.[97]

Finally, it seems to me that Dworkin and those who share his view[98]

96. See Dworkin, *supra* note 84, at 30; Sartorius, *supra* note 33, at 203.

97. See Paterson, *supra* note 4, at 194.

98. See Sartorius, "Social Policy and Judicial Legislation," 8 *Am. Phil. Q.* 160: "A 'legislator' who is not entitled to appeal to anything other than pre-established authoritative legal standards in justification of his decision is simply not a legislator." I don't agree. A legislature such as this is not an all-powerful legislature, but it is still a legislature. A primary legislature acting within the framework of a constitution or a secondary legislature operating within the framework of a statute are limited by standards, yet this does not negate their legislative character.

do not sufficiently distinguish between the existence of judicial discretion and its limitations. Dworkin is correct in saying that the judge is not entitled to weigh every factor he likes. He must not be arbitrary or discriminatory; he must act fairly and reasonably. Principles and policies restrict his discretion.[99]

Yet it does not follow that after these conditions are met, only one solution remains.[100] As we have seen, even if principles and policies obligate the judge, they do not negate judicial discretion, but rather they simply limit it. Professor Raz discussed this in the following terms:

> The thesis of judicial discretion does not entail that in cases where discretion may be exercised anything goes. Such cases are governed by laws which rule out certain decisions. The only claim is that the laws do not determine any decision as the correct one.[101]

Dworkin's error lies, in my opinion, in that from the existence of limitations on judicial discretion, he concludes the absence of discretion. Such is not the case. As Professor Tedeschi wrote,

> The existence of the statutory rules, because of their obscure nature, does not go so far as to establish only one solution as the correct solution for every problem—even if the faithful interpreter will have to view these rules as disqualifying certain solutions.[102]

One may, in this regard, liken the judge to a secondary legislature. The secondary legislature, too, operates in a given framework, has a limited number of possibilities open to it. The statute restricts the scope of considerations. Yet in the context of all of these, the secondary legislature exercises discretion. The same is true for the judge. He has limited, not absolute, discretion. Yet in the context of these limitations, discretion exists, for the limitations are neither sufficiently encompassing nor sufficiently clear to provide an answer to every question that arises.

---

99. See G. Gottlieb, *supra* note 32, at 110, 117.

100. See MacCallum, "Dworkin on Judicial Discretion," 60 *J. of Phil.* 638, 640 (1963).

101. See Raz, *supra* note 21, at 843; Greenawalt, *supra* note 20, at 386: "It is also wrong to suppose that judges have no discretion in deciding on results, even if they do have a duty conscientiously to search for the best possible results and even if there is some ultimate theoretically objective standard for determining which results are correct."

102. Tedeschi, *supra* note 27, at 41.

JUDICIAL DISCRETION—IN EVERY CASE?

The Problem

I have argued that the law recognizes judicial discretion, albeit limited. Thus, I rejected the approach of those who believe that for each legal problem there is one lawful solution, and that therefore judicial discretion does not exist. Now I must contend with another front. Assuming judicial discretion exists, in which cases does it exist? Is my approach, according to which it exists only in some cases—those I have called hard cases—correct, or does judicial discretion in fact exist in every judicial decision? Of course, this question is not important to those who hold, like Dworkin, that judicial discretion does not exist at all. Yet the question is important to those who maintain, as I do, that judicial discretion exists. For those who share this latter view, it is important to know whether they think judicial discretion exists in every judicial decision regarding the application of a norm or regarding a norm itself, or whether, even according to their view, judicial discretion is limited only to special situations and to special judicial decisions in hard cases.

My thesis is that judicial discretion does not exist in all judicial decisions, but only in some. Moreover, most judicial determinations—though they always entail a mental element of thought, balancing, and weighing—do not involve judicial discretion. These are the easy cases and the intermediate cases. Only in a minority of judicial decisions does the judge face not only a mental state of thought and weighing, but also judicial discretion. These are the hard cases. Thus, along the broad spectrum between those who hold that every judicial decision involves judicial discretion and those who argue that no judicial discretion exists, I find myself occupying a middle ground. According to my position, every judicial decision requires a mental condition of thought and weighing. Yet, in some decisions, the easy cases and the intermediate cases, no judicial discretion is involved. In these situations, I concur with those who deny the existence of judicial discretion, yet I do not agree with them completely. In my opinion, not every case is an easy case or an intermediate case. Indeed, I believe that in some judicial decisions, judicial discretion exists. These are the hard cases. In these situations, I share the view of those who hold that the judicial decision involves judicial discretion. We part ways when those who hold that view insist that every judicial decision involves discretion, whereas in my view only some judicial decisions involve judicial discretion.

Furthermore, as to the internal division between the different types of decisions, my view is that the majority of judicial decisions do not involve judicial discretion. In my opinion, most cases are easy or intermediate. Only a minority of judicial decisions involve judicial discretion. Indeed, this relationship is essential, in my view, in order to guarantee security and stability in the legal system, while allowing for change and renovation.

Judicial Discretion in Every Case

I do not know whether any philosophers take the view that every decision involves judicial discretion. Of course, some well-known philosophical approaches, accepted in Europe (for example, the "free law" movement[103]) and in the United States (for example, the "Realists"[104]), recognized judicial discretion. Yet I do not find in these schools support for a contention that discretion exists in every case. In the United States today, a neo-Realist approach—Critical Legal Studies—is gaining currency.[105] The members of this philosophical school hold that the text and the various rules of interpretation do not lead one to a single lawful solution. Instead, the court, through its exercise of discretion, which is guided by its political worldview, gives meaning to the legal norm. Yet I doubt that even the holders of this view would claim that all rules, in all cases, provide a basis for judicial discretion. After the Israeli Motor Vehicles Accident Compensation Law (1975) established absolute liability for the use of a motor vehicle, could any knowledgeable lawyer argue that a horse is a motor vehicle? Be this as it may, it seems to me that the commonly accepted view is that not every legal norm gives rise to judicial discretion in every situation. Indeed, any other view would result in chaos and would prevent normal social relations.[106] If every rule creates judicial discretion in every situation, then no person would have any rights. Such a state of affairs is inconceivable. Who would be foolish enough to carry out contracts, honor obligations, and act lawfully, if, irrespective of his behavior, he would have a colorable argument that the

103. The French "Libre recherche scientifique" and the German "Freirechtslehre": see J. Stone, *Legal System and Lawyers' Reasonings* 219 (1964).

104. See J. Harris, *Legal Philosophies* 83 (1980); Fuller, "American Legal Realism," 82 *U. Pa. L. Rev.* 429 (1934).

105. For bibliography see Kennedy and Klare, "A Bibliography of Critical Legal Studies," 94 *Yale L.J.* 461 (1984).

106. See J. Raz, *Practical Reason and Norms* 137 (1975).

opposing party lacked any right? One should bear in mind that the courts deal with only a small fraction of the legal activities that exist in a legal system at a given time. If the approach that postulates that no problem has only one lawful solution were correct, one would expect the courts to be flooded with lawsuits, since each side would have some chance of prevailing. This approach would change the psychology of the life of law into a pathological system. Indeed, just as there is life outside hospitals, so is there law outside courts. The majority of citizens obey the law and have no qualms about what is legal and what is illegal. Most legal norms do not generate any controversy, since the order they establish is clear, simple, and known, and there is no room for legitimate contrary views.

The Easy Cases

Indeed, many are the legal norms whose meaning with respect to a given system of facts is so simple and clear that their application involves no judicial discretion. Some of these norms require only the most cursory study and examination in order to realize that for the purpose of deciding in the conflict, there is no room for judicial discretion. These are the easy cases.[107] Once the Motor Vehicles Accident Compensation Law (1975) fixes absolute liability for the use of a motor vehicle, the judge has no discretion when asked to rule whether riding a horse and driving a car both constitute using a motor vehicle. The negative answer to the former case and the positive response to the latter are as clear as day to every lawyer. They are derived by means of logical deduction against the background of the purpose of the legislative text. Two options do not exist. There is only one possibility, only one lawful solution, and the judge must choose this solution.

One must not conclude from this view that the easy cases do not require interpretation. According to my approach, the judge arrives at the conclusion that he has no discretion only after going through a process of interpretation. Every legal norm necessitates a process of interpretation. As Professor Guido Tedeschi wrote,

> "In claris non fit interpretatio": Although this phrase is not classical Roman, it is hallowed because of its long tradition, and it is known to all the lawyers of the world. However, scholars of recent generations increasingly recognize the fact that the view embedded within it, that the rule—if only the "clear"

107. See Schauer, "Easy Cases," 58 *S. Calif. L. Rev.* 399 (1985).

rule—may speak for itself, is too facile. Someone else's idea cannot work within us unless we absorb it, unless we give the cooperation that constitutes the interpretive process; whether the interpretation is difficult and exhausting, or mere child's play. And, even in the latter case, whatever the interpretation, it is precisely the ease and confidence with which it is made, that permit us to conclude that the text or the behavior at issue is clear. The holding of the Latin saying we quoted is no more correct—if such a comparison may be permitted us—than that which asserts that light foods do not require digestion. For even here, the ease and speed of the digestion are exactly what prove the lightness of the food. Otherwise, no meaning whatsoever should be ascribed to a holding such as this.[108]

In Cr. App. 92/80, *Gov Ari Ltd. v. Local Council for Planning and Building, Netanya,*[109] I wrote, "Even the most simple and clear rule appears to us in its simplicity, only after we have passed it, consciously or unconsciously, through the melting pot of our interpretive conception." Indeed, "the meaning of the words of the statute is not self-evident, but rather they require interpretation. Each of us deals with interpretation all the time. Every text requires interpretation, and every statute requires interpretation."[110] To understand means to interpret. The determination that only one correct solution exists does not advance or dispense with the interpretive process. It constitutes the fruit and result of the process.

Therefore, a case is an easy case if, after a process of interpretation, the interpreter arrives at the clear conclusion that there is only one lawful solution to the controversy before him. What is unique to most of these cases is that the interpreter arrives at his inevitable conclusion through an unconscious process of interpretation, one that is based for the most part on logical deduction against the background of the clear purpose of the statutory goal. The result is reached as though it were self-evident. Indeed, every knowledgeable lawyer who dealt with the same question would reach the same result, immediately and without any need for detailed examination, since the legal question at issue has only one lawful solution. A judge who reached a different result would arouse amazement. The legal community would raise its eyebrows and wonder

108. Tedeschi, *supra* note 27, at 1.
109. 35 P.D.(4) 764, 769.
110. H.C. 47/83 *Tur Avir (Israel) Ltd. v. The Chairman of the Restricted Practices Board* 39 P.D. (1) 169, 174.

what had happened to the judge, for him to have made such a gross error,[111] and would say that in his ruling there was a "twisting of the written word, like calling day night and night day."[112]

In the context of precedent, there are also easy cases. This is the situation when the conflict is completely controlled within the borders of a precedent that is accepted by both the judge and the legal community as a correct one. In this event, there is no judicial discretion as to whether or not to deviate from that rule. The court must apply the earlier rule, and for the most part, it will do so unconsciously. At times, the ruling will be cited by name, primarily for the sake of brevity and for avoiding the need to go into detail. Justice Alfred Witkon, who also distinguished among different types of cases, discussed this:

> One group raises no problem at all because the judge's view fully coincides with the existing precedent. In those instances the earlier case is referred to not necessarily for its binding or persuasive authority, but merely by way of shorthand, in order to avoid repetition.[113]

Thus, in broad areas of law and life, the legal norm (whether statutory or common law) and its application do not give the judge freedom to choose among different possibilities.[114] It is clear to every knowledgeable lawyer, usually as an intuitive matter, that in the stated circumstances norm X applies, its meaning is Y, and its application in the circumstances of the case necessitates result Z. Justice Cardozo referred to this:

> In countless litigations, the law is so clear that judges have no discretion. They have the right to legislate within gaps, but often there are no gaps. We shall have a false view of the landscape if we look at the waste spaces only, and refuse to see the acres already sown and fruitful.[115]

It must be emphasized that the norm and its application are not clear in the abstract, but rather in relation to a particular set of facts, a given controversy. A change in the facts or a change in the evidentiary basis of the conflict may produce a situation of judicial discretion. Only by

111. See Edwards, *supra* note 2, at 390.
112. H.C. 1/50 *supra* note 39, at 70.
113. Witkon, *supra* note 17, at 480.
114. See Pound, "Discretion, Dispensation and Mitigation: The Problem of the Individual Special Case," 35 *N.Y.U.L. Rev.* 925, 930 (1960).
115. See Cardozo, *supra* note 67, at 129.

comparing the norm to the fact can one obtain an answer to the question whether or not judicial discretion exists. Furthermore, the norm and its application involve no judicial discretion only in relation to a given normative system. A change in the normative system—such as new legislation or new case law or a change in the approach to the rules of interpretation—may produce a situation of judicial discretion, such as the need for a judicial determination because of a conflict between different norms. Indeed, the "ease" of the case is always relative. The case is easy in relation to given facts and in relation to a given normative system. The legal norm operates in a given time and place.[116] A change in these may cause the easiest of cases to become the most difficult of cases.

Intermediate Cases

Intermediate cases are characterized by the fact that, in the final analysis, the judge has no discretion in deciding them. From this perspective, they are easy cases. What sets them apart from the easy cases is only that in the intermediate cases both sides appear to have a legitimate legal argument supporting their position. A conscious act of interpretation is needed before the judge can conclude that the argument is in fact groundless and that there is only one lawful solution.[117] Every lawyer who belongs to the legal community of which we spoke will come to this conclusion—that only one lawful solution exists—such that if a judge were to decide otherwise, the community's reaction would be that he was mistaken. Here are some typical situations: first, a legal norm (statutory or common law) is at first glance capable of two or more interpretations, but close analysis indicates that only one interpretation is possible. Take a statute whose words allow of several meanings. Yet examination of the purpose of the legislation indicates unambiguously that only one of the linguistic meanings is possible and that any other meaning is absurd. If the legal community reaches one clear conclusion in its determination, then one may say that the legal argument that is based solely on the statutory language and that arrives at an absurd conclusion is not correct, and there is no discretion in the interpretation of that rule; second, study

116. See Levi, "The Nature of Judicial Reasoning," 32 *U. Chi. L. Rev.* 395, 405 (1965).

117. See Edwards, *supra* note 2, at 393.

of the applicable normative system indicates that there exists a legal norm that, if it applied to the case, would support a certain possibility. Closer analysis, however, suggests that the norm does not apply. This is so, for example, when it is clear from the circumstances that a previous general statute is displaced by a more recent and more specific statute.[118] Or when it is evident from the circumstances that the "precedent" is not relevant and this latter determination is an easy case. In all these cases, and in many others, after a conscious balancing and weighing—which at times require a concerted, serious effort—and in the framework of the accepted rules, every knowledgeable lawyer will reach the conclusion that only one possibility exists and that there is no judicial discretion.

The Hard Cases

Alongside easy and intermediate cases are the hard cases.[119] In these—and only in these—the judge is faced with a number of possibilities, all of which are lawful within the context of the system. Only in these cases does judicial discretion exist. In these situations, the choice is not between lawful and unlawful, but between lawful and lawful.[120] A number of lawful solutions exist. To be sure, the discretion is limited, not absolute: the judge is not entitled to weigh any factor he likes. Yet within the framework of the limitations, and after they have been exhausted, there is freedom of choice,[121] that "sovereign prerogative of choice" Justice Holmes described.[122]

118. See F. Bennion, *Statutory Interpretation* 434 (1984).

119. As we saw this expression "hard cases," in the present context, comes from Professor Dworkin. Other writers used similar expressions. Thus, for example, Professor Weiler referred to "trouble cases": see Weiler, "Legal Values and Judicial Decision-Making," 48 *Can. Bar Rev.* 1, 30 (1970). Judge Edwards calls these cases "very hard" cases: see Edwards, *supra*, note 2, 395. Cardozo termed the decision in this type of cases a "serious business": see Cardozo, *supra* note 67, at 21, when he says: "It is when the colors do not match, when the references in the index fail, when there is no decisive precedent, that the business of the judge begins." On the other hand, Professor Raz calls these cases "unregulated disputes": see Raz *supra*, note 12, at 180, without giving any description of their degree of difficulty.

120. See Witkon, *supra* note 17, at 480: "It is always easy to decide between right and wrong; the difficulty begins where you have to decide between two kinds of right." See also Traynor, "*Le Rude Vita, La Dolce Giustizia,* Or Hard Cases Can Make Good Law," 29 *U. Chi. L. Rev.* 223, 239 (1962).

121. See MacCormick, *supra* note 20, at 250.

122. See O. Holmes, *Collected Legal Papers* 239 (1921).

This book focuses on the hard cases, and only on them. The troublesome questions about them are legion. What sets these cases apart, and how are they created? Is it possible to prevent them? Are they desirable? How can they be made to coalesce with the status of the judicial branch in the context of the separation of powers and the democratic system? How is the choice among the different possibilities made? Is it possible to develop a theoretical model for making the best choice? What is the role of judicial subjectivity and judicial intuition in making the choice? To what extent can one guarantee that the choice will be "objective," and to what extent will it be influenced by the personality and judicial worldview of the judge?

We have seen that classifying a case as an easy case is a relative issue. The same is true of classifying a case as a difficult case. A change in the facts or in the normative framework may quickly turn a hard case into an easy case. Nothing is hard in the abstract. The case is hard in relation to a given constellation of facts and norms. A case that is hard in a given normative-factual framework may cease to be difficult with a change in one of these components. Moreover, what turns a case into a difficult case is not the amount of thought that must be invested in it or in the quantity of weighing and study that must be accorded it. These may be great or small, according to the case. What makes a case hard is simply the fact that it does not have one lawful solution, and the judge is faced with the need to decide among a number of lawful solutions. The decision itself may, in the final analysis, be an easy one for the judge.

Judicial Discretion—In How Many Cases?

One might well ask about the internal division among the different cases, and especially about the frequency with which hard cases come before the court. The accepted view is that most of the cases that come before the courts are not hard cases.[123] In the words of Justice Cardozo, "Nine-tenths, perhaps more, of the cases that come before a court are predetermined—predetermined in the sense that they are predestined—their fate preestablished by inevitable laws that follow them from birth to

123. See Tate, "The Law-Making Function of the Judge," 28 *La. L. Rev.* 211 (1968); Llewellyn, *supra* note 28, at 25; Clark and Trubek, "The Creative Role of the Judge: Restraint and Freedom in the Common-Law Tradition," 71 *Yale L.J.* 255, 256 (1961); Friendly, "Reactions of a Lawyer-Newly Become Judge," 71 *Yale L.J.* 218, 222 (1961).

death.''[124] At the appeals level, the proportion of hard cases rises, although one gets the impression that most appeals fall into the category of easy cases or, even more often, intermediate cases. In the Supreme Court, the number of hard cases is even greater, and it is particularly large if the appeal is by permission only, since the courts sometimes tend, in their granting of permission, to give priority to hard cases. From this standpoint, the Israeli Supreme Court is atypical of the highest instance in most systems, since a sizeable part of its jurisdiction over appeals is obligatory jurisdiction. Although more hard cases come to the Supreme Court than to other levels, most of the matters it deals with still do not fall into the category of hard cases.

The typical situation, in which a significant percentage of the decisions of a system's supreme court fall into the group of hard cases, creates the impression that a substantial share of all the legal decisions in the system are within the realm of the hard cases. This is an unfortunate optical error. Only a small part of all the decisions in a system are in the sphere of hard cases, and only a small percentage of all the cases that are brought before the various instances raise problems of judicial discretion. The great resonance given to the decisions of the system's highest instance in the hard cases need not obscure the balance of the complete picture.

The Distinction among the Three Types of Cases

We saw that classifying a conflict as an easy case or a hard case—and of course also as an intermediate case—is a relative matter. A small change in the facts or in the law may move the conflict from one category to another. Moreover, the borderlines among the different categories are not precise. It is impossible to specify exactly where the border between the easy cases and the intermediate cases lies, for the standard for distinguishing between them—consciousness and the apparent existence of arguments—is itself inexact. The distinction between these two and the hard cases is also difficult. We do not possess an instrument that lets us distinguish in a precise manner between a lawful possibility and an unlawful possibility. The terminology of the legal community does not permit sharp distinctions. Indeed, we are dealing not with an enduring and precise physical structure, but rather with a fragile and obscure

124. Cardozo, *supra* note 6, at 60.

theoretical structure.[125] A change in the facts, a change in the law, a change in the conception of the legal community all produce a change in categorization. Furthermore, it is not only that the bridges among categories are not solid, but also that the categories themselves are not fixed. We are dealing with a normative creation that is in constant flux and with normative categories that have wide margins of uncertainty. Yet there is in these categories also a solid nucleus of certainty. Around these solid nucleii rotates the entire structure, with all its broad spectrum.[126]

A Retrospective Look

One may observe the process of the exercise of judicial discretion from the point of view of the judge after he has ruled on the law. At this stage there exists, with respect to the facts that were before him, only one lawful solution. Each judge is convinced either that this is the appropriate solution (if he is in the majority) or that it is an inappropriate solution and that there exists another, appropriate solution (if he is in the minority). Any solution other than that at which the judge arrived is inappropriate. Justice Cardozo described this well:

> The curious thing is that sometimes in the hardest cases, in cases where the misgivings have been greatest at the beginning, they are finally extinguished and extinguished most completely. I have gone through periods of uncertainty so great, that I have sometimes said to myself, "I shall never be able to vote in this case either one way or the other." Then, suddenly the fog has lifted. I have reached a stage of mental peace. I know in a vague way that there is doubt whether my conclusion is right. I must needs admit the doubt in view of the travail that I suffered before landing at the haven. I cannot quarrel with anyone who refuses to go along with me; and yet, for me, however it may be for others, the judgment reached with so much pain has become the only possible conclusion, the antecedent doubts merged, and finally extinguished in the calmness of conviction.[127]

A retrospective look is dangerous, for it may create the erroneous impression that a hard case turned into an easy case or into an intermediate case. Even in retrospect, and after the judge has become convinced of the correctness of a certain solution, he must not deny the existence of an

125. See B. Cardozo, *The Paradoxes of Legal Science* 2 (1928).
126. See MacCormick, *supra* note 20, at 198; Raz, *supra* note 12, at 206.
127. Cardozo, *supra* note 125, at 80.

additional lawful solution. Therefore we must not view the process in retrospect, but rather from the point of view of one observing its outset. For even the experience of Justice Cardozo shows how important it is to be aware of the different stages of thought and of the difficulties that characterize each one of them. Only then is it possible for the judge to reach the mental peace and calmness that Justice Cardozo described. Only by doing intellectual battle at the beginning of the process will he experience intellectual satisfaction at its end.

Chapter 2
The Substantive
Sources of
Judicial Discretion

TYPES OF SOURCES

Formal, Substantive, Extralegal, and Legal Sources

The question What are the sources of discretion? has four aspects. The first concerns the legal basis for the judge's authority to choose among lawful alternatives. This aspect answers the question Who authorized the judge to exercise discretion? It examines what may be called the formal legitimacy of the judge's exercise of discretion. The second aspect concerns the analytical-legal basis for the existence of the freedom of choice. This aspect grapples with the following question: What causes there to be judicial discretion? It examines the nature of the judicial norm itself, in order to deal with the reasons for judicial discretion. The third aspect deals with the extralegal basis for the existence of judicial discretion. This aspect seeks to answer the question Is it desirable from a societal standpoint to grant discretion to the judge? It examines the various factors that are to be taken into account in deciding the sociological question of whether it is desirable to give discretion to judges. The fourth and final aspect also has a legal basis. The aim of this aspect is to answer the question In a situation where the judge is given discretion, how should he exercise it? The fourth aspect lies at the heart of this book, yet before dealing with that, I must examine the other three aspects. In this chapter I will address the second aspect, which concerns the analytical-legal basis for judicial discretion.

Substantive Sources

Why is there, in the substantive plane, judicial discretion in the establishment and application of the legal norm? Why is it that there are hard
cases? Why isn't every case an easy case or an intermediate case? Is there
something in the legal norm and in law in general that makes judicial
discretion unavoidable? Is it possible—even if it were desirable—to
prevent the existence of judicial discretion? Are the human mind, which
does not delve deep enough, and the human eye, which does not see far
enough, at the basis of judicial discretion? In order to respond to these
questions, I will examine the legal norm itself and the ways it is created,
beginning with the statutory norms and going on to deal with the other
norms. In this discussion, I will not pretend to undertake a comprehensive analysis covering all the possibilities. It is enough to emphasize
those issues that are important for our purpose.

SUBSTANTIVE SOURCES OF JUDICIAL DISCRETION
IN THE STATUTORY NORM

The statutory norm—such as a constitution, statute, or regulation—is a
general and binding legal norm created by a body authorized to do so, not
as an incidental consequence of adjudication. Every statutory norm has a
linguistic element. It is expressed in words. In addition, it has a "normative" component that establishes permission, prohibition, power, or
immunity. This summary description points to two substantive sources
that may serve as the basis for judicial discretion: the language of the
norm and its normative element.

The Uncertainty of Language

The statutory norm is expressed in the language of humans,[1] which is
composed of signs or symbols that have no independent internal meaning,[2] but rather constitute descriptions that are accepted by people who
speak the same language.[3] These descriptions do not always conjure up a

---

1. See Glanville Williams, "Language and the Law," 61 *Law Q. Rev.* 71, 293, 384
(1945); 62 *Law Q. Rev.* 387 (1946); Moore, "The Semantics of Judging," 54 *S. Cal. L.
Rev.* 151 (1981).
2. See A. Ross, *On Law and Justice* 111 (trans. M. Dutton, 1959).
3. See Ross, "Tu-Tu," 70 *Harv. L. Rev.* 812 (1957).

single, unitary image in the minds of all who use the same language, but rather they occasionally produce several images within the same user and occasionally different images within different users.[4] This is why the language of the statute is at times ambiguous,[5] vague, obscure,[6] and open-textured.[7]

Expressions such as "reasonable," "negligent," "good faith," "vehicle," and thousands of others fill the statute books. These are expressions that have multiple meanings. As a result, the content of the legal norm does not always produce only one possibility. As I said in one Supreme Court judgment,

> Indeed, the expression "concerning" is general, and it does not have an unambiguous content. It has an "open texture." Like it, there are many expressions in our language that are composed of words that constitute signs or symbols lacking in independent internal meaning. When this language is absorbed in our thinking, it does not conjure up a single, unitary image that is common to all those who use the language. Due to this very nature of the language, these descriptions generally produce a number of images. No one image is always, under all circumstances, dominant and exclusive. As a result, a number of meanings are attached to the statutory language.[8]

About this very same concept President Agranat said,

> Neither the spoken language nor the written language is a perfect means of communication. The meaning that the sender intended when he spoke or wrote them is not always, or is not necessarily, the meaning that the receiver gives them when he hears or reads them. The explanation for this phenomenon is that words, being only symbols, are simply like a meaningless empty vessel.[9]

These characteristics of language create a situation of uncertainty and raise a number of possibilities, all of which have a linguistic anchor. Of

---

4. See Chafee, "The Disorderly Conduct of Wards," 41 *Colum. L. Rev.* 381 (1941).

5. On ambiguity, see Empson, *Seven Types of Ambiguity* (1947); Williams, *supra* note 1; Moore, *supra* note 1, at 181; Ross, *supra* note 2, at 115; Miller, "Statutory Language and the Purposive Use of Ambiguity," 42 *Va. L. Rev.* 23 (1956).

6. On vagueness, see Christie, "Vagueness and Legal Language," 48 *Minn. L. Rev.* 885 (1964).

7. On the open texture of language see Hart, *supra* note 12, ch. 1, at 124; Raz, *supra* note 12, ch. 1, at 74; Moore, *supra* note 1, at 200.

8. H.C. 47/83 *supra* note 110, ch. 1, at 174.

9. Agranat, "The Contribution of the Judiciary to the Legislative Endeavor," 10 *Tel-Aviv U. L. Rev.* 233 (1984).

course, not all words are uncertain in all circumstances. If this were the case, it would be impossible for humans to communicate. The uncertainty varies with the different linguistic expressions. In addition, the lack of certainty is a function of the context. In some contexts uncertainty exists, while in others it disappears. The uncertainty of a text is always a function of a given system of facts and norms. Professor Julio Cueto-Rua emphasized this, saying, "[E]very rule of law may be clear with reference to certain facts but ambiguous or vague with reference to a different set of facts."[10]

Thus, despite the lack of certainty in language, people understand one another, and despite the lack of clarity of the statutory language, most statutory norms do not raise doubt. The reason for this is that we are constantly interpreting the language. "In order to get to the depth of the words' meaning," says President Agranat, "the addressee must interpret them."[11] "The meaning of the words of the statute are not self-evident; rather, they require interpretation. Each of us deals all the time with interpretation. Every text requires interpretation, and every statute requires interpretation."[12] To understand means to interpret. As a result of the act of interpretation, the lack of certainty embedded in the human language is eliminated, and communication between creator and reader is made possible.[13] The trouble is that legal interpretation cannot eliminate the uncertainty in every circumstance. As a result, a situation is created in which, alongside the statutory rules whose uncertainty the

10. Cueto-Rua, *supra* note 51, ch. 1, at 95.

11. Agranat, *supra* note 9, at 237.

12. H.C. 47/83, supra note 110, ch. 1, at 174.

13. This proposition raises difficult hermeneutic problems. This book is not the place to examine these problems, which are not unique to law. The literature on this subject is particularly vast. For everything having to do with interpretation in literature, see especially Jehl, *Interpretation: An Essay in the Philosophy of Literary Criticism* 198; Eagleton, *Literary Theory* (1983); Hirsch, *Validity of Interpretation* (1967); Hirsch, *The Aims of Interpretation* (1976); S. Fish, *Is There a Text in this Class?* (1986). On the connection between interpretation and literary interpretation, see *The Politics of Interpretation* (W. Mitchell, ed., 1983). Volume 60 of the *Texas Law Review* (pages 373–586) was devoted entirely to a symposium on law and literature. On the connection between interpretation in law and interpretation of a nonlegal text in general—not necessarily literary—see volume 58 of the *Southern California Law Review* (1985), which dedicated two issues (pages 1–725) to these questions. See also Herman, "Phenomenology, Structuralism, Hermeneutics and Legal Study: Applications of Contemporary Continental Thought to Legal Phenomena," 56 *U. Miami L. Rev.* 379, 402 (1982).

rules of interpretation succeeded in removing in certain circumstances, there are other rules, as to which the rules of interpretation were unable to remove the uncertainty in given circumstances. As a result, a situation of judicial discretion is created. The lack of certainty within the text is not eliminated—or is only partially eliminated—and one is left with a situation in which the statutory legal norm has a number of meanings, all of them lawful in the context of the system.

This state of affairs can be described by means of three concentric circles. In the innermost circle, closest to the core, are those circumstances as to which the meaning of the language is clear and simple. This follows from the unconscious application of the rules of interpretation. Only a single solution exists. These are the easy cases. In the middle circle one finds those circumstances as to which a situation of uncertainty may arise, yet after a conscious interpretive process, the uncertainty disappears. The application of the language of the statute in those circumstances becomes clear. There is only one lawful solution. These are the intermediate cases. In the outermost circle are all those circumstances as to which application of the statute creates a situation of uncertainty. This is the penumbra of which a number of authors have written.[14] In the framework of this outer circle, there are a number of possibilities, not just a single solution. Judicial discretion exists. Of course, the borderline between the various circles is not unambiguous. There are borderline cases along the border and even borderline cases on the borders of the borderline cases. Moreover, the circles are determined by the given factual[15] and normative system. If these change, a change also occurs in the circles themselves.

It is possible, of course, to undertake to minimize the uncertainty embedded in the language. The legislator generally tries to do so. Yet this effort cannot do away completely with the lack of certainty. Pro-

14. On the distinction between the "core" and the "penumbra" in interpretation, see Dickinson, "Legal Rules, Their Application and Elaboration," 79 *U. Pa. L. Rev.* 1052, 1084 (1931); Williams, *supra* note 1; Hart, *supra* note 12, ch. 1; Hart, "Positivism and the Separation of Law and Morals," 71 *Harv. L. Rev.* 593 (1958); Ross, *supra* note 2, at 114; Moore, *supra* note 1, at 181.

15. One should not, in my opinion, attribute to Professor Hart the view that there are expressions that are understood in all circumstances. From his writings, it emerges that his approach is only relative. For another view, see Fuller, "Positivism and Fidelity to Law— A Reply to Professor Hart," 71 *Harv. L. Rev.* 630 (1958).

fessor Hart wrote about this in the following terms: "In all fields of experience, not only that of rules, there is a limit, inherent in the nature of language, to the guidance which general language can provide."[16] Sometimes, the lack of certainty is intended: the legislator employs vague expressions knowing full well that they create uncertainty, because he wants to give the court the power to choose the appropriate alternative. Thus, regardless of whether the legislator seeks to avoid uncertainty or to create it, the statutory language cannot be fully certain in all circumstances. Uncertainty, inherent in language, cannot be eliminated. In order to prove this thesis, it would be necessary first to delve into the doctrine of language and then into the doctrine of interpretation. The framework of my book does not allow this search for proof. I shall limit myself, therefore, to focusing attention on a number of important sources of uncertainty both in the language and in the rules of interpretation.

Language that Expresses Principles

Principles are rules of behavior that are based on ethical values such as fairness, justice, and morals. Principles serve various functions in the law.[17] For example, they play an important role in the interpretation of legal norms. Here we are dealing with statutory language that expresses a principle. An example of this is Section 30 of the Israeli Law of Contracts (General Part), 1973, which stipulates that an immoral contract is void. Another example is Section 31 of the Law of Contracts (General Part), which authorizes the court to exempt a party from the duty of restitution in an illegal contract "if it appears just to do so." These two rules contain within them two principles (morality and justice). Additional examples are scattered plentifully throughout the statute books.

Principles do not come equipped with a list of the situations to which they will apply in the future. They constitute the starting point for balancing and weighing. In the words of Professor Roscoe Pound,

---

16. See Hart, *supra* note 12, ch. 1, at 123.

17. For the place of principles in law, see Dworkin, *supra* note 16, ch. 1, at 14; Raz, *supra* note 21, ch. 1; MacCormick, *supra* note 20, ch. 1; Hart and Sacks, *supra* note 26, ch. 1; Wellington, *supra* note 20, ch. 1; Tur, "Positivism, Principles and Rules," in *Perspective in Jurisprudence* 42 (Attwood, ed., 1977); Tapper, "A Note on Principles," 34 *Mod. L. Rev.* 628 (1971).

These principles do not attach any definite detailed legal result to any definite, detailed state of fact. They do not threaten any definite official action in case of any definitely described conduct. They do not provide any patterns for definite situations. They are starting points from which to proceed according to the received technique.[18]

The determination as to the situations to which the principles will apply is in the hands of the judge. He frequently is faced with a number of possibilities (narrow or broad discretion), with the principle being a general factor to consider in the choice among the possibilities. On the strength of this factor, some of the possibilities may fall, and what at first appears to be broad discretion may evolve into narrow discretion. In certain cases, however, no principle is sufficiently specific under the circumstances, so the judge is left with discretion in making the choice among the different (narrow or broad) possibilities. Professor Raz described this in relation to a specific type of principle:

> Principles of the second group, on the other hand, do not stipulate what considerations should be acted on. They merely specify the type of considerations which may be taken into account and leave the rest to the officials or the courts addressed by the principles. Rather than negating discretion, they presuppose its existence and guide it. What is "unjust" or "for the general good" is a matter of opinion and the courts or officials concerned are instructed by law to act on their own views. The law does not impose its own views of justice or the common good. Rather it leaves the matter to the discretion of the courts or the officials.[19]

The discretion is not arbitrary. It must satisfy the fundamental elements of judicial discretion. Judicial discretion is always limited, yet within the framework of the limitations that the law places on the discretion, and after these have been exhausted, there remains freedom of choice among several possibilities, all lawful in the context of the statutory norm. Moreover, at times the rules of interpretation will be able to provide a principle with sufficient concretization, so that in the circumstances of a given case, discretion will no longer exist. Yet this will not always be within the power of the rules of interpretation. Thus, for example, it may be that the rule of interpretation that concerns the case and that is meant to clarify the principle embedded in the language is itself based on a

18. Pound, *supra* note 114, ch. 1, at 925.
19. Raz, *supra* note 21, ch. 1 at 847.

principle and has embedded within itself the very same uncertainty. Frequently, indeed, one can clarify a generalization only by using another generalization. This use is not without value. Some of the questions become clearer, some possibilities are eliminated. Yet at times, in particular circumstances, the uncertainty is not eliminated, and the discretion remains in place.

Language that Expresses Policy

At times the legislated norm contains within it expressions that reflect policies,[20] such as "the existence of the state," "the democratic character of the state," "the security of the state," "the public welfare," "the benefit of the child," and other "policy expressions"[21] contained in the language of the statute. Yet these expressions, like their twin brothers[22] the principles, do not include a list of facts to which they apply, and they, too, constitute only a starting point for balancing and weighing. Expressions of policy create, by the nature of things, a wide range of uncertainty, as they contain a number of meanings, each of them possible from the semantic standpoint and permissible, under certain circumstances, from the legal standpoint. Consider, for example, the expression "the good of the adoptee," which appears in the Child Adoption Law (1981). In the context of the Adoption Law, it may have various meanings.[23] For example, there is the question of the relationship between the good of the child in the short run and in the long run. What is the proper trade-off between material advantage and emotional harm? Not infrequently, the application of this principle to a given set of facts creates a broad discretion. Is the "best interest" of a physically handicapped child better served by returning him to his natural, single-parent family, which agreed in the past to the child's adoption, or by leaving him with the family that wants to adopt him and with which he has lived since birth?

20. On the place of policy in law, see MacCormick, *supra* note 20, ch. 1, at 263; Hughes, *supra* note 41, ch. 1, at 430; Hart and Sacks, *supra* note 26, ch. 1, at 159; Tur, *supra* note 17; Tate, *supra* note 123, ch. 1.

21. See Summers, "Two Types of Substantive Reasons: The Core of a Theory of Common-Law Justification," 63 *Cornell L. Rev.* 707 (1978).

22. There are those who distinguish sharply between principles and policies: see Dworkin, *supra* note 17. Others believe that this distinction is artificial. Principles also reflect policies, and both may be seen as policies: see Raz, *supra* note 21, ch. 1; MacCormick, *supra* note 20, ch. 1, at 263; Hughes, *supra* note 41, ch. 1, at 419.

23. See J. Goldstein, A. Freud, and A. Solnit, *Beyond the Best Interests of the Child* (1973); J. Goldstein, A. Freud, and A. Solnit, *Before the Best Interests of the Child* (1979).

This question does not have just one lawful answer. There are a number of lawful solutions. In making the choice among them the judge exercises judicial discretion. To be sure, the rules of interpretation can sometimes clarify the obscure and negate a number of possibilities. But they cannot clarify the obscure in every case. In those cases in which, notwithstanding the application of the rules of interpretation, the uncertainty in the language of the statutory norm expressing a policy remains, the judge is given judicial discretion.

Language that Expresses a Standard

Not infrequently, a legal norm contains expressions that reflect a standard of conduct,[24] such as reasonable care, negligence, "in an acceptable manner and in good faith," and other expressions that reflect standards for appropriate or inappropriate behavior. What is common to all these expressions, as it is to principles and policies, is that the legal norm does not itemize the set of factual situations to which it applies. With respect to the "reasonable person" standard of conduct, the Supreme Court said,

> This standard of conduct is determined by the court, and the reasonable person is none other than the court itself. (See *Glasgow v. Muir*, [1943] A.C. 448, 457) Here, as in the matter of the duty of care itself, the statute establishes only a general standard that does not list the set of factual circumstances to which it applies. Indeed, these situations cannot be foretold. This set of situations is not to be established on the basis of physical standards (of size, distance, or weight). The scope of application of the "reasonable person" standard is determined by the level of the approving or disapproving response of the judge vis-à-vis the result. This reaction is based primarily on the judge's human experience, on the one hand, and on principles and policies, on the other hand. Not infrequently, two judges may reach different conclusions with respect to the reasonableness of the conduct, for their personal experiences, and the set of principles and policies, are different.[25]

In this, the standard differs from the normal rule.[26] The set of situations to which the standard applies is not capable of being determined in

24. On the nature of standards, see Hart and Sacks, *supra* note 26, ch. 1, at 157; Dickinson, *supra* note 14, at 1086; Pound, "Hierarchy of Sources and Forms in Different Systems of Law," 7 *Tul. L. Rev.* 475 (1933).

25. C.A. 243/83 *The Municipality of Jerusalem v. Gordon*, 39 P.D. (1) 113, 137.

26. As to the distinction between rules and standards, see Hart and Sacks, *supra* note 26, ch. 1, at 157.

advance. In explaining the characteristics of the standard, Professor Pound said,

> For three characteristics may be seen in legal standards: (1) They all involve a certain moral judgment upon conduct. . . . (2) They do not call for exact legal knowledge exactly applied, but for common sense about common things or trained intuition about things outside of everyone's experience, (3) They are not formulated absolutely and given an exact content, either by legislation or by judicial decision, but are relative to times and places and circumstances, and are to be applied with reference to the facts of the case in hand. They recognize that within the bounds fixed each case is to a certain extent unique.[27]

One cannot hide the fact that in some circumstances, the application of a standard is simple and certain. The life experience and worldview of the legal community draw everyone to the same result. These are the easy cases. In other circumstances, the application of the standard is not self-evident, since there appear at first to exist arguments for several different ways of applying it. Yet in the end, after weighing and thinking, every knowledgeable lawyer would realize that there is only one way to apply it. These are the intermediate cases. But there will be cases in which the judge's life experience and the set of principles and policies that are taken into account will not produce an unambiguous solution, but will rather leave the judge with a number of possible courses of action. In these cases the judge has judicial discretion. Take, for example, the standard of reasonableness.[28] In the application of this test, the judge must consider various social goals, such as freedom of action and protection of property and life. Principles of fairness and justice also must be taken into account. All of these create a large set of possibilities that, in the appropriate factual circumstances, leave room for broad judicial discretion.

DISCRETION IN THE STATUTORY NORM: THE UNCERTAINTY OF THE NORMATIVE SCHEME

I dealt earlier with a judicial discretion whose origin is in the language of the statutory norm. At times the scope and means of application of a

---

27. R. Pound, *An Introduction to the Philosophy of Law* 58 (Rev. ed., 1954).

28. Lloyd, "Reason and Logic in the Common Law," 64 *Law Q. Rev.* 468, 475 (1948); MacCormick, "On Reasonableness," in *Les Notions A Contenu Variable En Droit* 131 (Perelman and Vander Elst, ed., 1984).

particular norm do not create any judicial discretion. However, there is judicial discretion as a result of the lack of certainty as to its normative power. Thus, for example, there may be uncertainty as to whether subsidiary legislation was enacted *intra vires* a statute. On occasion, two norms contradict one another, and there is doubt as to the question of which one takes precedence.

In these situations, and in many others, the question of the normative force of the norm may raise situations of judicial discretion. It seems to me that we need not dwell on this matter or consider it as a separate issue, because in the majority of cases, the uncertainty may be traced to the lack of certainty stemming from the wording of another norm or from uncertainty as to the rules of interpretation themselves. For example, the doubt surrounding the question whether a regulation was enacted *intra vires* may result from a lack of certainty in the drafting of the enabling statute. The doubt as to the outcome of the confrontation between two norms may result from a lack of certainty in the rules of interpretation that are meant to resolve this doubt. Sometimes the origin of this uncertainty is in another statutory norm, sometimes in another common law rule.

DISCRETION IN THE STATUTORY NORM: UNCERTAINTY IN THE RULES OF INTERPRETATION

The Rules of Interpretation: Rules to Remove Uncertainty

I considered language as a source of the uncertainty of the statutory norm and as a source of judicial discretion in the choice among different possibilities regarding the scope and application of the norm. Yet language alone does not determine the meaning of the statutory norm. "The interpreter is not simply a linguist."[29] Rules for statutory interpretation exist in every legal system, and they are intended, inter alia, to remove the lack of certainty and the doubt that stem from the wording of the statutory norm. Where the words of a statutory norm, in the circumstances of a given case, raise more than one possibility, the function of

---

29. H.C. 118/63 *Batzul v. The Minister of Interior,* 19 P.D. (1) 337, 350 (Berenson J.); Cr. App. 787/79 *Mizrachi v. State of Israel,* 35 P.D. (4) 421, 427: "The words of the statute are not fortresses, to be conquered with the aid of the dictionary, but are the wrapping of a live idea which changes with the circumstances of time and place so as to realize the basic purpose of the statute."

the rules of interpretation is to guide in the choice of the one and only lawful possibility. In the words of Professor J. Kohler,

> Interpreting a statute means not only to find the meaning concealed behind the expression, but also to select from the various meanings which the text may bear that meaning which must be held to be the correct and authoritative one.[30]

Frequently, the rules of interpretation accomplish their mission. What appears at the outset to be a rule that confers judicial discretion may be revealed after study and examination not to impart judicial discretion, but rather to dictate only one lawful solution. Thus, the question is not whether a given statutory norm confers, by its terms, judicial discretion, but rather whether the same rule confers discretion after it has passed through all the interpretive filters.

From this flows the importance of the rules of interpretation. Bishop Benjamin Hoadly discussed this in the eighteenth century: "Whoever hath an absolute authority to interpret any written or spoken law, it is he who is truly the lawgiver to all intents and purposes, and not the person who first wrote or spoke them."[31] What the learned bishop omitted to note is that the judge never has absolute discretion to interpret the statute. His discretion is always limited.

The Rules of Interpretation: Can Judicial Discretion Be Eliminated?

In theory, one can imagine a legal system whose rules of interpretation would eliminate judicial discretion. For this purpose, a long and detailed list of rules of interpretation would not suffice, since judicial discretion might survive in the cracks between the rules. For this goal to be accomplished, it seems the system would have to adopt a sweeping rule, stipulating that in situations where the "normal" rules of interpretation leave room for judicial discretion, that interpretation must be given which negates judicial discretion. It is interesting to speculate whether, even with this rule, judicial discretion would disappear. Whatever the answer, legal systems have not opted for this method, apparently because judicial discretion is not perceived as an evil that must be expunged at any cost and in all circumstances.

---

30. Kohler, "Judicial Interpretation of Enacted Law," 9 *Science of Legal Method* in *The Modern Legal Philosophy Series,* 187, 190 (1917).

31. See J. Gray, *The Nature and Sources of the Law* 102, 125, (2d ed., 1921).

In the absence of a sweeping rule of interpretation, the accepted rules of interpretation, by their structure, are not sufficient to eliminate all judicial discretion in the interpretation and application of a statutory norm.[32] The simple reason for this is that the rules of interpretation are themselves legal rules.[33] Like any other legal rule, they too are expressed in words, and the uncertainty that characterizes the words of the norm being interpreted also characterizes the wording of the interpreting norm. Professor Hart spoke of this in the following terms:

> Canons of "interpretation" cannot eliminate, though they can diminish, these uncertainties; for these canons are themselves general rules for the use of language, and make use of general terms which themselves require interpretation. They cannot, any more than other rules, provide for their own interpretation."[34]

This is especially true in those cases in which the rule of interpretation is itself based upon terms that express principles, policies, and standards. Professor Josef Raz emphasized this, noting,

> Vagueness is inherent in language. It is a problem courts have to face very frequently. As noted above, principles as well as rules of interpretation can sometimes solve problems of vagueness without leaving room for discretion. But principles themselves are vague, and discretion in cases of vagueness cannot be dispensed with so long as courts are entitled to render judgment in such cases.[35]

On occasion, a legal system develops "second-level" rules of interpretation that serve to interpret the ordinary rules of interpretation. Yet these, too, require interpretation. It is the fate of the legal norm that it always requires interpretation, even if it constitutes a norm of interpretation itself. From this flows the natural lack of certainty of the interpretive norm, which cannot be completely eliminated. To be sure, the development and refinement of the rules of interpretation may limit the scope of judicial discretion, yet they will never be able completely to eliminate it. It is wishful thinking to aspire to perfectly clear rules of interpretation. As a result, many criticize rules of interpretation and dismiss them as

32. See Reig, "Judicial Interpretation of Written Rules," 40 *La. L. Rev.* 49, 65 (1979).
33. See R. Cross, *Statutory Interpretation* 27 (1976).
34. Hart, *supra* note 12, ch. 1, at 123.
35. Raz, *supra* note 21, ch. 1, at 846.

useless.[36] But rules of interpretation are essential for every legal system. They establish the legitimacy of the judicial enterprise, and they solve most of the conflicts. But they cannot solve every case.

For every rule of interpretation, as for every other legal rule, there are simple and intermediate situations, in which its scope of application is clear in given circumstances. However, as with all other legal rules, there also exist with respect to the rules of interpretation hard cases within a penumbra in which their scope of application, in certain circumstances, is not clear, leaving the judge with discretion. When this penumbral area in the norm of interpretation is the relevant one for eliminating uncertainty in the penumbra of the norm being interpreted, the state of uncertainty persists and judicial discretion remains. Judicial discretion in one realm (the interpreting norm) leaves in place judicial discretion in another realm (the norm being interpreted).

To demonstrate the judicial discretion that exists in the rules of interpretation themselves, I shall turn now to a number of selected issues. They do not represent a complete list of the cases in which judicial discretion exists in the rules of interpretation. For this it would have been necessary to provide a systematic survey of the rules of interpretation. Still, they are sufficient to indicate types of cases, and typical cases, of judicial discretion in the context of the statutory rules of interpretation.

UNCERTAINTY AS TO THE CIRCUMSTANCES OF APPLICATION OF A RULE OF INTERPRETATION

In a significant number of rules of interpretation, uncertainty exists as to the occurrence of the circumstances and the conditions that activate the rule. Thus, for example, the application of the rules of interpretation established in the Israeli Law of Interpretation (1981) is conditioned upon the absence, in the issue under consideration or in connection with

36. A well-known statement by a judge holds that there are two types of books he does not read: "books about spiritualism and books about interpretation": see Landis, "A Note on 'Statutory Interpretation,' " 43 *Harv. L. Rev.* 886 (1929–30). Lord Wilberforce labeled interpretation "a non-subject": see 277 H. L. Deb. Ser. 5 Cole. 1254, 6th November 1966. Those who sought to do a favor noted that interpretation is an art, which must be felt more than understood, and one must perform it more by intuition than by rules: see Barak, "On the Judge as An Interpreter," 12 *Mishpatim* 248, 249 (1982).

it, of anything "that is inconsistent with" the Law of Interpretation.[37] This expression—"that is inconsistent with"—has very wide margins of uncertainty and includes within it uncertainty as to the very applicability of the rules of interpretation themselves. The applicability of a number of rules of interpretation is conditioned upon two statutes being *in pari materia*. This terminology is not clear in every circumstance, and as a result the very applicability of these rules of interpretation is given to the discretion of the court.

Some rules of interpretation apply only if the statutory language is not clear and unambiguous or if the clear and unambiguous language of the statute yields an absurdity or an outcome that is manifestly illogical. When these conditions exist, one may draw upon the title of the provision, weigh considerations of logic, add or subtract words, consult the legislative history, and seek help in the intent of the legislator. As Justice Bach wrote in HCJ 249/82, *Wagnin v. The Military Appeals Court*,[38]

> All of the arguments about the intent that should or should not be ascribed to the legislator have merit, yet they should be taken into account only when the wording of the statute is obscure and its language susceptible of differing interpretations.

On the other hand,

> When the language is clear and when the proposed interpretation does not lead in practice to an absurd or illogical result, then there is no room for engaging in speculations about the presumed policy of the legislator.[39]

According to this interpretive approach, in case of doubt one may turn to the legislative purpose in order to remove the doubt. However, the legislative purpose cannot be consulted in order to create the doubt. This approach entails two main foci of uncertainty as to its applicability. The first concerns the determination that the language is not obscure but rather clear and that it is not susceptible of two interpretations; the second has to do with the determination that an absurdity exists and that the result is manifestly illogical. Of course, there are cases that every knowledgeable lawyer would agree are clear or obscure and produce a logical or illogical result. In these cases, there is no discretion as to the applica-

37. Sec. 1 of the Interpretation Law, 1981.
38. 37 P.D. (2) 393, 416.
39. Ibid.

bility of these rules of interpretation. But there are many cases in which one cannot say that the expression is clear. Sometimes it is not at all clear whether the order is clear,[40] and the answer to the question whether the order is obscure, itself is obscure. Judge Roger Traynor has noted that "plain words like plain people are not always so plain as they seem."[41] Indeed, clear words do not always have a clear meaning, and if the meaning is unclear, one may have to refer for their explication to the same rules of interpretation. Justice Frankfurter spoke of this, saying, "The notion that because the words of a statute are plain its meaning is also plain, is merely pernicious oversimplification."[42] And, a number of years later, he addressed this issue in stronger language: "The notion that the plain meaning of the words of a statute defines the meaning of the statute reminds one of T. H. Huxley's gay observation that at times 'a theory survives long after its brains are knocked out.'"[43] The same holds true for the question of the absurdity, and whether the lack of logic is manifest. Indeed, these expressions—*clear, obscure, absurd, illogical, manifestly*—are themselves obscure and open-textured. Where the application of a rule of interpretation is conditioned upon them, the very application of the rule of interpretation naturally brings with it uncertainty as to the legal norm itself, and as a result, uncertainty as to the existence of judicial discretion.

UNCERTAINTY AS TO THE CONTENT OF THE RULE OF INTERPRETATION: "LEGISLATIVE PURPOSE"

The Problem

Sometimes no discretion exists as to the applicability of a rule of interpretation. Nonetheless, questions arise about its content. Here, too, circumstances are plentiful in which the content of the rule of interpretation raises no doubt whatsoever in the mind of every knowledgeable lawyer; yet there are other situations in which the very nature of the guideline established in the rule of interpretation is uncertain, and thereby a situa-

---

40. See *Barbee v. United States,* 392 F.2d 532.

41. Traynor, "No Magic Words Could Do It Justice," 49 *Calif. L. Rev.* 615, 618 (1961).

42. *United States v. Monia,* 317 U.S. 424, 431 (1943).

43. *Massachusetts Bonding and Ins. Co. v. United States,* 352 U.S. 128, 138 (1956).

tion of judicial discretion is created. Judicial discretion, which flourished in the soil of the uncertainty of the interpreted norm, is not eliminated. It continues to exist. There are two key examples in this area. One has to do with the concept of *legislative purpose*. The second deals with *acceptable values* that are used in interpretation.

Legislative Purpose—How?

The statutory norm is a purposeful norm. The statute is a normative creation meant to realize a social goal, and it is an expression of policy. The interpreter must uncover, from among the spectrum of linguistic possibilities, that meaning which will accomplish the purpose of the statute. "The statute is an instrument for executing a legislative goal, and therefore it must be interpreted according to the purpose it embodies."[44] "The judge, when he comes to interpret the statute, should ask himself: what normative social goal does this statute seek to attain?"[45] Indeed, it is an established rule of interpretation in most systems that a statute is to be interpreted in light of its legislative purpose and with a view to effecting its accomplishment. Yet how are the legislative purpose and goal to be determined, and how can the judge ascertain the intent of the legislator?

Examination of the case law reveals no rules in this matter that are acceptable to the legal community. The minimalists hold that the goal and purpose of the statute may be gleaned only from its language. The maximalists contend that one may learn about the purpose of the statute from any reliable source. Such a source is, first and foremost, the language of the statute itself, but it is not the only source. Every question of interpretation begins with the statutory language, yet does not end with it.

So one may learn about the aim of the statute from sources external to the statute, such as the rules that existed before the statute was enacted and the relevant legislative and parliamentary history. Between these two poles are several intermediate positions, according to which it is permissible, in certain circumstances, to rely upon particular external sources. Thus, for example, one finds the approach that if the statutory language is unclear and permits of two meanings, reference may be had

---

44. C.A. 481/33 *Rosenberg v. Shtesel*, 29 P.D. (1) 505, 516 (Sussman, J.).
45. Cr. App. 71/83 *Sharon v. The State of Israel*, 38 P.D.(2) 757, 770 (Levine, J.).

to the parliamentary history. Thus, the lack of agreement about the content of the legal norm in this matter may produce varying fields of application of the norm that is being interpreted, all in accordance with the sources from which one can learn about the legislative intent.

Legislative Purpose—Only from the Statutory Language

We turn first to the judge who holds that the purpose of the statute may be learned only from its language. This judge will find himself facing many situations of uncertainty because in most cases the statute does not indicate its purpose. The judge must draw his own conclusions about the legislative purpose. How is he to do so? In many systems, there are no standards acceptable to the legal community for deriving the statutory purpose from the language of the statute. Not infrequently, the judge will discover that the statute is based upon two contradictory purposes. What should he do then? Often, the legislative purpose emerges from the statutory language, yet this purpose may be expressed in varying levels of abstraction, from the lowest, which repeats the statutory language, to the highest, which embraces the accepted values. There are no agreed-upon standards in many systems to guide the minimalist judge in the choice he has to make. As a result, the minimalist judge frequently finds himself faced with a situation of judicial discretion, for in the absence of direction he may choose one of several paths. In this one recognizes the existence of judicial discretion. Thus, the interpretive norm holding that the statutory purpose may be learned only from the language of the statute is itself an open-textured norm.

Legislative Purpose—Not Only from the Statutory Language

A judge who does not content himself with the statutory language in his effort to learn about the legislative purpose will seek guidance from every reliable source. He will study the legal situation that preceded the enactment of the statute, read the reports of public committees, gain an impression from legislative bills and the parliamentary record. Sometimes all of these will be enough to point to the legislative purpose and thereby to constitute a key to the interpretation of the statutory language. At times, the judge who goes beyond the language of the statute to learn about the legislative purpose may find a solution to his problem and discover the legislative purpose in circumstances in which the minimalist judge did not succeed in doing so. In this event, the minimalist judge has discretion, while the judge who is not a minimalist does not. Frequently, however, the abundance of sources and their lack of clarity will place before the judge many alternatives for concretizing the statutory purpose. The maximalist judge may discover many and varied legislative purposes, with different levels of abstraction and different indications of reliability. Thus, the norm of interpretation holding that one may learn about the legislative purpose from any reliable source is itself a vague norm and leaves a significant penumbra, in which judicial discretion is possible.

The Usefulness of Legislative Purpose

One should not conclude from all this that the legislative purpose concept should not be used in the interpretation of statutes. For all its weaknesses, I do not believe that the alternatives are any better or clearer. Legislative purpose as a means to interpret a statute must guide the judge. It follows from the doctrine of the separation of powers and from the status of the legislature and of the judge. Moreover, one should not conclude that legislative purpose is like clay in the hands of a potter: the judge does not invent purposes or create history. Justice Frankfurter had the following to say about this:

> Legislation has an aim; it seeks to obviate some mischief, to supply an inadequacy, to effect a change of policy, to formulate a plan of government. That aim, that policy is not drawn, like nitrogen, out of the air; it is evidenced in the language of the statute, as read in the light of other external manifestations of purpose. That is what the judge must seek and effectuate, and he ought not to be led off the trail by tests that have overtones of subjective design. We are not concerned with anything subjective. We do not delve into the mind of legislators or their draftsmen, or committee members.[46]

Thus, the search for legislative purpose is the analysis of the statute in light of its goal, and not the psychoanalysis of the legislator in light of his intent.[47] This analysis has clear, objective elements, but nonetheless, one must admit that this standard of legislative purpose is obscure and vague. It leaves the judge with room not only for weighing and balanc-

---

46. Frankfurter, "Some Reflections on the Reading of Statutes," 47 *Colum. L. Rev.* 527, 538 (1947).
47. See *United States v. Public Utilities Commission of California*, 345 U.S. 295, 319 (1953).

ing, but also for judicial discretion. Its borders are not clear, and within it there exists a broad area of uncertainty. Part of the uncertainty is inherent in legislation. The legislature frequently exhibits contradictory legislative tendencies; often one finds indecision in legislation. Not even the most successful legislator can predict the unforeseeable. Part of the uncertainty stems from negligent legislation. Be this as it may, one cannot deny that in certain circumstances the terminology of legislative purpose confers broad judicial discretion upon the judge. He faces several lawful possibilities, and this standard does not guide him in choosing among them.

UNCERTAINTY AS TO THE CONTENT OF THE RULE OF INTERPRETATION: "GENERAL PRINCIPLES"

Legislative Purpose and Accepted Values

Sometimes the judge encounters a situation in which he cannot formulate, from the material before him, a legislative purpose capable of solving the interpretive problem at hand. If he is a minimalist judge, the language of the statute does not indicate the relevant legislative purpose for solving his problem. If he is a maximalist judge, the extralegislative material (such as the preparliamentary and parliamentary history) does not help him formulate a legislative purpose to solve the problem facing him. The statute has a purpose, and this purpose may even be discovered, but it sheds no light on the specific problem of interpretation with which the judge is faced. What should the judge do? Some think that in this situation the judge should ask himself what the purpose of the legislature would have been had it thought about the legal question that is now before the judge.[48] This approach has its advantages and its disadvantages. Suffice it to say that this approach is fictional. In reality, the court does not ask itself, "What would the legislature do if . . . ?" since for the most part the judge has no answer to this question. In any event, the only possible honest answer might be that the legislature would act as it in fact acted, for it cannot act otherwise given the balance of forces. Thus, in reality the judge does not ask himself, "What would the legislature do if . . . ?" but rather, "How should I, as a judge, act?"

48. See Cohen, "Judicial 'Legisputation' and the Dimensions of Legislative Meaning," 36 *Ind. L. Rev.* 414 (1961).

Linked to the legislative purpose, the question becomes, "What should he, as a judge, establish as the legislative purpose?" If one does not want to connect this question to legislative purpose, the question is, "How should he, as a judge, act when the legislative purpose rule does not assist him?"

One of the most important rules of interpretation to aid the judge in this situation is that a statutory enactment is to be interpreted against the background of the accepted values of the system and in such a way as to further them. One may ground this rule of interpretation in the rule of legislative purpose. According to this approach, one must posit that the legislature's purpose was to advance the fundamental values of the system, not to negate them. "In the absence of a specific instruction," said Supreme Court President Izhak Olshan, "one should not assume that the legislature intended to be harsh and to deviate from the principles that one may call axiomatic."[49] The same notion finds expression in the words of Justice Haim Cohn:

> And when we speak of an enlightened democratic legislature, for whom the good customs and the highest principles and the concepts of justice are its guiding light, not only must we not assume that it eliminated and annuled them, but rather the legislature's words themselves cannot be faithfully interpreted without assuming that the statute was the product of its hands but was adapted to the framework of the existing "law," with its many and varied components.[50]

The same rule may be grounded on the background of the more general approach, according to which a legislative act in general, and fundamental rules in particular, are not a one-time act cut off from the general experience. The statute forms flesh and bones in the context of a given political and legal system. It constitutes one brick of an overall structure that is built on given foundations of system and law. The statute is, in the words of Justice Sussman, "a creation that lives in its environment."[51] This environment includes not only the immediate legislative context, but also wider circles of accepted principles. Justice Frankfurter spoke of this, saying, "An enactment is an organism in its environment. And the environment is not merely the immediate political or social context in

49. H.C. 163/57 *Lubin v. Municipality of Tel-Aviv,* 12 P.D. 1041, 1050.
50. Cohn, "Faithful Interpretation—Three Dimensions," 7 *Mishpatim* 5, 6 (1976).
51. H.C. 58/68 *Shalit v. The Minister of Interior,* 23 P.D. (2) 477, 513.

which it is to be placed, but the whole traditional system of law and law enforcement."[52] The interpreter must seek to attain "harmony of legislation" while fitting the chapters of the various statutes into the overall web of legislation. He must, therefore, interpret the individual statute against the background of the general principles of the system, "in order to bring it into harmony with the fundamentals of the constitutional regime that exists in the state."[53] These principles constitute a sort of normative umbrella covering all the legislative acts.

The Accepted Values of the System

A statute is to be interpreted against the background of the accepted values of the system. Justice Shneor Heshin stressed this: "A statute in which the intent of the legislator was not expressed clearly enough, must be interpreted so as to manifest an intent that is consistent with convenience, logic, justice and accepted principles."[54] Among the accepted principles in Israel, for example, is the Declaration of Independence, which expresses—in the words of Supreme Court President Zmora[55]— "the vision of the nation and its 'articles of faith'," and the Parliament's statutes must be interpreted in its light. From here one also gets the concept that a statute is to be interpreted in light of the fundamental values of the democratic regime and of the legal system. These fundamental values include, among others, accepted principles such as equality, justice, and morality. They include policies such as the existence of the state, its democratic character, separation of powers, personal freedom, freedom of expression, freedoms of procession, religious worship, property, and occupation, human dignity, integrity of the judicial process, and public welfare and safety. These fundamental values include within them standards of good faith, natural justice, fairness, reasonableness, impartiality, lack of conflict of interest. Justice Menachem Elon discussed this in the following terms:[55a] "We have an important rule, that a legal system cannot sustain itself on the body of the law alone. The body of the legal system needs a soul, and perhaps even a super-soul.

52. Frankfurter, "A Symposium on Statutory Construction: Forewords," 3 *Vand. L. Rev.* 365, 367 (1950).

53. Landau, *supra* note 17, ch. 1, at 306.

54. H.C. 282/51 *Histadrut Haovdim v. The Minister of Labour*, 6 P.D. 237, 245.

55. H.C. 10/48 *Ziv v. Gubernik*, 1 P.E. 33, 36.

55a. C.A. 391/80 *Lasarson v. Shikun Ovdim*, 30 P.D.(2) 237, 264.

The legal system will find this soul in the character and image of various value norms."

This rule of interpretation concerning accepted values is crucial in that it applies as an aid in interpreting the statute in every case where the judge fails to discern a specific legislative purpose. It helps in the search for the broad legislative purpose, which includes, in addition to a specific purpose, the fundamental values of which we spoke. Close examination of this rule of interpretation indicates that its content is for the most part obscure. The rule is meant to interpret an open-textured legislative text, yet is itself open-textured to a large extent. As a result, there is, in this rule of interpretation, a significant degree of judicial discretion.

Judicial Discretion: What Are Accepted Values?

What is included in the framework of accepted values? The standard established in the case law on this issue is extremely vague. "The law of the nation," said Justice Agranat,[56] "is to be learned in the perspective of the complex of its national life," and the accepted values should be drawn, in the words of Justice Landau,[57] "from our sources—the sources of the consciousness of the nation in whose midst the judges sit." This includes among other things, basic concepts of democratic-liberal government. In many areas, deriving these accepted values will not pose any problem. But there will surely also be difficult borderline cases. Do we, for example, recognize the principle that a statute is to be interpreted in light of the principle of "privacy"? The list of accepted values is clearly not closed. Yet how does one gain admission to this select club, and under what conditions is one forced to leave? The answers to these questions are not clear. Surely, these values are not only those expressed in the existing statutes, but also those that the judge channels into the law from the life of the nation. But what level of consensus must these values enjoy before they are recognized? Thus, there exists, after all, substantial room for judicial discretion.

Judicial Discretion: What Is the Scope of the Accepted Values?

The scope of application of the accepted values is unclear. Each value has a core of application that does not pose any problems, yet it also has a

56. H.C. 73/53 *"Kol Haam" v. The Minister of Interior*, 7 P.D. 871, 884.
57. Landau, *supra* note 17, ch. 1, at 306.

penumbra that raises difficulty and doubt. Not infrequently we find ourselves interpreting the penumbra of a rule by means of the penumbra of a value. This state of affairs naturally creates a situation of uncertainty and judicial discretion.

Judicial Discretion: Balancing Accepted Values

Quite often, a number of accepted values apply in the circumstances of a given case. As long as all these values lead to the same conclusion, there is no difficulty: the case is thus easy or intermediate. Yet frequently the accepted values pull in different—and opposing—directions. More than once we find a principle right next to its opposite, and alongside a thesis we find its antithesis. In the words of Justice Cardozo, "Again the task of judging is found to be a choice between antithetical extremes. We seem to see the workings of an Hegelian philosophy of history whereby the tendency of every principle is to create its own antithesis or rival."[58] Indeed, the accepted values of the system often march in pairs, each in its own direction. As Professor John Dickinson said,

> The question . . . is always at what point to draw the line between two basic legal principles of opposing tenor. . . . The conditions of human life and association being what they are, every such interest if carried beyond a certain point is bound to come into conflict with some other interest or interests of a kind which the law also protects, and will thus come to conflict with a competing legal principle of equal validity.[59]

Thus, for example, the values of the security of the state and public order and safety may compete with freedom of expression, freedom of demonstration, freedom of religion and worship, and freedom of information. The principles of the integrity of the legal process and a person's good name may at times conflict with the principle of freedom of expression.

Sometimes, the legislature itself balances and decides between these opposing tendencies. Thus, for example, it was established in Israel[60] that in the clash between personal freedom and the security of the state, with respect to revealing classified evidence, the balance is to be determined by the test of whether "the need to reveal it for doing justice

58. Cardozo, *supra* note 125, ch. 1, at 62.
59. See Dickinson, "The Law behind the Law," 29 *Colum. L. Rev.* 285, 298 (1929).
60. See the Evidence Ordinance (New Version) (1971), sec. 45.

outweighs the interest in not revealing it.'' But frequently the legislator does not take any position regarding conflicting principles, or the standard he provides is so vague that it is the practical equivalent of leaving the balancing in the hands of the judge.

Sometimes the point of balance is evident and simple. The case being contested falls so plainly to one side or the other of the border, that the one and only solution is obvious to every knowledgeable lawyer. Yet at times the point of balance is not at all clear. The judge is faced with a situation of judicial discretion such as Professor Hart described:

> In these cases it is clear that the rule-making authority must exercise a discretion, and there is no possibility of treating the question raised by the various cases as if there were one uniquely correct answer to be found, as distinct from an answer which is a reasonable compromise between many conflicting interests.[61]

Frequently, the borderline between the principles that are competing for primacy is not at all obvious and may fluctuate among a number of points. The judge must pin down the border to be able to decide the case before him. Justice Frankfurter said the following about the complexity of this task:

> The core of the difficulty is that there is hardly a question of any real difficulty before the court that does not entail more than one so-called principle. . . . Judges cannot have such contradiction between two conflicting ''truths'' as ''part of the mystery of things.'' They have to adjudicate. If the conflict cannot be resolved, the task of the Court is to arrive at an accommodation of the contending claims. This is the core of the difficulties and misunderstandings about the judicial process. This, for any conscientious judge, is the agony of his duty.[62]

In establishing the borderline, the judge sometimes has nothing more to go on than the principle that he must strike the balance reasonably. This standard may point to one and only one lawful solution in a number of situations, yet in many other cases there is more than one lawful solution. The judge has no choice but ''to exercise the sovereign prerogative of choice,'' about which Justice Oliver Wendell Holmes said,

> I think it most important to remember whenever a doubtful case arises, with certain analogies on one side and other analogies on the other, that what really

61. Hart, *supra* note 12, ch. 1, at 128.
62. Frankfurter, *supra* note 7, ch. 1, at 43.

is before us is a conflict between two social desires, each of which seeks to extend its dominion over the case, and which cannot both have their way. The social question is which desire is stronger at the point of conflict. . . . [W]here there is doubt the simple tool of logic does not suffice, and even if it is disguised and unconscious, the judges are called on to exercise the sovereign prerogative of choice.[63]

In this activity, the judge exercises judicial discretion.

Judicial Discretion: Balancing Values by Their Weight

The "sovereign prerogative of choice" grows when the judge is required, as a precondition to locating the point of balance, to assign relative weights to the accepted values that are competing for the upper hand. It must be understood that values have relative weights.[64] They are not all equal before the law. Their weight determines their status in the ultimate balance. "The process of placing competing values on the scales," said Justice Meir Shamgar,[65] "describes the starting line of interpretation, but it is not sufficient for formulating a scale or value-weights with whose help the work of interpretation will be done." At times, the legislature itself performs the task of assigning the weights. Thus, for example, in the area of adoption, where the interests of the child, his natural parents, and his "psychological" parents all compete, the legislature established a policy of giving decisive relative weight to the benefit of the child. Frequently, however, in the absence of legislative guidance as to the relative weight to be given to the competing values, the judge is left with this task: within the borders of the test of reasonableness, he applies judicial discretion. Referring to judicial discretion in this matter, Professor Raz wrote,

> Though principles sometimes limit the scope of the courts' discretion, they tend on the whole to expand it. . . . [T]he law usually determines with precision the relative weight of rules. Not so with principles. The law characteristically includes only incomplete indications as to their relative weight and leaves much to judicial discretion to be exercised in particular cases. The scope of discretion is in fact doubly extended, since not only must the relative importance of principles be determined, but also the importance

63. Holmes, *supra* note 122, ch. 1, at 239.
64. See Dworkin, *supra* note 16, ch. 1, at 14; Raz, *supra* note 12, ch. 1, at 57; Pound, "A Survey of Social Interests," 57 *Harv. L. Rev.* 1, 2 (1943); Dias, "The Value of a Value-Study of Law," 28 *Mod. L. Rev.* 397 (1965).
65. F.H. 9/77 *Hevret Hachashmal v. Haaretz*, 32 P.D.(3) 337.

relative to each principle of deviating from it or of following it on particular occasions. This matter is usually entrusted to judicial discretion.[66]

The task of assigning weights to the competing values is both natural and essential. Without it, the judge cannot carry out his balancing activity. At times the judge is not conscious of the need to do this and may simply attach equal weight to every value. Or he may give certain values greater relative weight, without explaining to himself or to others why he did so. At times the judge is aware of the need to assign relative weights. In either case, he exercises judicial discretion. Justice Holmes spoke of this:

> Behind the logical form lies a judgment as to the relative worth and importance of competing legislative grounds, often an inarticulate and unconscious judgment, it is true, and yet the very root and nerve of the whole proceeding. . . . Such matters really are battle grounds where the means do not exist for determinations that shall be good for all time, and where the decision can do no more than embody the preference of a given body in a given time and place.[67]

Thus, this process of placing various values on the scales frequently carries with it judicial discretion.

Judicial Discretion in General Principles

So we see that the principle of interpretation that requires taking into account the accepted values sometimes leads to judicial discretion. This stems from the fact that frequently there is no way of escaping a choice between competing principles, a choice that must balance the competing principles according to their weight and their importance. Often, there is no normative guidance—beyond the need to balance among the values *reasonably*—as to the weight to be given the various competing principles and as to their relative importance. At times a certain specific guidance exists, yet it has wide margins and leaves room for a number of possibilities. In these circumstances, the judge, acting within the framework of the test of reasonableness, must make the choice among the competing principles on the basis of his discretion. There is more than one lawful solution. Discretion exists. As Professor Hart wrote,

> Judicial decision, especially on matters of high constitutional import, often involves a choice between moral values, and not merely the application of

---

66. Raz, *supra* note 21, ch. 1, at 846.
67. Holmes, *supra* note 122, ch. 1, at 181.

some single outstanding moral principle; for it is folly to believe that where the meaning of the law is in doubt, morality always has a clear answer to offer. At this point judges may again make a choice which is neither arbitrary nor mechanical. . . . No doubt because a plurality of such principles is always possible it cannot be *demonstrated* that a decision is uniquely correct; but it may be made acceptable as the reasoned product of informed impartial choice. In all this we have the ''weighing'' and ''balancing'' characteristic of the effort to do justice between competing interests.[68]

Judicial discretion reaches its peak when the judge strikes a balance between competing principles, according to their weight and their strength at the point of confrontation.

UNCERTAINTY ABOUT THE VALIDITY OF THE RULE OF INTERPRETATION

Does a Certain Rule of Interpretation Exist?

The vast majority of the rules of interpretation established in a system are known and recognized. Yet this phenomenon is not without exceptions. Not infrequently, the judge finds himself in a situation in which he does not know whether or not a certain rule of interpretation applies in his system. This occurs primarily with respect to rules of interpretation that are either old—for then the judge does not know whether they are still valid, or whether they have been replaced by newer rules; or new—for then the judge does not know if they are already in force, or whether they do not yet constitute a binding interpretive-legal norm.

Thus, there is a rule of interpretation in Israel according to which a tax statute is to be given a restrictive interpretation. One can find many decisions that attest to the existence of this rule.[69] Yet in other decisions, reservations are expressed.[70] It seems that this rule was indeed accepted in the past, as it reflects the literal interpretive approach then current in England. But with the gradual change in the general approach to rules of interpretation in the Western world, other rules are being developed that put pressure on the old ones, raising doubts as to whether the old rules are still valid.

68. Hart, *supra* note 12, ch. 1, at 200.
69. C.A. 120/52 *Komprovski v. Director of Land Taxes,* 7 P.D. 141, 153, based on *Cape Brandy Syndicate v. I.R.C.* [1921] 1 K.B. 64, 71.
70. C.A. 165/82 *Kibutz Hazor v. Tax Authority,* 39 P.D.(2) 70.

Contradictory Rules of Interpretation

The Phenomenon and Its Explanation At times the judge encounters rules of interpretation that are mutually incompatible.[71] This incompatibility may be only apparent, for the system has rules ("second-level rules of interpretation") that decide between the conflicting rules of interpretation. Reality teaches us that such "decisional rules" are not numerous in the field of interpretation, and that the phenomenon of conflicting, valid rules is more prevalent. Professor Karl Llewellyn noted that "[t]here are two opposing canons on almost every point."[72] These words seem to contain an element of exaggeration, for the number of contradictory rules is not great. Frequently, what appear to be conflicting rules are simply rules that apply to different sets of facts. Yet one cannot deny that this phenomenon of contradictory rules of interpretation exists in many legal systems. There are those who say it stems from the nonlegal nature of the rules of interpretation.[73] Others argue that it is linked to the fact that the rules of interpretation are principles and not rules.[74] I do not accept either of these explanations. Rules of interpretation are legal rules. Some of them are rules and some are principles, and this does not suffice to answer the question of contradiction.

One explanation for the phenomenon of conflicting rules of interpretation has its origin in the changes taking place in all legal systems. These changes occur first and foremost in certain special laws. Yet together with the change in the law, sometimes a change in the laws of interpretation—which are the laws of laws—is also required. This latter change is, for the most part, slow and continuing, since it involves an alteration of the basic conceptions themselves, of the "operative jurisprudence." As a result, we are witness to a long transition period in which one finds, one next to the other, rules of interpretation from different historical strata, without the system attempting to choose among them. This leaves the decision to a lengthy process of gradual change.

This appears to have been the pattern in England.[75] In the sixteenth

71. See Llewellyn, "Remarks on the Theory of Appellate Decision and the Rules of Canons About How Statutes Are to be Construed," 3 *Vand. L. Rev.* 395 (1950).

72. Ibid., at p. 401.

73. See Ross, *supra* note 2, at 153.

74. See Cross, *supra* note 33, at 27.

75. Ibid., p. 8.

and seventeenth centuries the "mischief rule"—also known as Heydon's rule—prevailed. In the eighteenth and nineteenth centuries and with the change in the status of legislation itself, there began a transition to the "literal" or "plain meaning" rule, out of which later grew the "golden rule." This transition took place slowly, without any attempt to force a clear decision among the competing rules. In twentieth-century England there was an attempt to synthesize all of these rules, and this effort, too, is progressing without one being able to point to winners and losers. Yet one has the impression that the "purposive approach," which takes the statutory purpose into account and which constitutes something of a return, in a broader form, to the mischief rule, is gaining the upper hand.[76]

A similar process is taking place in Israel.[77] Upon the founding of the state in 1948, we essentially adopted the British rules of interpretation. This approach was not unbending, but flexible, and it took into consideration the legal reality as it existed at independence. The Supreme Court noted[78] that "it is preferable for the time being to continue to rely on the British rules of interpretation for the needs of Israeli law-making." The phrase "for the time being" was used with knowledge of the system of legislation and its processes, and of the terminology that characterized it, all of which were influenced by their British counterparts. In the words of Justice Sussman, "The drafter of Israeli statutes is in the habit of continuing to use, when necessary, terms borrowed from English law, in 'Hebrew dress,' and it is only natural that the Israeli interpreter will turn to the rules of interpretation of that same law."[79] Thus it was said[80] that "only when Israeli legislation increases in quantity will experience be able to teach us what are the Israeli rules of interpretation, that can take the place of the English rules." Through the years, a change took place in our legislation. It multiplied. It distanced itself from the British ways of thinking and drafting. The "independence" of the legislation was increasingly emphasized. Obligatory referrals to English law for purposes of interpretation evolved into permis-

76. See Bennion, *supra* note 118, ch. 1, at 657.
77. See Barak, "Interpretation and Adjudication," 10 *Tel-Aviv U. L. Rev.* 467 (1984).
78. H.C. 15/56 *Sopher v. The Interior Minister*, 10 P.D. 1213, 1221 (Sussman J.).
79. H.C. 163/57 *supra* note 49, at 1077.
80. H.C. 15/56 *supra* note 78, at 1221.

sive referrals. The formal link to English law was cut. All of these produced a slow change, leading to a cautious and gradual formulation in the case law of rules of interpretation to match our needs. Given this slow journey, it is only natural to find, side by side, rules of interpretation that reflect old and new, British and Israeli conceptions, that occasionally contradict one another, without the system having decided the outcome of that contradiction. As a result, a judge is faced with a number of rules of interpretation, each of which is legitimate and valid and leads to a result of its own in the interpretation of the statute. When a judge chooses among the conflicting rules of interpretation, he exercises judicial discretion. Whichever possibility he chooses is lawful, and the choice itself is not determined by any legal norm.

Examples Our system recognizes the "literal" interpretation as well as the "purposive" interpretation. The former holds that if the language of the statute is clear, provided it does not lead to an absurdity, one should not consult the legislative purpose in interpreting the statute. The other holds that one should always look to the purpose of the legislation, whether or not the language is clear. These are contradictory rules for the interpretation of statutes. Frequently, this conflict does not lead to a difference in result, since the two rules point in the same direction. Yet at times they lead in different directions, and the selection of interpretive method determines the outcome. This state of affairs confers discretion upon the judge, who is entitled to choose the rule that appears to him to be best.

There is also disagreement about the extent to which legislative history—especially the Knesset record—may be consulted. Some hold that reference to Knesset debates is prohibited. Others say it is permitted, but only when the statutory language is unclear. Still others believe that consulting the Knesset record is always permitted. Each of these three schools finds support in the case law. None of them is preferable to the others from a normative viewpoint, and none can negate the others. Their use is given to the discretion of the judge.

The case law is unclear as to the interpretive value of "legislative silence." Some argue that legislative silence constitutes a factor according to which statutes should be interpreted. Thus, for example, it was held that if the legislature remains silent after a judicial ruling, that silence is evidence that the judicial ruling interpreting the legislation matches the legislative purpose. The lack of a legislative initiative in the matter at hand leads to the conclusion that at least in retrospect, the legislature accepted the interpretation of the commission and adopted it as its own. According to others, legislative silence has no interpretive significance.

A third view takes the middle ground. According to this view, the legislature's silence has limited interpretive significance. This significance is not normative; the legislator does not legislate by not legislating. The significance is factual; the silence of the legislator is a fact that should be taken into consideration in formulating the legislative history, which in turn influences the determination of the legislative purpose. The three views are all possible. They are all legitimate. In making the choice among them, the judge has discretion.

A number of rules of interpretation are derived from the way the judge perceives the professionalism of the drafting of legislation. A judge who assumes professional legislation will employ a rule of interpretation according to which one can, when the legislature permits something, learn from this about what is prohibited, and when it prohibits something, one can learn from this about what is permitted, since one presumes that the legislature does not use its words for nought and that every expression has a meaning of its own that either adds or subtracts something. From this, one also learns that words and expressions in one statute may be interpreted as having the same meaning they were given in another statute dealing with the same material. A judge who sees a lack of professionalism in legislation takes a different approach. He does not derive any ''no'' from the legislature's ''yes,'' and he assumes that at times the legislature uses its words for nought and that there are many expressions in legislation that neither add nor subtract anything.

SUBSTANTIVE SOURCES OF DISCRETION IN THE CASE LAW

A case law rule is a general and binding legal norm created by a body authorized to do so, as an incidental consequence of adjudication. It establishes a rule containing a normative element that determines its application. Does judicial discretion also exist in the context of case law? The reader will not be surprised to find that even in the context of case law—perhaps especially in this context—judicial discretion exists. Thus, the reasons for the existence of judicial discretion in the case law are for the most part, and in their general sense, the same reasons that produce discretion in the statutory law—namely, the lack of clarity in the terms. These reasons are, moreover, sometimes stronger in the area of precedent than in the field of statutory law, and as a result one may say that judicial discretion exists with greater force in the case law. There is, in any event, nothing in the character of case law that either negates or narrows discretion in comparison to the statutory law.

DISCRETION IN THE CASE LAW:
THE UNCERTAINTY OF THE TERMS

In statutory law, the language is the law. In case law, the language is evidence of the law. The law is the rule that emerges from the holding. This rule is generally expressed in words, yet its normative strength is not derived from the words.[81] Thus, a rule might exist even if it were not couched in words. So the problem of precedent is not just the words themselves, but also the concepts that the creator wants the words to communicate to the reader. These concepts have clear implications in one type of case, yet they have a penumbra in another type of case. Indeed, case law, like statutory law, expresses principles, policies, and standards. The uncertainty that exists in the statutory law also exists in case law, and with greater force, precisely because there is no binding text to guide the delineation of the borders of the concepts. Thus, for example, the common law principle that an unreasonable administrative act is void creates problems of uncertainty regarding the concept "reasonable," similar to the problems that would arise in the interpretation of the same norm were it clothed in statutory dress. Thus, the problems in understanding the word *reasonable* when it appears in a statute are not much different from the difficulties in understanding the same concept when it appears in the case law. In any event, understanding concepts is no easier—and it is frequently more difficult—by virtue of the fact that they are phrased in a text that brands their language.

Case law is interlaced along its entire length and width by a terminology that expresses principles, policies, and standards.[82] These concepts constitute the main axis on which the common law turns. At times case law, by its very nature, has difficulty using rules that establish the factual circumstances to which they apply, and so it uses instead the

81. See L. Fuller, *Anatomy of the Law* 92 (1968).
82. See Summers, *supra* note 21.

terminology of principles, policies, and standards. Thus, for example, a common law judge cannot establish that driving at a certain speed is prohibited. He can, however, determine that driving unreasonably is prohibited.[83] Not infrequently, the need for legislation arises precisely because of a desire to arrange a certain subject by rules that establish the set of facts to which they apply, rather than by principles that make this impossible.

Therefore, what we said in the context of statute law about the uncertainty of language applies with even greater force to case law as well. Here the emphasis is not on the language, but rather on the concept. Most of the legal literature that we cited and analyzed on the uncertainty embedded in principles, policies, and standards does not distinguish between case law and statute, and all that we said there applies, with added vigor, here.

On occasion, in the process of establishing a common law rule, the judge is required to strike a balance among conflicting principles, policies, and standards. Thus, for example, when the judge assesses the reasonableness of the conduct of a governmental authority, he must balance the authority's freedom of action for the sake of the general good and the personal freedom of the individual. Not infrequently, the court must assign weights to the different values in order to perform this balancing. Everything we said about balance and weight in the field of statutory law applies to the case law as well.[84] Therefore, in balancing the court must seek the most reasonable solution, and if this standard has proven unavailing, the court must adopt the solution that seems to it to be best. Its discretion is limited, yet within the limitations that the law imposes, and after these have been applied, the court has freedom of action. It has discretion.

DISCRETION IN THE CASE LAW: UNCERTAINTY IN THE NORMATIVE ORDER

The *Ratio Decidendi*

In statute law the judge has an agreed-upon starting point for interpretation: the language of the statute. In case law no such starting point

---

83. See Hart and Sacks, *supra* note 26, ch. 1, at 138.

84. Professor Stone showed the importance of ''Categories of Illusory Reference'' in the development of the common law: see J. Stone, *The Province and Function of Law* 171 (1950); Stone, *supra* note 103, ch. 1, at 235.

exists. The role of the judge is to interpret[85] the judgment and to fashion the rule contained in it.[86] He must extract the rule from the judgment. For this, creativity is required. In truth, the number of possibilities is not unlimited. Yet within the bounds set by the natural limitations, a number of possibilities exist. This is so because there is no clear and binding rule concerning the manner in which one is to determine the binding holding[87] and the nonbinding dictum. Throughout judicial history, judges have refused to tie their hands in this matter,[88] and for the most part, the legislature has not intervened. The result is that there are a number of methods for finding the *ratio decidendi,* all of them legitimate in the context of the system. From a given judgment, then, one may sometimes derive a number of holdings.[89] In other words, there is judicial discretion with respect to the very existence of the judicial norm.

Not only is there no agreement about the rules for determining the holding, but even within the context of a given set of rules, one may often reach different outcomes. All agree that the facts of the case are important for determining the holding. The holding is the rule within the boundaries of the facts. Yet the facts are infinite. The judge must distinguish between "important" facts and "unimportant" facts. This distinction is not made on the basis of precise standards, and thus a certain judicial leeway is possible. Freedom in sorting the facts also means freedom in culling the rule that arises from the judgment. To be sure, this freedom is not complete. There are facts that every knowl-

---

85. In general the term *to interpret* is used in the matter of a statutory norm and not in the matter of a common law norm. In my view, there is no justification for this. To interpret means to determine the scope of application of a norm. This process of determination exists with respect to the statutory rule as well as with respect to the case law rule. See Greene, *supra* note 42, ch. 1, at 11: "Interpretation in this connection means to my mind exactly the same thing fundamentally in the case of interpretation of precedents as it does in the case of the interpretation of statutes. There is a superficial distinction between the two things. . . . When a judge 'interprets' a precedent he discovers and enunciates the true meaning of a principle in its relation to the particular set of facts before him. Similarly, when he interprets a statute he discovers and enunciates the true meaning of the statute in its relation to the particular facts before him." On the "interpretation" of the common law norm, see also Dworkin, *supra* note 16, ch. 1, at 111.

86. See Goodhart, "Determining the Ratio Decidendi of a Case," 40 *Yale L.J.* 161 (1930); Stone, "The Ratio of the Ratio Decidendi," 22 *Mod. L. Rev.* 597 (1959).

87. See R. Cross, *Precedent in English Law* (3d ed., 1977).

88. See D. Lloyd, *Introduction to Jurisprudence* 1119 (4th ed., 1979).

89. See R. Wasserstrom, *The Judicial Decision* (1961).

edgeable lawyer would recognize as important and there are facts that every knowledgeable lawyer would identify as unimportant. Between these two extremes is a substantial network of facts about which it cannot be said at the outset whether or not they are important. In this determination, there is judicial discretion.

So we see that there is judicial discretion, however limited, in determining the holding. As Professor Hart noted,

> Any honest description of the use of precedent in English law must allow a place for the following pairs of contrasting facts: *first*, there is no single method of determining the rule for which a given authoritative precedent is an authority. Notwithstanding this, in the vast majority of decided cases there is very little doubt. The head-note is usually correct enough. *Secondly*, there is no authoritative or uniquely correct formulation of any rule to be extracted from cases. On the other hand, there is often very general agreement, when the bearing of a precedent on a later case is in issue, that a given formulation is adequate.[90]

Thus, the legal community may agree that certain propositions surely do not constitute the holding, and that other propositions surely do comprise the holding. Between these two poles there is a broad area of judicial discretion.

Distinguishing the Holding

The rule of binding precedent imposes an obligation to rule on the basis of the holding of certain judgments. Yet within the framework of the rule of binding precedent, it is accepted that every court has the power to distinguish a binding judgment. The act of distinguishing constitutes a determination that the holding of the earlier judgment does not apply to a given set of facts. The court that distinguishes does not determine that the earlier judgment has no binding effect at all. It simply determines that the holding of the earlier case is restricted to a certain network of facts. By distinguishing, therefore, the court brings about a change in the law as it narrows the holding.

Just as there are no hard and clear rules regarding the determination of the holding, neither are there hard and clear rules with respect to the ways of distinguishing. Here, too, there are simple and obvious cases, but there are also borderline cases, in which there is judicial discretion

90. Hart *supra* note 12, ch. 1, at 131.

about whether and how to distinguish. Distinguishing is not to be done however one likes. There are rules. Professor Raz, for example, notes that distinguishing is subject to the following two conditions: "(1) The modified rule must be the rule laid down in the precedent restricted by the addition of a further condition for its application. (2) The modified rule must be such as to justify the order made in the precedent."[91] However, these conditions do not dictate one sole distinction in every case. Not infrequently, the judge can choose among a number of ways of distinguishing, all of them lawful in the context of his system. In this state of affairs, judicial discretion exists.

Deviating from the Holding

A number of legal systems that recognize the system of binding precedent sometimes permit deviations from it. The most prominent examples are those legal systems that allow the Supreme Court to deviate from its own precedents.[92] This is the law in Israel, where "A holding of the Supreme Court binds every court, except the Supreme Court."[93] Opinion is divided as to the meaning of this rule. I think the correct position requires one to distinguish among different situations. First, if the initial judgment is correct and acceptable to the court, it will follow it, and no question of deviation will be raised. Second, if the previous judgment is undoubtedly wrong, it should not be followed. In this case one should not speak of self-binding or of the restrictions of precedent. The judge is required, I believe, to deviate from the precedent. In the expression "undoubtedly wrong" I include all those cases in which there is only one lawful solution, but the court, in the initial case, did not adopt it and chose an unlawful solution instead. Such will be the case if the court completely ignored a statute and ruled in opposition to it. In this case, even within the framework of a system of binding precedent, deviation is permitted, for the original judgment was *per incuriam*. Yet in my opinion, the same rule must apply when a statute was quoted and interpreted by the previous court, but the interpretation was obviously erroneous. In this case, too, the court is under an obligation to deviate from the first precedent.

Another case belongs in this category: when the first decision was

91. Raz, *supra* note 12, ch. 1, at 186.
92. See Cross, *supra* note 87.
93. Sec. 20(b) of Basic Law: Judging.

handed down, it was lawful, but since that time changes have taken place
that make it no longer lawful. These changes may have been in the
normative plane, such as changes in the law (statutory or common law).
Then the case resembles the *per incuriam* example, yet the two are not
identical. The changes may also have been in the social plane, to the
extent that it is relevant for the formulation of the common law. This has
been recognized as an exception to the rule of controlling precedent, and
it seems to me that it continues to stand in the context of the existing
order, in the sense that in this case the judge is bound to deviate from the
earlier judgment. The third situation arises when the first judgment chose
one out of a number of lawful possibilities—in other words, the judges
who issued the first judgment were faced with using their discretion—
and these possibilities remain lawful today. Then the court may follow
the first judgment (and thus adopt the first court's use of discretion), but it
may also choose not to follow it (and thus to adopt another possibility
among those that are open to the court). In deciding whether or not to
follow the previous holding, the court must weigh the fact that the first
decision exists and consider the damage to the public's expectations and
its confidence in the courts that a deviation from it will produce. The
court must balance between this harm and the benefit of a deviation from
the first decision. Only if the benefit outweighs the harm is there room to
deviate from the first rule.[94]

This analysis indicates that where a court is not bound by a prior
decision (of its own or of another court) it may at times face a dilemma
about whether to bind itself by that earlier decision and to follow in its
path, or to cut itself off from it. This will be the case, for example, if in
the earlier decision the court chose from among a number of lawful
possibilities, and that same freedom of choice (perhaps with additional or
fewer possibilities) persists. The judge must choose among the various
possibilities in a reasonable manner. Sometimes this requirement will be
enough to indicate one solution (such as leaving the old ruling in place).
Yet in other cases this standard will not suffice to negate judicial discretion, as each of the possibilities is consistent with the test of reasonableness. Then the court will have freedom of choice, without the law

94. See ch. 9. See Sprecher, "The Development of the Doctrine of Stare Decisis and
the Extent to which it Should Be Applied," 31 *A.B.A.J.* 501 (1945); Schaefer, "Precedent
and Policy," 34 *U. Chi. L. Rev.* 3 (1966).

imposing upon it a duty to act one way or another, other than the obligation to choose that solution which appears to the court to be the best. This freedom of choice entails judicial discretion. Thus, in deviating from a precedent from which the court is permitted but not required to deviate, judicial discretion may exist.

This judicial discretion becomes broader if, in addition to the basic question of deviation, another question—whether or not the deviation shall be retroactive—also arises. At times this option does not present itself to the court, for even if the court deviates from precedent, the deviation must be retroactive. Yet there are legal systems in which the law permits prospective deviation or overruling. In other legal systems, the question has not yet arisen, and it is unclear whether the law permits prospective overruling. In all these situations the range of discretion becomes wider, for in addition to the question, To deviate or to uphold? there is also the question, To deviate as of when?[95]

SUBSTANTIVE SOURCES OF DISCRETION: THE LACK OF A LEGAL NORM ("LACUNA")

The Question

Is there judicial discretion where no legal norm exists? This is a difficult question. It raises fundamental problems of jurisprudence,[96] and it raises complicated issues in Israeli law. In order to examine this question, one must first define its parameters. As I indicated, the question assumes a state of affairs in which no legal norm is found that decides a particular conflict, and it concerns the scope of judicial discretion in such a situation. What does this assumption mean insofar as the absence of a statutory norm and the absence of a common law norm are concerned?

The Absence of a Statutory Norm—When?

From the perspective of the statutory norm, this assumption means that the decision in a particular controversy falls outside the field of application of any statutory norm. For this one must, of course, examine every statutory norm, for a given case might fall outside the field of application of one norm, yet within the bounds of the field of application of another

95. See ch. 9.
96. See Raz, *supra* note 12, ch. 1, 70, 180.

norm. Therefore, our assumption requires that the conflict fall outside the field of application of all the statutory norms. This assumption does not exist—and thus a statutory norm that regulates the case exists—if (a) the dispute falls within the area regulated in a "negative arrangement" by a certain statutory norm, or (b) the dispute falls within the area of judicial discretion in the context of interpreting a statutory norm. In these cases, the judge finds a statutory norm that regulates the conflict, although his discretion is required in order to determine its scope of application.

In situation (a), a statutory norm is found. It establishes a certain arrangement—the granting of a right or power, or the imposition of an obligation, or the recognition of an immunity—with respect to the matters it encompasses ("a positive arrangement"), and it establishes a certain arrangement—the lack of a right or obligation, or the lack of a power or an immunity—with respect to matters that are not included in it ("a negative arrangement"). What distinguishes this state of affairs is that the positive arrangement finds expression in the explicit language of the norm, while the negative arrangement either is inferred from the language or stems from something established in other norms. Thus, for example, the norms of the criminal law establish responsibility (a positive arrangement) if the conditions stipulated in the criminal laws are fulfilled, and they establish a lack of responsibility (a negative arrangement) if the conditions established by the criminal laws are not fulfilled. This stems from a combined activity of interpreting the specific criminal laws and applying the general principle of *nullum crimen sine lege*. Every case that falls within the boundaries of one of these arrangements, whether positive or negative, is controlled by the statutory norm, and the question of judicial discretion in the absence of a statutory rule does not arise. Sometimes, of course, it is difficult to know whether a norm establishes only a positive arrangement or whether it also creates a negative arrangement. Some statutory norms establish a positive arrangement for certain issues, and no arrangement whatever—neither positive nor negative—for other issues. For example, a rule stipulating that a manufacturer bears strict liability in tort for any harm caused by the use of a defective product does not establish that the manufacturer is not responsible, or that he is absolutely liable, in other cases. Similarly, the norm establishing that under certain conditions the tortfeasor is liable for "malicious prosecution" does not contain a negative arrangement respecting tort liability (for example, in negligence) in the absence of these specific conditions. The aforementioned statutory norms established a certain positive arrangement if certain conditions were met, but took no position regarding the question of liability if the conditions were not met (that is, they created no negative arrangement). At times it is easy to say whether a particular arrangement is only positive or is also negative. At times the answer to this question is difficult and involves judicial discretion. But this is judicial discretion in the interpretation of a given statutory norm, which we discussed elsewhere. It is not connected to the question with which we are currently concerned, namely, the question of judicial discretion in the absence of a statutory norm.

In situation (b)—a matter within the scope of judicial discretion in the interpretation of a statutory norm—a statutory norm exists. But the field of application of that norm is not clear. There are several possibilities, each of them lawful. The judge must determine, through his use of discretion, the controlling option. This state of affairs is "covered" by a statutory norm, but the content of the norm is determined by the exercise of judicial discretion. For example, the Israeli Contracts Law (General Part) (1973) stipulates that a contract must be carried out in good faith. But the concept of good faith is obscure and open-textured. Some hold that its meaning is subjective ("no malice"), while others argue that its meaning is objective ("act honestly"), and still others say it has both subjective and objective elements.

The judge, exercising judicial discretion, decides whether the contract was executed in good faith. Nonetheless, the question is "resolved" by the statutory norm. Judicial discretion in the absence of a norm is not involved. Rather, what is at issue is judicial discretion in the interpretation of an existing norm.

Thus it follows that the question with which we are dealing—judicial discretion in the absence of a statutory norm—arises only in disputes that fall outside the field of application of a given statutory norm. True, in many cases the field of application of the norm may not be clear (that is, the case is neither easy nor intermediate), and the judge may have discretion in establishing its scope (a hard case)—whether with respect to the content of the arrangement (only positive or also negative) or from other perspectives (objective or subjective good faith)—yet in the final analysis, there is a statutory norm in whose framework the dispute will be decided.

At times there is a statutory rule in a given system that establishes how the judge should act in the absence of a statutory rule. One may, of course, argue that in such a case a statutory order resolving the case in fact exists, and thus the question of judicial discretion in the absence of a statutory norm does not arise. However, one must distinguish between a case in which there is a statutory rule whose field of application is unknown and can be determined only through the exercise of judicial discretion, and a case in which no statutory rule exists, and judicial discretion is required in order to establish the rule itself. To understand this distinction, we may adopt the terminology developed by Professor Hart. He distinguishes between "primary rules" and "secondary rules." Primary rules establish a particular set of norms that regulate the life of the individual in society. Secondary rules establish ways to recognize (rules of recognition), change (rules of change), or decide a case (rules of adjudication) in respect of a primary rule. When we are dealing with the interpretation of an extant statutory norm, a primary rule already exists, and the judge, through the use of his authority to decide the case, gives it its correct meaning. But when no statutory norm exists, and the judge creates it on the strength of a rule in the law that regulates this, there is no primary rule, and the court, through its authority to decide in the case and to change the existing law, creates it. Of course, these two situations have much in common. In both cases, the judge may exercise discretion. In both cases, he acts on the basis of a secondary norm. In both cases, he ultimately decides the conflict. Nonetheless, there is an important difference between the two scenarios. In one, a primary norm exists, although its scope is unknown. In the other, a primary norm that did not exist previously is created.

The critical question, from our perspective, is whether the difference between these two situations—interpretation of an existing statutory norm and creation of a new norm—is relevant for the matter of judicial discretion. Is judicial discretion in the interpretation of a statutory norm identical to judicial discretion in the creation of a new norm on the basis of a statutory norm empowering the judge to do so?

The Absence of a Case Law Norm—When?

We already posed the question What is judicial discretion in the absence of a legal norm? We analyzed the importance of this question in the matter of a statutory norm. What significance does this question have from the perspective of the case law norm? It seems to me that from the point of view of the case law norm, the "absence of a legal norm" means that the legal conflict falls outside the bounds of the "holdings" of the binding precedents in that legal system. If the controversy is controlled by the holding of one precedent or another, one cannot say that there is no legal norm that determines the outcome of the conflict. On the other hand, if there is no holding that applies to the case, then the question with which we are dealing arises.

What if the case law in a given legal system establishes, in the context of the holding, the method of resolving cases as to which there is no precedent? The analysis here must, in my opinion, be the same as my analysis of the statutory norm. Thus, there is no existing rule, and we are faced with the question occupying us regarding judicial discretion in the creation of a new judicial rule.

Judicial Discretion in the Creation of a New Norm

Is there judicial discretion in the creation of a new norm where a lacuna exists in the system? Every modern legal system, it seems, has norms relating to the filling of lacunae, and these undoubtedly confer judicial discretion, albeit limited. But the scope of this discretion varies from one system to the next. Every legal system has its own general normative direction for this issue. Judicial discretion in a system in which the judge fills a lacuna as the legislature would have had the problem arisen before it differs from judicial discretion in a system in which lacunae are to be filled by analogy from the existing laws.

What is the normative direction in whose context the (American or British) common law develops? It seems that no clear norm (secondary rule) has yet crystallized that permits the court to draw an analogy from a statutory norm.[97] In any event, even if the practice is not unknown it is extremely limited. As for the case law itself, it certainly develops according to the standard of analogy,[98] although this is not the only rule the common law recognizes.[99] It seems that this system, in an effort to retain

97. See Landis, "Statutes and the Sources of Law," in *Harvard Legal Essays* 213 (1934); Atiyah, "Common Law and Statute Law," 48 *Mod. L. Rev.* 1 (1985).

98. See Parke J. In *Mirehouse v. Rennell* (1832) 8 Bing. 490, 515.

99. See Lord Halsbury in *Keighley, Maxstead and Co. v. Durant* [1901] A.C. 240, 244.

maximum flexibility, refused to limit itself by any fixed norms.[100] Thus in case of a lacuna, the judge is permitted to draw an analogy, but he is also entitled to employ other principles, such as justice, reasonableness, common sense, morality, and other general principles accepted in the system. Of course, these principles may sometimes conflict. The judge then balances them by assigning appropriate weights to the competing values. Thus we see that when a lacuna in the common law system arises, the judge is given broad discretion.

A similar broad discretion is given to the civil law judge. Swiss law, for example, stipulates[101] that in the event of a lacuna, the judge is to supply what is missing as though he were the legislature. Surely there is in this a grant of broad discretion to the judge, with the normative limitation—requiring him to act as though he were the legislature—as weak as can be. In practice, it appears that only limited use is made of this discretion.

Austrian law establishes[102] that where a problem cannot be solved by interpretation or analogy, it is to be solved in accordance with the natural principles of justice. The Italian code provides[103] that where a problem is not solved through interpretation or analogy, the decision should be made according to the general principles of the legal order of the state. A similar directive is found in the Mexican code,[104] which also refers (370a) to general legal principles.

Does a Lacuna Exist When There Is a Norm Regarding Filling a "Lacuna"?

It may be argued that in a legal system containing secondary rules that determine how to fill the vacuum created by a lacuna no lacunae exist. To be sure, there is no lacuna in this system as to how lacunae are to be filled. Yet this system has other lacunae that require filling. Of course, over time a certain number of spaces will be filled, but additional spaces may simultaneously be created. Therefore, one has to distinguish be-

100. See Lucke, *supra* note 70, ch. 1, at 67.
101. Sec. 1(2) of the Law of Obligation, 1907. See also von Overbeck, "Some Observations on the Role of the Judge Under the Swiss Civil Code," 37 *La. L. Rev.* 681 (1977).
102. Sec. 7 of the Civil Code of 1811.
103. Sec. 12 of the Civil Code of 1942.
104. Sec. 19 of the Mexican Code of 1928.

tween a legal system's potential for filling lacunae, and the actual filling of these spaces by the court. As long as the court has not filled the lacunae, we say that there are lacunae in the system, even if the system has a normative potential that enables it to fill them.

Judicial Discretion in Israel in the Filling of a Lacuna: The Foundations of Law Law

The Foundations of Law Law, 1980, repealed Section 46 of the King's Order in Council (1922) and established a new normative order in its place. The decree is worded thus:

> If the court sees a legal question requiring decision, and found no answer to it in a statutory norm, in the case law, or by means of analogy, it will decide it in light of the principles of freedom, justice, equity and peace of the heritage of Israel.''

This provision does not explicitly rank the normative system, yet it appears that a proper interpretation would say that one should proceed according to the order set in it. The court must examine first and foremost whether the question is resolved by a statutory norm. Then it examines whether there is an answer to the question in the case law. Only if the court does not find an answer in these two does it turn to the ''means of analogy,'' and if this method, too, fails to resolve the question, ''it will decide it in light of the principles of freedom, justice, equity and peace of the heritage of Israel.'' Thus, one should not consult the named principles of the heritage of Israel if the question may be solved by analogy, nor seek an analogy if the legal question has an answer in statutory or case law, and one should not look to the case law if there is an answer to the question in a statute.

This rule is among the most central in the Israeli system. It grants broad judicial discretion to the judge. Like any judicial discretion, this discretion is limited. The scope of the limitations depends, of course, on the interpretation given to the provisions of the statute. Like any other statutory rule, this rule, too, must be interpreted. Unfortunately, its vagueness outweighs its clarity, and many basic questions are left without clear answers. Even here, therefore, the exercise of judicial discretion cannot be avoided.

Chapter 3
The Formal
Sources of
Judicial Discretion

JUDICIAL DISCRETION AND JUDICIAL LAW-MAKING

Basic Terminology

Judicial discretion, according to our definition, is the power given to the judge to choose from among a number of possibilities, each of them lawful in the context of the system. In the interpretation of a statutory rule, this power means the carrying out of one of the various possibilities that are embedded in the language of the statute. In the interpretation of case law, this power means the determination of the *ratio decidendi* of a case. In a deviation from an existing common law rule, this power is used to replace the existing rule with another rule. Where no previous legal norm exists, the significance of this power lies in filling the void by the creation of a new norm. In all these situations, a new normative reality is created through the use of the hidden power of judicial discretion. On the strength of the principle of binding precedent, this new normative reality is imbued with a general character.

"Law-making" is the creation of general legal norms. As Professor Hans Klinghoffer said, "Making general norms is law-making in the functional sense, without distinction as to the organ creating the general norm."[1] In the modern democratic state, law-making is, first and foremost, the work of the elected political body, the legislative branch. The

---

1. H. Klinghoffer, *Administrative Law* 7 (1957).

main—if not the only—task of the legislative branch is to enact laws. The requirements of society demand that the executive authority also make laws. This is secondary legislation. But the judge, by deciding a case, is also involved in the creation of general legal norms. The judge, too, is occupied with law-making: judicial law-making.[2]

Judicial law-making is, therefore, the creation of general legal norms by the judge in the process of adjudication. Judicial discretion is the power and the authority to choose and to create. Judicial law-making is the result obtained by the application of this power and authority. Lord Diplock said:

> It is the second function of the judicial process, deciding whether what really happened amounted to a breach of one man's duty to his neighbour, with which I am concerned. This must entail legislation whenever there is room for dispute as to what man's duty to his neighbour is. In the majority of cases there is none. Once it has been found what really happened—there is no dispute as to its legal consequences; the relevant rule of conduct is plain. But there are also cases—many more than one would expect—where there is room for dispute as to what the rule of conduct really is. This is so as much with rules laid down by Act of Parliament as with those which have evolved at common law.[3]

There are, of course, substantive differences between judicial law-making and other forms of law-making. Thus, for example, judicial law-making is always the by-product of the act of adjudication. It does not stand on its own. True, all three branches of government are involved in law-making, but they make law in different ways, and therefore their law-making is, by its very nature, different.[4] Yet this difference is not enough to blur the similarity nor to erase the reality that the judge, incidentally to deciding the controversy, also is involved in law-making.

Discretion, Law-Making, and the Principle of Binding Precedent

I defined judicial law-making as the creation of general legal norms by the judge through adjudication. When the judicial branch creates an

2. See Barak, "Judicial Legislation," 13 *Mishpatim* 25 (1983).

3. K. Diplock, *The Courts As Legislators* 5 (Holdsworth Club, Presidential Addresses, 1965).

4. See Dickson, "The Judiciary—Law Interpreters or Law Makers?" 12 *Manitoba L.J.* 1, 5 (1982): "The judiciary and the legislature both make law—but it is not the same kind of law nor is it made for the same purposes."

individual legal norm—that is, a norm that binds only the parties before it—it is not involved in judicial law-making, but rather in simple adjudication. According to this analytical approach, there is a direct link between judicial law-making and the principle of binding precedent. This connection means that only in those cases where the judgment of the court has the status of binding precedent does judicial law-making exist.[5] When a precedent is binding, the rule embedded in the judgment binds not only the parties to the conflict, but the entire public. The judicial creation of the court thereby acquires general validity. From this one gets the acknowledgment of the judicial rule as a legislative act in its functional sense. As Lord Diplock stated:

> Yet implicitly every judgment delivered not under a palm tree but in a Court bound by the rules of precedent speaks to the future and speaks generally. It says not only to the particular party to the action but to all to whom the judgment becomes known: "If anyone does this kind of thing in the future this kind of consequence will follow". It is by that implicit content of every judgment that the Court is performing a judicial function exercise—a legislative power.[6]

The fact that the Supreme Court is not bound by its own precedents is irrelevant to this issue. As far as the legislative character of the act of adjudication is concerned, it is enough that the public is bound by Supreme Court precedents. Similarly, the fact that the legislature can change a judgment by its own act of legislation does not detract from the legislative character of the judgments.

This connection between judicial law-making and binding precedent may surprise, given the common view that judicial restraint curbs judicial discretion and therefore limits the scope of judicial law-making. Indeed, judicial restraint does curb the scope of the judicial creation to some extent. Yet it imparts legislative authority to the limited judicial creation that it recognizes.

Despite the formal link between the functional concept of judicial law-making and the principle of binding precedent, one cannot ignore the social-legal reality, which also attaches significant weight to rulings

---

    5. See Krindle, "The Law Making Process," 2 *Manitoba L.J.* 167 (1967); Hiller, "The Law-Creative Role of Appellate Courts in the Commonwealth," 27 *Int'l & Comp. L. Q.* 85 (1978).

    6. Diplock, *supra* note 3, at 3.

of the court whose holdings are not binding. Naturally, this is the view of those who, like Holmes,[7] hold that the law is only the prophecy of the judgments of the courts. According to this approach, a judicial ruling about which one can predict with a high degree of certainty that it will be followed is of itself law, even if it does not have the power of a binding precedent. But even someone such as myself, who does not share Holmes's view, cannot ignore, from the standpoint of social dynamics, the place of judicial rulings that the public follows in practice, yet that are not binding from the formal viewpoint, such as Supreme Court dicta or judgments of the district or magistrate courts. As Professor Tedeschi said:

> Even when there is no binding precedent, in the custom of the world it raises a certain expectation that it will be followed in the future. This is so especially in those legal systems that have rules intended to guarantee unity in the case law, so that one cannot say that the judgment is exhausted by its relevance for the parties in the case and that is all, and that any stranger who takes into account its ratio decidendi will resemble an eavesdropper who hears, through a wall, speech that is not meant for his ears.[8]

Thus, the speech of the case law, even when it is not binding, is meant not only for the parties in the case, and all its rulings constitute legislation, albeit not in the formal sense. Moreover, as far as the lowest courts are concerned, without their activity the highest court would not be able to carry out its function properly. Establishing the factual base, raising the various legal options, and setting them up for the highest court's decision are important roles in the development of judicial law-making.

Judicial Discretion in the Application of a Norm and Judicial Law-making

The object of judicial discretion might be the norm itself or it might be the application of the norm to the particular controversy. In the former case, we seek to learn what the norm is (What is negligence?). In the latter case, we want to know how to apply the norm to a given set of facts (Is driving at a certain speed at a certain time negligent behavior?). By its very nature, then, judicial discretion as to the application of the norm cannot constitute a precedent for other cases. It represents only a deci-

7. Holmes, *supra* note 17, ch. 1, at 461.
8. G. Tedeschi, *supra* note 27, ch. 1, at 30.

sion in the particular case. It follows that judicial discretion whose object is the application of a given norm to a given set of facts does not constitute judicial law-making. However, in order to establish the particular decision, the judge must determine (consciously or subconsciously) the scope of the norm. This determination, to the extent it contains judicial discretion, will constitute law-making: it is of a general character, and on the strength of the principle of binding precedent, it becomes an act of law-making. So we see that of the three objects of judicial discretion (facts, application of the norm, and the norm itself) only the third-—the force of the norm itself—serves as a basis for judicial law-making.

Judicial Law-making in the Absence of Judicial Discretion

The connection between judicial discretion and judicial law-making is not inevitable. On the one hand, there can be judicial discretion without judicial law-making. This is the situation wherever the exercise of judicial discretion does not create a general rule. On the other hand, judicial law-making can exist in the absence of judicial discretion. This is the situation when the judge creates a general legal norm, without any other lawful possibility being open to him. In the interpretation of a statute, this situation arises when a judge gives the norm the only possible interpretation. When dealing with case law, there is judicial law-making in the absence of judicial discretion when the court repeats a ruling that was handed down lawfully or when it deviates from a ruling that was clearly erroneous. When there is no legal norm, this is the case when there is only one lawful solution for filling the lacuna. In all these cases, judicial law-making takes place without the judge having judicial discretion.

Indeed, most acts of judicial law-making do not involve any judicial discretion. Only one lawful option exists, with no possibility of choosing among different situations. In many cases, Montesquieu's description, which sees the judge as the mouthpiece that repeats the language of the statute, is valid. In many situations, the so-called phonograph theory, according to which[9] the judge repeats the words with which the statute speaks to him, is correct. Similarly, in many cases, the judge repeats a holding that was decided lawfully and does not innovate at all. The declaratory theory, according to which the judge does not create new law but rather simply declares the existing law, is, in this type of case,

9. M. R. Cohen, *Law and the Social Order* 112, 113 (1933).

faultless. The difficulties begin when one fails to make the necessary distinctions and instead holds that what is true in most cases is true in all cases—that if in the majority of cases judicial law-making is carried out without judicial discretion, this is an indication that judicial law-making is done without judicial discretion in every case. Not so. One must distinguish carefully between easy and intermediate cases, on the one hand, and hard cases, on the other. In the first two types, there is no judicial discretion, and to the extent they involve judicial law-making— that is, a general norm by virtue of precedent—they do so without judicial discretion. In the hard cases, however, there is judicial discretion, and to the extent they involve judicial law-making—that is, a general norm on the strength of precedent—they do so through judicial discretion. The field of the law is not unitary. It has mountains as well as plains, and whoever navigates it must distinguish among its paths. In the words of Justice Sussman,

> The image of the judge, in Montesquieu's eyes, is the image of a person extremely capable of finding his way in the hidden paths of the forest of legislation, yet Montesquieu's view is flawed by the common error, that these paths always exist and all your capability lies only in discovering them. Montesquieu did not realize that sometimes the paths were not paved by the legislature at all, and the judge himself has to pave them.[10]

Cases in which there is no judicial discretion—even if there is balancing and weighing in their mental sense—lie outside the scope of this book, as do cases in which there is no judicial law-making—even though they involve decision in a controversy by means of a particular act. This book is concerned with judicial law-making that follows the exercise of judicial discretion. The reason for this self-limitation is that in this type of case, difficult problems arise as to the substantive legitimacy of the act of legislation, the status of judges in a democratic society, and the relationship between judicial law-making and the separation of powers.

THE FORMAL SOURCES OF JUDICIAL DISCRETION AND JUDICIAL LAW-MAKING

The Problem

What is the source of judicial discretion, and of the judicial law-making that follows in its footsteps? There are several aspects to this question. In

10. Sussman, *supra* note 44, ch. 1, at 213.

the present context, the question arises in its formal aspect: What is the legal basis for the authority and power of the judge to choose among a number of possibilities and thereby to perform an act of establishing the legal norm or establishing the scope of its application? This examination is extremely important, since the judicial branch—like the other branches of government—must anchor its activities in the law. The judicial branch has nothing more than what the law gives it. This is the formal principle of the rule of law. Judicial law-making is permissible only if it is recognized in the law and only to the extent recognized by law. It follows that the authority for judicial law-making and its scope must be anchored in the law. This is the principle of formal legitimacy. It applies to the activity of every governmental body, in particular to the activity of the judicial branch because it examines whether the other bodies are acting within the law. Someone who examines and checks whether others are acting lawfully must first and foremost insist that his own activity be lawful.

In the matter of the formal authority of the judge to exercise judicial discretion and to create judicial law, one must distinguish between two legal situations: one, in which there is an explicit rule granting the judge discretion to establish the legal norm or its scope of application; and the other, in which no such rule exists.

The Formal Sources: An Explicit Rule

In the first situation, the statutory norm explicitly stipulates that the judge has discretion as to the determination of the legal norm or the scope of its application. An example of such an explicit authorization may be found in the Foundations of Law Law, which grants the judge power to create new rules "by means of analogy" or, where this proves impossible, to make rules "in light of the principles of freedom, justice, equity and peace of the heritage of Israel." Similar rules exist in many legal systems. In general, however, the statutes rarely give the court explicit authority to establish the norm or the scope of its application. This issue is usually left to jurisprudence and to the case law itself.

The Formal Sources: In the Absence of an Explicit Rule

Natural or Delegated Authority In the second legal situation, there is no explicit rule giving the judge authority to exercise judicial discretion in the determination of the legal norm or its scope of application. What is the source of his authority to do so in this state of affairs? The answer is that the authority is a necessary corollary of the need to decide in the controversy. In order to rule in the conflict, the court must determine the facts and apply the legal norm to these facts. To do this, it must first establish what that legal norm is and determine its scope of application. The judge cannot decide the case unless he has before him a legal norm according to which the case will be decided. The authority to decide in the dispute carries with it, as a natural result, the authority to determine the legal norm according to which the case will be decided and the scope of its application. This determination is for the parties, but because of the principle of binding precedent it is given general normative force in cases in which it applies. It becomes an act of lawmaking.

Of course, where the law contains only one lawful possibility, the judge must apply the law according to that possibility. He is not authorized to exercise judicial discretion in easy or intermediate cases. Yet where the law contains a number of lawful options, there is no alternative to choosing, consciously or subconsciously, among the various possibilities. This is a hard case, which authorizes the exercise of judicial discretion. The judge cannot decide the case without selecting the lawful, binding norm.

One can reach the same conclusion, with respect to a statutory norm, in the following manner as well. "Every legislated rule, as a natural and self-evident matter, contains a bestowal of interpretive authority on the court."[11] It follows that even if there is no explicit authorization to use judicial discretion, implicit authorization is always present.[12] The judge cannot judge on the basis of a statutory norm without interpreting it.[13] To judge means to interpret. "The application of a law frequently—and in practice always—involves taking a position as to its substance and its content."[14] Whoever enacted a given norm thereby implicitly authorized the judge to interpret it[15] and to determine its areas of application. Whoever authorized the judge to decide the controversy implicitly autho-

11. H.C. 73/85 *Kach v. The Speaker of the Knesset,* 39 P.D.(3) 141.

12. See Calabresi, *supra* note 11, ch. 1, at 92.

13. See Fiss, *supra* note 37, ch. 1.

14. H.C. 306/81 *Sharon v. The Parliamentary Committee,* 35 P.D.(4) 118, 141 (Shamgar, J.).

15. See Curtis, "A Better Theory of Legal Interpretation," 3 *Vand. L. Rev.* 407, 424 (1950).

rized him to establish the norm according to which he is to decide the case and the areas of its application. Enactment of a statute is the bestowal of discretion upon the judge to interpret it.

The need to determine the norm or the scope of its application, as an essential condition of an act, is not unique to the judicial branch. Every person or body that acts on the basis of a legal norm must, incidentally to its action, decide for itself—knowingly or unknowingly—the norm according to which it is acting and the scope of its application. We live in a normative world. Each of us, at all times, acts on the basis of legal norms, and thus must—again, consciously or unawares—determine for himself the norm and its scope. This is particularly striking in the matter of governmental bodies. These bodies have only what the law bestows upon them. Each of their actions must, therefore, be anchored in the law. It is only natural, then, that before they act, and as a precondition to their action, they will take a stand regarding the law that applies to them and the scope of its application. The legislative body, before it legislates, must take a position as to the norm fixed in the constitution, according to which it acts and from which it is prohibited to deviate. It is also required to take a position regarding the norms established in other statutes, which it may not breach. Similarly, the executive branch, which acts under the laws, must—knowingly or unknowingly—determine for itself before exercising its legislative, executive, or judicial powers the norm according to which it is acting and the scope of its application. The same holds true for the judicial branch. Every judge, parenthetically to his decision in the controversy, must establish the legal norm and the area of its application.

The Uniqueness of the Judge's Authority Every person must decide for himself, consciously or otherwise, the legal norm according to which he acts, and the field of its application. How, then, is the judge different from any other person? The answer is that every person determines the legal norm for himself and for those who are willing or obliged to accept his determination. As long as no one challenges him, they act according to this determination. Yet occasionally one person's decision conflicts with someone else's decision. For example, the citizen believes that by virtue of a certain legal norm he enjoys a right or immunity. The government believes that the same legal norm does not bestow a right or immunity. Thus a conflict is created, which the court is called upon to decide. The court applies its discretion, while deciding between the positions of the various parties. Once it has decided, its decision—and only its decision—is binding. It follows that the judge's discretion in establishing the legal norm or the area of its application differs from the discretion of others, in that the judge's discretion binds them, whereas their discretion does not bind him. In other words, the need to decide in the case includes, as a natural and pendent issue, the need to establish the legal norm and its field of application. This decision binds the parties, whoever they may be. As Justice Meir Shamgar noted,

> Each governmental authority is called upon, at appointed times, to interpret legislation, for the application of the statutory law frequently—and in theory always—involves taking a position as to its substance and content. But the ultimate and decisive interpretive determination regarding a statute, its validity at any given time, is in the hands of the court, and as for cases that are brought for examination within the legal system, it is in the hands of the Supreme Court.[16]

By the principle of binding precedent, this determination acquires general normative validity and becomes an act of judicial law-making in the functional sense. I discussed this elsewhere in the following terms:

> Thus, every governmental organ—and for this matter also every individual—is involved in statutory interpretation, in order to guide its steps. Occasionally the practice is to give the interpretive authority for a certain organ to one bureaucrat or another. Thus, for example, the authority to interpret the law for the executive branch is given to the Attorney-General, and his interpretation binds it internally. If a question of interpretation arises in court and the court has the power of interpretation, its interpretation is what binds the parties, and if it is the Supreme Court that provides the interpretation, it binds the entire public (by virtue of the principle of binding precedent: Section 20 (b) of the Basic Law: Adjudication).[17]

This formal approach to the source of the (natural or implicit) authority of the judge to exercise judicial discretion draws its sustenance from its conception of the modern democracy. At its core stands the principle of the rule of law. Every person and every private or governmental body is subject to the law. When a conflict arises as to the content of the law, the authority to decide is placed in the hands of the judicial branch. This is the principle of the separation of powers, which gives the judicial

16. See *supra* note 14.
17. H.C. 73/85 *supra* note 11, at 152.

branch—and to it alone—the authority to decide in the dispute. In making this decision, the judicial branch is independent and is not instructed by any person or body as to how it should interpret the law. It must decide alone, and it is responsible for its decision. Of course, in many situations there is no discretion in this matter. Only one lawful possibility exists. But in other situations, the law itself creates a situation of discretion. The judge must choose from among a number of lawful possibilities. The power to choose is in the hands of the judge, and in this choice he has no master other than the law. The executive branch[18] and the legislative branch[19] cannot instruct him how to apply his discretion in the interpretation of the statute. I discussed this elsewhere, saying,

> In the relations between the judicial branch and the executive branch, as well as in the relations between the judicial branch and the legislative branch, the principle is that whatever the interpretation of the other authorities may be, the binding interpretation is that of the court.[20]

The same principle is accepted by enlightened democratic states. Thus, for example, the United States Supreme Court held in *Powell v. McCormack:*

> Our system of government requires that federal courts on occasion interpret the Constitution in a manner at variance with the construction given the document by another branch. The alleged conflict that such an adjudication may cause cannot justify the courts avoiding their Constitutional responsibility. . . . It is the responsibility of this Court to act as the ultimate interpreter of the Constitution.[21]

"These words are not unique to a legal system that has a formal constitution and that recognizes judicial review of the constitutionality of legislation. These words are fundamental truths in every legal system in which an independent judicial branch exists."[22]

This does not prevent the legislature—if it is not bound by a constitutional provision—from lawfully changing these fundamental truths. Accordingly, the legislature may declare in a statute that the authority to interpret a statute in a certain matter is vested not in the court deciding the

18. See *United States v. Nixon,* 418 U.S. 683 (1974).
19. See *Powell v. McCormack,* 395 U.S. 486 (1969).
20. H.C. 73/85 *supra* note 11, at 152.
21. See *supra* note 19, at 549.
22. H.C. 73/85 *supra* note 11, at 153.

conflict but rather in a nonjudicial body, whose interpretation is binding upon the court. But rules such as this are rare. In general, they are linked to the denial of the court's jurisdiction to deal with the merits of the case. Indeed, sometimes it is more convenient to negate the court's authority to consider and decide the case than to deny the court its natural authority to interpret the statute according to which it adjudicates in the dispute. Yet negation of the court's jurisdiction is also a rare occurrence. Thus, where the legislature is dissatisfied with the way the court exercised its discretion, its primary tool is to change the general norm that emerges from the case law.

THE SCOPE OF JUDICIAL LAW-MAKING— "THE ZONE OF FORMAL LEGITIMACY"

The scope of judicial law-making is a function of the scope of judicial discretion. As we saw, judicial discretion is limited, never absolute. Therefore, judicial law-making is also limited. Absolute judicial law-making does not exist. Not every option that the judge would prefer is possible; not every consideration is permissible. When the discretion involves the interpretation of a statute, the statute itself limits the scope of judicial law-making. The words of Justice Holmes apply to this type of law-making: "I recognize without hesitation that judges do and must legislate, but they can do so only interstitially; they are confined from molar to molecular motion."[23] Justice Moshe Landau discussed the same principle: "Even after such legislation the courts go back and weave anew the web of their interpretation around the sections of the statute or within its cracks (interstitially), as in Justice Holmes' famous phrase."[24] The material is statutory; only its adaptation is judicial. The notes are statutory; only their rendition is judicial.[25] The legal blocks— to use Justice Landau's imagery[26]—are statutory; their rearrangement is judicial. The words of the statute, on the one hand, and the legislative purpose, on the other, determine the scope of judicial law-making. When the judge fills a lacuna in the law, the scope of his judicial law-making is

23. *Southern Pacific Co. v. Jensen,* 244 U.S. 205, 221 (1917).

24. Landau, *supra* note 17, ch. 1, at 297.

25. See Frank, "Words and Music: Some Remarks on Statutory Interpretation," 47 *Colum. L. Rev.* 1259 (1947).

26. Landau, *supra* note 17, ch. 1, at 292.

like the scope of the gap the law creates. This gap is not infinite. It is a gap within a given normative framework, a "closed gap."[27] It follows that the judicial law-making that fills it is also "closed law-making." Justice Cardozo discussed this, noting,

> If you ask how he is to know when one interest outweighs another, I can only answer that he must get his knowledge just as the legislator gets it, from experience and study and reflection; in brief, from life itself. Here, indeed, is the point of contact between the legislator's work and his. The choice of methods, the appraisement of values, must in the end be guided by like considerations for the one as for the other. Each indeed is legislating within the limits of his competence. No doubt the limits for the judge are narrower. He legislates only between gaps. He fills the open spaces in the law.[28]

Similar—if not identical—limitations apply to judicial discretion and to judicial law-making in case law. Principles, policies, and standards all create judicial discretion, yet they also limit it, and with it judicial law-making. Thus, judicial discretion outlines a zone—the zone of formal legitimacy. Every option within this zone is lawful and a subject for judicial discretion, while every option outside this zone is unlawful and not a subject for judicial discretion. Judicial law-making is possible only within the borders of the zone.

Judicial Law-Making and Law-Making by the Primary Legislator

It bears repetition and emphasis that although the judge is involved in law-making, his law-making differs from that of the legislative branch. In the absence of a constitution, the legislature can legislate at will. The judge can never do so. Moreover, the institutional characteristics of the legislature and the judge, which influence legislative content, differ. The judge legislates incidentally to his adjudication and only for its purposes. His law-making does not stand on its own. Not so the legislator, whose law-making is his main function and stands alone. Justice Brian Dickson said in this connection, "The judiciary and the legislature both make law—but it is not the same kind of law nor is it made for the same purposes. The primary function of the judge is to decide the case before him, to 'trancher le litige'—cut through the issue."[29] Thus, judicial law-

27. Compare Tammelo, "On the Logical Openness of Legal Order," 8 *Am. J. Comp. Law* 187 (1959).

28. Cardozo, *supra* note 67, ch. 1, at 113.

29. Dickson, *supra* note 4, at 5.

making has special characteristics that set it apart from the law-making of the primary law-maker.

Judicial Law-Making and Law-Making by the Secondary Legislator

There is a certain similarity between judicial law-making and the secondary legislation of the executive branch. Justice Sussman addressed this, saying, "The judge who decides according to his interpretation is none other than a sort of secondary legislator with reduced powers, and the limit of his authority is the expressed intent of the legislature."[30] In both administrative secondary legislation and judicial law-making in interpreting a statute, the law-making is drawn from the statute. Both put into effect the normative potential embedded in the statute. The statute establishes a certain zone of options, which the judge and the administrator concretize. In both cases the law-making—judicial or administrative—must act within the bounds of the statute, not outside it. In both cases, the law-making cannot cancel or change the statute, only "carry it out" and give expression to what is latent in it.

Nonetheless, there is a substantive difference between judicial law-making and administrative law-making. As we have seen, judicial law-making is incidental to adjudication. Administrative law-making is not incidental to adjudication. From this fact we get another, institutional difference. Just as the institutional characteristics of the judge differ from those of the primary legislator, so too do they differ from those of the secondary legislator. There is also a substantive difference between the two in the formal realm. Judicial law-making interprets a legislative act and becomes part of it. Its status in the normative hierarchy is coequal with the status of the legislative act that it interprets. On the other hand, the position of the administration's law-making in the normative hierarchy is below that of the statutory rule that it carries out. Thus, judicial law-making that comes from the interpretation of a constitution has the same normative standing of the constitution itself, and only a change in the constitution—or in the judicial rule itself—can alter it. Similarly, judicial law-making that comes from the interpretation of a statute has the hierarchical standing in the normative system of the statute itself, and only a change in the statute—or in the judicial rule itself—can change it. Lord Diplock said the following about this: "But whoever has final authority to explain what Parliament meant by the words that it used

30. Sussman, *supra* note 15, ch 1, at 158.

makes law as much as if the explanation it has given were contained in a
new Act of Parliament. It will need a new Act of Parliament to reverse
it."[31]

The Scope of Judicial Law-Making and
the Formal Sources of Judicial Discretion

The scope of judicial law-making is determined by the limited scope of
the judicial discretion. This scope changes from one issue to the next,
and one should not try to lay down hard and fast rules. For example, one
cannot say that in a common law legal system, judicial discretion and
judicial law-making are always broader than in civil law systems. Indeed, in a common law legal system, in which there is a rigid rule of
binding precedent that applies even to the highest court, judicial discretion may be more limited than in a civil law system, in which there is a
rule granting the court broad judicial discretion. True, in a common law
legal system, most of the law comes from the case law, yet the individual
judge may find himself at any given moment more limited than a judge in
a civil law system, in which most of the law comes from the legislature.

When in a given legal system, legislation replaces case law in a
certain matter, one cannot know in advance whether judicial discretion
will increase, decrease, or remain the same.[32] The effect depends upon
the scope of judicial discretion before the statute was enacted and upon
the scope of judicial discretion within the framework of the statute. For
example, in the absence of the statute, the judge may have had—
according to the rules of the system—broad discretion. The statute, on
the other hand, is drafted in detailed and casuistic language, and the
legislative purpose is crystal clear. As a result, judicial freedom is
restricted. In this state of affairs, the legislation brought in its wake a
narrowing of the judicial discretion. But one can also imagine the opposite situation. In the absence of statutory law, the field may have been
strewn with judicial precedents, so that judicial freedom, in the context
of the rules of the system, was extremely limited. The statutory rule, in
contrast, employs general, broad, open-textured language, and it operates within the framework of a very broad legislative purpose, so that the
judicial freedom in it is also extremely broad.

31. Diplock, *supra* note 3, at 6.
32. See Traynor, "Statutes Revolving in Common-Law Orbits," 17 *Cath. U.L. Rev.*
401 (1968).

At times the enactments of the legislative branch are in a field that was already covered by statutory law. The legislature repeals old laws and enacts new laws in their place. One cannot foretell what influence this will have on judicial discretion and judicial lawmaking. Judicial discretion may decrease as a result, yet it may also increase. The effect depends on the legislative policy of the legislature. For example, the new statutes that comprise Israel's civil codification are in the main drafted in a concise and summary form. They are based on general language that sometimes is vague and open-textured and on a highly general legislative goal that leaves the work of concretization to the court, which must balance among general principles. This gives the court broad judicial discretion and establishes a wide area for judicial lawmaking. Indeed, if we consider the civil codification together with the Foundations of Law Law, we find that the Israeli legislature tends to grant broad powers of judicial lawmaking to the judicial branch.

JUDICIAL DISCRETION—CREATING LAW OR DECLARING LAW?

The Problem

Judicial discretion means that not every legal problem has one lawful answer, and that in some situations the system contains a number of lawful solutions, among which the judge may choose. Is this approach consistent with the declaratory theory of law? According to this doctrine, the judge does not create new law, but simply declares the existing law that is "hidden" in the system. Even when a later judicial ruling cancels an earlier judicial rule, the new rule does not establish that the previous ruling was mistaken, but rather that it was not law at all.[33] In his writings, Professor Dworkin seeks to give renewed momentum to the declaratory doctrine.[34] Is my approach, which opposes Dworkin's, incompatible with the declaratory theory?

Judicial Discretion and Law-Declaring

I do not see any contradiction whatsoever between my approach to judicial discretion and the declaratory theory. The latter would refer to

33. See W. Blackstone, *Commentaries on the Law of England* 88 (13th ed., London, 1796); Friedmann, "Limits of Judicial Lawmaking and Prospective Overruling," 29 *Mod. L. Rev.* 593 (1966); Mishkin, "The High Court, the Great Writ, and Due Process of Time and Law," 79 *Harv. L. Rev.* 56 (1965–66).

34. Dworkin, "Natural Law Revisited," 34 *U. Fla. L. Rev.* 165 (1982).

judicial discretion as the putting into effect of the system's hidden potential. According to this approach, when a judge interpets a statute whose language is vague and obscure, and that is open-textured, he puts into effect a lawful possibility that is already in the text, and therefore he is proclaiming the text. When a judge draws an analogy from an existing rule, he gives effect to what is hidden in the rule from which he draws the analogy. When he deviates from existing case law or when he establishes a new rule, he develops the radiating power of the existing rule. Thus, from a dogmatic standpoint, there is no contradiction between the declaratory theory and judicial activity according to a statutory rule that stipulates that the judge may do as he sees fit. In this latter case, too, the judge puts into effect the limitless potential that is latent in that rule. Professor Tedeschi dealt with this as follows:

> Even when one explicitly gives the judge substantial authority to decide the case as he sees fit, in the eyes of many his activity should nonetheless be viewed as declaratory, since even the unformulated rule was already hinted at by the legislature, by virtue of its determination as to how and in what manner and by whom that rule would be given expression. In other words, even in these cases some see the judge as acting within the framework of the statute, though that framework be extremely wide.[35]

However, my approach to judicial discretion suggests the fictitious nature of the declaratory doctrine. True, the judge puts into effect the potential embedded in the system, but this potential is unrefined, and its formulation as binding law, defining what is permitted and what is forbidden in human relations, is accomplished by the act of adjudication. One could argue that the common law is embedded in the English law and that the judges simply exposed this treasure to the light of day. But this would be a fiction,[36] just as it is a fiction to say that a statute is hidden in a constitution or that secondary legislation is embedded in the statute. Thus, one must distinguish between the finding that a concrete solution is hidden in the system and the holding that the system has hidden within it ways to solve concrete cases. Insofar as the declaratory theory equates the two, its approach is faulty and its view fictitious.

True, the declaratory theory of law can be squared with my approach to judicial discretion. But it is difficult to square the theory with reality.

35. Tedeschi, *Studies in Israel Law* 143 (2d ed., 1959).
36. See Jessel M.R. *In Re Halle's Estate* (1879) 13 Ch. 696, 710.

Most legal scholars, representing different and opposing philosophical trends,[37] and most judges refer to it as a fiction.[38] The following quote from Lord Reid is representative:

> There was a time when it was thought almost indecent to suggest that judges make law. They only declare it. Those with a taste for fairy tales seem to have thought that in some Aladdin's cave there is hidden the Common Law in all its splendour and that on a judge's appointment there descends on him knowledge of the magic words Open Sesame. Bad decisions are given when the judge has muddled the password and the wrong door opens. But we do not believe in fairy tales any more. So we must accept the fact that for better or for worse judges do make law.[39]

Take a simple case. On the basis of a given set of facts, a certain rule was established. In a future case, that same rule is applied to a different set of facts. The declaratory theory holds that the judge in the second case only activated in the new case what was already concealed in the system.[40] Indeed, this is so, but when he does so he creates a new rule, for the rule is a function of the facts. Or, take a specific statutory rule—outside the Civil Wrongs Ordinance—that imposes absolute liability upon shipowners. The rule says nothing about contributory negligence of the injured party. The court decides[41] that this silence constitutes a lacuna and that it is to be filled by means of analogy from the laws of contributory negligence in the Civil Wrongs Ordinance. The declaratory theory would hold that the court which filled the void merely activated the system's hidden potential. Both the statute from which it drew the analogy (the Civil Wrongs Ordinance) and the statute that determines the analogy (the Foundations of Law Law) are part of the system. Yet by the same token, one may say that a new rule—one that had not existed previously—was created. Before, there was doubt about whether a gap existed; now there is no doubt, and the gap has been filled. Moreover, it might have been

---

37. See Friedmann, *supra* note 17, ch. 1.

38. See Diplock, *supra* note 3, at 2; Scarman, "Law Reform—Lessons from English Experience," 3 *Manitoba L.J.* 47 (1968); Edmund-Davies, "Judicial Activism," 28 *Curr. Legal Probs.* 1 (1975); Fox, "The Judicial Contribution," in *Law Making in Australia* 3 (Erb Soon Tay and Kamenka, eds., 1980).

39. Reid, "The Judge as Law Maker," *J. Soc'y Pub. Teachers of Law* 22 (1972).

40. See Lord Esher in *Willis v. Baddeley* [1892] 2 Q.B. 324, 326.

41. C.A. 804/80 *Sider Tanker Corporation v. Ailat-Ashkelon Pipe Line* 39 P.D. (1), 393, 421, 441.

possible to fill the gap in other ways, such as by applying the Torts Ordinance directly, yet this path was not chosen. These and other examples suggest that all that appears to remain of the declaratory theory is the determination that the judicial decision must be legitimate and that it must be based on certain formal sources. The judge cannot act outside the zone of formal legitimacy. This proposition does not seem to be disputed.

I underscored the fictional character of the declaratory theory. This fiction is particularly sharp when no primary rule exists, and judicial discretion, operating in the context of a secondary rule, establishes that primary rule. It is a fiction to say that the primary rule is hidden in the secondary rule; on the other hand, it is correct to say that the primary rule draws its legitimacy from the secondary rule. The fiction of the declaratory theory is less extreme when a primary rule exists, and the judicial discretion—here, too, operating in the framework of a secondary rule—establishes the scope of its application. In this case there is a certain validity to an approach that says the judge puts into effect the potential hidden in the primary rule. However, the difference between the two situations is only in the degree of the fictitiousness, not in its existence. Thus, the trouble with the declaratory theory is that it is one-dimensional, it does not provide an overall view of judicial discretion. True, the judge declares the law, but in doing so he sometimes also creates the law. Declaring the law and creating it are not contradictory functions. Rather, they are two sides of the same coin. If one views the declaratory theory in this light and sees that it represents only a part of the picture, then the theory may not only give legitimacy to judicial discretion, but it also may help solve various legal problems, such as the problem of the retroactivity of judicial norms and that of judicial objectivity.

Judicial Discretion and Law-Creating

Judicial discretion means the creation of law by the judge. The judge chooses from among the lawful options and establishes the sole and binding option, thereby creating new law. This is the case in the interpretation of a statute. The role of the interpreter is to choose the appropriate possibility from among the possibilities arrayed before him. This choice is not a mechanical act, but a creative one. And this creativity does not exist only in the mental plane, but also in the normative plane. A new norm is created. This is also the case in the interpretation of a case law norm and in the exercise of judicial discretion in the absence of a norm. In all these cases, the judge creates new law, the scope of his creation being conditioned upon the scope of judicial discretion given to him.

Jurists are not eager to recognize this state of affairs. More than once one finds in the case law a judicial determination that the judge does not create law, but simply declares existing law. This approach may draw its character from the declaratory theory. At times it is simply an expression of the view—which I do not contest—that the judicial creation must be anchored in law. Others use such ''declaratory'' terminology only in order to express the idea—which I also accept—that the scope of judicial discretion and judicial lawmaking is limited, because not every option that is available to the legislative branch is also available to the judicial branch, and because judicial lawmaking differs from lawmaking by the legislature. Thus, the determination that the judge's discretion must be formally anchored in law, that it is never absolute, and that it differs from the discretion of the primary or secondary legislator is acceptable to me. However, there is no contradiction between this determination and the proposition that in the exercise of his limited discretion within the framework of the law the judge creates new law. Thus, the judge declares the law, and at the same time he also creates law.

The notion that judicial discretion causes law to be made is by now quite common. The words of Lord Radcliffe on this issue are typical:

> There was never a more sterile controversy than that upon the question whether a judge makes law. Of course he does. How can he help it? The legislative and the judicial process respectively are two complementary sources of law-making.[42]

The same idea recurs in the words of Lord Simon:

> In this country it was long considered that judges were not makers of law but merely its discoverers and expounders. The theory was that every case was governed by a relevant rule of law, existing somewhere and discoverable somehow, provided sufficient learning and intellectual rigour were brought to bear. . . . But the true, even if limited, nature of judicial law-making has been more widely acknowledged of recent years.[43]

42. C. Radcliffe, *Not in Feather Beds* 216 (1968).
43. *Jones v. Secretary of State* [1972] 1 All E.R. 145, 198 (H.L.).

And in a similar spirit, Justice Alfred Witkon wrote,

> Today it is well recognized that the judicial function consists not only in the interpretation and application, but also in the creation of law. Whether we rejoice in this recognition or have our misgivings about it, it has come to be accepted as a fact. There is no longer any novelty in this statement, nor is there a need to elaborate.[44]

These observations are reiterated by scholars in articles[45] and books[46] and by judges in opinions[47] and essays.[48]

44. Witkon, *supra* note 17, ch. 1, at 475.

45. See Keeton, "Creative Continuity in the Law of Torts," 75 *Harv. L. Rev.* 463 (1962); Stevens, "The Role of a Final Appeal Court in A Democracy: The House of Lords Today," 28 *Mod. L. Rev.* 509 (1965); Veitch, "Some Examples of Judicial Law Making in African Legal Systems," 34 *Mod. L. Rev.* 42 (1971); Hiller, "The Law-Creative Role of Appellate Courts in the Commonwealth," 27 *Int'l & Comp. L. Q.* 85 (1978); Koopman, "Legislature and Judiciary: Present Trends," in *New Perspectives for A Common Law of Europe* (M. Cappelletti, ed., 1978); Hall, "Law Reform and the Judiciary Role" 10 *Osgoode Hall L.J.* 399 (1972); Cappelletti, "The 'Mighty Problem' in Judicial Review and the Contribution of Comparative Analysis," 53 *S. Cal. L. Rev.* 409 (1980); Clinton, "Judges Must Make Law: A Realistic Appraisal of the Judicial Function in a Democratic Society," 67 *Iowa L. Rev.* 711 (1982).

46. See Stone, *supra* note 40, ch. 1; Keeton, *supra* note 11, ch. 1.

47. See J. Bell, *Policy Arguments in Judicial Decisions* 4 (1983).

48. See F. Hodson, *Judicial Discretion and Its Exercise* (Holdsworth Club, Presidential Addresses, 1962); Traynor, "Better Days in Court for A New Day's Problem," 17 *Vand. L. Rev.* 109 (1963); Stevens, "*Hadley Byrne v. Heller:* Judicial Creativity and Doctrinal Possibility," 27 *Mod. L. Rev.* 121 (1964); Traynor, "The Courts: Interweavers in the Reformation of Law," 32 *Saskatchewan L. Rev.* 201 (1967); H. Friendly, *Benchmarks* 41, 96 (1967); Traynor, "The Limits of Judicial Creativity," 29 *Hastings L.J.* 1025 (1978); Traynor, "Transatlantic Reflections on Leeways and Limits of Appellate Courts," *Utah L. Rev.* 255 (1980); Barwick, "Judiciary Law: Some Observations Thereon," 33 *Curr. Legal Probs.* 238 (1980); Easterbrook, "Legal Interpretation and the Power of the Judiciary," 7 *Harv. J. L. & Pub. Pol.* 87 (1984).

Part Two
Limitations of
Judicial Discretion—
The Zone of
Judicial Reasonableness

Chapter 4
The Zone of
Reasonableness

HOW ARE THE HARD CASES TO BE SOLVED?

The Problem

In part 1 I sought to show that alongside the easy cases and the intermediate cases, in which there is no judicial discretion, there are hard cases, in which judicial discretion exists. I analyzed the formal sources and the substantive sources of this judicial discretion. I attempted to demonstrate that in these cases the judge does not merely declare the existing law, but also creates it. I pointed to the existence of "judicial lawmaking" and noted that judicial discretion is not absolute, but limited. Further, I discussed generally the procedural limitations (fairness) and the substantive limitations (reasonableness) that are imposed on judicial discretion. I noted that these limitations notwithstanding, there remains an area in which the judge is free to choose from among a number of possibilities the lawful possibility that seems best to him.

Now I am faced with the question of how judicial discretion is to be exercised. What is the meaning of the substantive limitations on judicial discretion? How is the "zone of reasonableness" established? The question I deal with in part 2 is not, therefore, whether limited judicial discretion exists or whether there is judicial creativity in making law. Of course limited judicial discretion exists, and of course there is judicial creativity in making law. The questions that interest me are: What is the meaning of the substantive limitations that are imposed on the discretion? How is the discretion to be exercised in the context of these limitations? No longer preoccupied with the question of whether the judge has power to choose, I am concerned now with the question of how the judge is to exercise his power to choose. As Lord Reid said, "We must accept the fact that for better or worse judges do make law, and tackle the question how do they approach their task and how should they approach it."[1] Judge Dickson reiterated this idea: "I do not for a moment doubt the power of the court to act creatively—it has done so in countless occasions: But manifestly one must ask—what are the limits of the judicial function."[2] These questions are raised not only by judges, but by academics as well. Professor Wolfgang Friedmann writes, "The policy element in the judicial decision may be refined, it may be pushed back further and further; the area of uncertainty may be reduced. But there must always remain a point at which a choice has to be made, and it is necessary to determine the factors guiding that choice."[3] Indeed, how is the choice to be made? What is it that establishes the zone of reasonableness?

The Importance of the Problem

I introduced the question of how the hard cases are to be resolved, or how the reasonableness of the judicial discretion is to be determined. This question is extremely important, for two reasons: first, because an unreasonable decision by the judge is an unlawful decision and contravenes the limitations imposed on judicial discretion. Just as one wants to know where the lawful frontiers of legislative and administrative discretion lie, one is also interested in knowing the lawful boundaries of judicial discretion. We have a special interest in this, precisely because judicial discretion is frequently exercised in review of administrative or legislative discretion, and one can imagine no greater mishap than the improper exercise of discretion in review of a proper exercise of discretion. Moreover, when the judicial discretion is that of the highest court in a given legal system, there is no judicial review of that discretion. Hence the great importance of establishing standards to direct the highest court in the use of its discretion and in its power to review itself.

The second reason the question is important is that the issues in which judicial discretion is exercised are for the most part issues of great public

---

1. Reid, *supra* note 39, ch. 3.
2. *Harrison v. Carswell* (1978) 2 S.C.R. 200, 218.
3. Friedmann, *supra* note 17, ch. 1, at 827.

importance. At the core of judicial discretion is the "open terminology."
Discretion exists in those situations in which the judge is required to
balance among contradictory and conflicting principles, lines of policy,
and standards. Judicial discretion is exercised in an area that is entirely
the realm of values, ideology, and politics. At times no consensus
surrounds the exercise of discretion. It may be the subject of political
competition among the parties for the vote of the electorate. The judge
must weigh general considerations of justice, morality, utility, and social
interests. Logic alone is not enough. He must weigh considerations of
policy. All these factors determine the dynamic framework of the law,
how it is changed and how it is renovated. A new norm is born because
an existing norm acquires a new form, or because the court distinguishes
or deviates from an existing norm, or because the court fills a gap in the
law. A change takes place in the legal system. The hard cases, therefore,
determine the dynamism of the law. They determine the direction in
which the law will develop in the future and whether that development
will be slow and gradual or rapid and sweeping. They define the relation
between stability and change in a given legal system. Judicial discretion
in these situations is intended to permit, from the functional standpoint,
stability through change and change through stability.[4]

All this places the judge in a complex and difficult reality of strug-
gling with ideological considerations that are sometimes the subject of
public debate. An unreasonable exercise of judicial discretion might
harm not only the parties, but the entire public. It might injure the standing of the judicial branch itself, its relations with the other branches, its
place in society, and the public's faith in it. Given these consequences,
one sees the great importance of the question of how the hard cases
should be resolved.

The Zone of Reasonableness

The fundamental duty of the judge is to exercise his discretion reasonably. An unreasonable option is an unlawful option. The judge may
choose only an option that is reasonable. Sometimes only one reasonable
option exists, and thus there is no judicial discretion, yet sometimes

4. See R. Pound, *Interpretation of Legal History* 1 (1923); "Law must be stable and
yet it cannot stand still. Hence all thinking about law has struggled to reconcile the
conflicting demands of the need of stability and of the need of change."

more than one exists: the judge has before him a number of reasonable options. A zone of reasonableness is created. Within this zone, every option is reasonable. How is the choice to be made? In this second part, I discuss the various factors that the judge must take into account when he chooses among the reasonable options in the zone of reasonableness.

I begin with the objective element. The choice among the different options must be made objectively. The judge must exercise his discretion as a reasonable judge. In order to do so, he must be conscious of the fact that he has discretion, of the meaning of discretion, and of the various factors that he must weigh in the context of this discretion. But once the judge is aware of the existence of judicial discretion and alert to the need to exercise it objectively, how should he act? What additional guidance does the principle of reasonableness provide?

Reasonableness is a standard against which behavior is measured.[5] In the present connection, it is the standard according to which judicial discretion is examined. At the basis of every standard lies an evaluation of behavior, according to tests of common sense, taking into account the special circumstances. In order to conduct this evaluation of judicial discretion, we must know the special circumstances of this discretion. So far, I have discussed the individual norm that constitutes the object of judicial discretion. I have examined the characteristics of structure (open terminology) and of content (values) that are at the basis of judicial discretion. This examination was essential for an understanding of the sources of judicial discretion. But this examination does not of itself determine whether the exercise of discretion was reasonable, because this test deals only with the question, Why does judicial discretion exist? It does not deal with the question, How is the judicial discretion to be exercised? The exercise of judicial discretion involves a process and motion, and these require consideration of ''environmental'' factors within whose framework those processes and motion take place. One cannot discuss the reasonableness of judicial discretion without examining three issues: first, the normative system (the law) within whose boundaries the individual norm that constitutes the object of the judicial discretion operates; second, the institutional system (the court) that activates the norm; and third, the reciprocal relations among all the institutional systems (the separation of powers) in the context of the

5. See MacCormick, *supra* note 28, ch. 2.

fundamental values of the state (democracy). Of course, these three components are interconnected. Nevertheless, each of them deserves to be considered separately.

Judicial Discretion and the Zone of Reasonableness

The zone of reasonableness distinguishes the easy cases and the intermediate cases from the hard cases. It represents a concentration of the hard cases and frames the options that are open to the judge with respect to these cases. As I noted, the distinction between the easy and intermediate cases, on the one hand, and the hard cases, on the other, is not sharp. From this reality flow the difficulties in determining the borders of the zone of reasonableness. There is substantial judicial discretion in establishing the border of the zone itself. The reason for this is that the various considerations that we will discuss—whether normative, institutional, or interinstitutional—do not provide a clear answer and do not distinguish clearly between the reasonable and the unreasonable. They establish a spectrum of possibilities, some of them more reasonable and some of them less so. For example, the normative principle that strives for the coherence and organic development of the system does not provide a clear solution to the choice among the options open to the judge. Two conflicting possibilities may be reasonable according to this principle, and a number of possibilities may be near each other on the broad spectrum between the reasonable and the unreasonable. The same is true for the test of consensus and for the other tests, such as the institutional suitability of the court, whether from the perspective of its inability to plan matters in advance, or from the perspective of the information at the court's disposal, or from the perspective of the resources it commands. In all of these issues, one finds not only black and white, but also a wide gray area. As a result, there is broad judicial discretion in establishing the zone of reasonableness itself. There is no one right answer to the question of what is located within the zone and what is located outside of it. A broad gray area connects the zone inward with the zone outward. The zone itself moves, therefore, among several points.

As a result, one finds not infrequently within the zone a number of possibilities that satisfy the fundamental considerations—both normative and institutional—in a stronger or weaker manner. Thus, for example, two possibilities may be reasonable from the point of view of the need to maintain coherence with the rest of the system, although this coherence is greater in one option than in the other. Similarly, two possibilities may be reasonable from the standpoint of the means at the court's disposal, although the means of the one option are more conventional than those of the other. Indeed, the fundamental problems that I discussed create—each of them separately and all of them together—a spectrum of possibilities. One may compare this to a series of nets, one under the other, through which the different possibilities seep. Each of the nets filters through more than one possibility. Within the zone of reasonableness, a number of possibilities coalesce, each of them satisfying the demands of the normative and institutional considerations, yet each bearing a different intensity of suitability to the various fundamental considerations.

Choosing the Reasonable Possibility within the Zone: Reasonable Considerations

The reasonable exercise of judicial discretion requires the choice of one of the possibilities located inside the zone. The judge is not entitled to choose a possibility situated outside the zone. But may he select—by his subjective discretion—any of the possibilities located within the zone? Does the restriction of judicial discretion end with the determination of the zone, so that within it, the judge is given a free hand? The answer, I think, is no. The zone establishes a set of possibilities, the choice among which—and not simply their inclusion in the zone—must be made in a reasonable manner.

The judge cannot be arbitrary. He must be rational. He is not entitled to choose among the different possibilities by flipping a coin. He must weigh relevant considerations related to the structure and development of the normative system, to the institutional system, and to the reciprocal relations between the institutions. A judge cannot say, "I choose possibility X simply because it advances Y's _____ ." This is an unreasonable choice, for there is not necessarily any relevant connection between the two. Similarly, a judge is not entitled to say, "I reject possibility A because it is not accepted in legal system B." This is an unreasonable rejection, as long as the judge fails to provide rational and relevant reasons to support the rejection of possibility A in his system. The connection with another system, by itself, is not a reason. Another system may serve as an inspiration for the judge, but he must ultimately weigh the considerations of his own system.

A judge takes an unreasonable factor into consideration if he says, "I refuse to deviate from precedent because I believe that any deviation by definition is undesirable from the point of view of the system." Such self-restraint is unreasonable. It fails to take into account the special circumstances of each particular case. Reasonableness is a flexible concept that necessitates taking changed circumstances into consideration. Similarly, a judge considers an unreasonable factor if he says, "I am not prepared to recognize a new cause of action, X, because it is not my function as a judge to recognize new causes of action. My job is to declare the existing causes of action." As we have seen, the role of the judge sometimes is to recognize new causes of action. A blanket claim denying the power of the judge to recognize new causes is inconsistent with the conception of the judge's role that is accepted today, and it is therefore not reasonable.

What of a judge who says, "I am aware that I am entitled to deviate from a previous ruling, but in the circumstances of the case, and in order to maintain the coherence of the system, I prefer the existing situation"? And what if the judge writes, "In the circumstances of the case, and within the context of the institutional limitations, I do not find it appropriate to recognize a new cause of action, X"? In both of these cases, the judge considers relevant factors. He assigns them weights and he balances among the various considerations according to what he finds appropriate. In these circumstances, the discretion seems to me to be reasonable. To be sure, I might reach a different conclusion. I might think that it is possible to maintain a lesser degree of coherence and to obtain a greater degree of adaptation of the law to society's needs, and thus that it is appropriate to deviate from the precedent. Similarly, I might believe that the existing institutional limitations do not justify a refusal to recognize a new cause of action. Yet my different approach notwithstanding, I cannot say that the factor the other judge weighed is unreasonable. Thus, different judges may weigh different factors, without any of the judges acting unreasonably. Two solutions may be reasonable, although only one of them is correct from the point of view of the decision-maker.

I mentioned a number of considerations that appear to me to be unreasonable, and a number of considerations that seem reasonable. The main difficulty is defining these situations with more specificity than the general term *relevant considerations*. The theory of reasonableness was developed more fundamentally in the field of administrative law than in the field of adjudication. The primary difficulty lies in the indecisiveness of the principles upon which the choice is based. In the final analysis, it is the personal experience of the chooser, and his basic conception of the nature of his choice, that determines whether or not a particular choice is reasonable. For our purposes, the determination of the reasonableness of a possibility is made according to the personal experience of the judge and his conception of the judicial function. These two operate on a broad spectrum of possibilities. It seems to me that in accordance with what is acceptable to the legal community—and this, it will be recalled, is the major criterion to be employed—a judge who thinks he must never deviate from precedent because such deviation is always undesirable from the perspective of the system does not properly conceive his judicial role. Similarly, it appears to me that the legal community is united in the view that a judge misunderstands the judicial function if he thinks he is prohibited from ever recognizing a new cause of action. Yet these are extreme examples. It is in the middle ground one finds most of the situations that arise, and in these there is no uniform conception of the judicial task. As a result, adequate guidance is lacking, and different judges may reach different results without acting unreasonably.

The Reasonableness of the Choice Reasonableness is a standard for choosing among different possibilities. In one case, I said the following about this standard:

> The scope of application of the "reasonable person" standard is determined by the degree of the judge's reaction of agreement or disagreement vis-à-vis the outcome. This reaction is based principally on the judge's human experience, on the one hand, and on social principles and goals, on the other.[6]

These general words apply also to the matter of the reasonable choice among various possibilities in the context of judicial discretion. The reasonableness of the choice is determined by the judge's worldview. This, in turn, is based on his human experience and on social principles and policies, which establish his conception of the judicial function. These two determine the weight the judge gives to the various possibilities and the balance he strikes among them. A different human experience and a different conception of the function produce, by the nature of things, a different reasonable choice.

6. C.A. 243/83 *supra* note 25, ch. 2, at 137.

The Reasonableness of the Choice: Personal Experience

A decisive component in the determination of the reasonableness of the choice is the judge's personal experience: his education, his personality, and his emotional makeup. There are judges who are more cautious and judges who are less cautious. There are judges whom a certain argument influences more than other judges. There are judges who insist on a heavy burden of proof before they will deviate from the existing law, and judges who are satisfied with a light burden of proof in deviating from existing law. There are judges who are more impressed by the writings of authors, scholars, and other judges, and there are judges whom these impress less. Every judge has a complex human experience that influences his approach to life and therefore also his approach to law. A judge who experienced the Weimar Republic will not have the same attitude toward the activity of undemocratic political parties as someone who did not experience it. There are judges for whom security considerations count much more than for other judges. There are judges for whom considerations of freedom of expression count much more than for other judges. There are judges whose personality makeup demands order and discipline, and as a result they also insist upon organic growth and ordered development of the law. There are judges whose personality makeup causes them to take interinstitutional considerations into account to a lesser or to a greater degree. All these considerations—and many others—determine the judge's personality and his human experience. One cannot ignore this factor. It seems that we would not want to operate in a system in which this factor did not carry substantial weight.

It should be emphasized that we are dealing with an area in which there is not just one lawful solution. We are not dealing with easy cases or intermediate cases. We are dealing with a hard case. In this field, in which tests of reasonableness hold absolute sway, there is no alternative but to give expression to the personal experience of the decision-maker. Moreover, the objectivization of judicial discretion means that an exceptional personal experience will not be taken into account. Yet one is left with a broad range of the judge's personality as a human being that influences the choice he makes. Again, our approach is not the one that is sometimes attributed to the American Realists, according to which personal considerations are decisive in every case. As I said, we are dealing with the hard cases and with the boundaries of the zone of reasonableness, after a complex set of objective factors has been applied. At the very end comes that stage that exists only in a small fraction of the cases—those in which the personal experience of the judge is decisive.

The Reasonableness of the Choice:
The Conception of the Judicial Function

Alongside human experience is a second factor: the conception of the judicial function—in other words, how the judge perceives his judicial role in the hard cases. What, in his view, is the relation between the individual decision that solves the immediate controversy before him and the normative decision that creates a new rule? President Agranat discussed this as follows:

> Based on my judicial experience, I can attest that when the judge who must decide a case is faced with the choice between creating a general legal norm, and refraining from doing so, a certain tension may stir within him. The mental tension that is created is due, on the one hand, to his desire to be daring and to choose the first alternative, in order to arrive at the result that seems to him just in the circumstances of the case; and on the other hand, to his desire to exercise redoubled judicial caution and to choose the second alternative, lest he slip into the domain of the sovereign legislative authority and thereby violate the principle of the separation of powers. In my opinion, the ideal solution to this dilemma is to strive for maximum balance, insofar as possible, regarding the _____ of the amounts of judicial daring and judicial self-restraint.[7]

I concur with these words. But do other judges agree? I would not be surprised to find judges who would argue that they must above all give a solution that is just in the specific case, and only then begin to worry about the general rule. Moreover, even if everyone agreed with President Agranat's approach, what is the "maximum balance" of which he spoke?

The conception of the judicial function does not focus exclusively on the relation between the general norm and the individual case. It involves the entire scope of the judicial function. Does the judge see it as his duty and his right to adapt the law to the changing reality, and does he endeavor to do so, or does he view this instead as a major complication that he sometimes cannot avoid? Does he see it as part of his function to apply society's values, or does he avoid doing this? Does he believe that

7. Agranat, *supra* note 9, ch. 2, at 256.

only values as to which there is societal agreement are worthy of judicial recognition, or is he prepared to be the standard-bearer for values as to which there is no consensus? The answers to all of these questions determine the conception of the judicial function and the choice of the reasonable possibility. Judge Walter Schaefer discussed this, referring to deviation from precedent:

> If I were to attempt to generalize, as indeed I should not, I should say that most depends upon the judge's unspoken notion as to the function of his court. If he views the role of the court as a passive one, he will be willing to delegate the responsibility for change, and he will not greatly care whether the delegated authority is exercised or not. If he views the court as an instrument of society designed to reflect in its decisions the morality of the community, he will be more likely to look precedent in the teeth and to measure it against the ideals and the aspirations of his time.[8]

It should be emphasized that I am not speaking of conceptions of the judicial function that are unacceptable to the legal community. I am referring to different emphases and different nuances or shades of a conception that is accepted by the legal community.

"The Possibility that Appears to Him to Be the Best"

Within the framework of reasonableness, and on the basis of reasonable considerations, every judge is entitled to choose the possibility that seems to him to be the best. The weight he gives to the various considerations and the balance he strikes among them are the fruits of his personal experience and his worldview as a judge. Judge Schaefer spoke of this in the following terms:

> The forces and factors which I have mentioned are not weighed in objective scales. Each judge will have his individual reaction to the value of a particular precedent. Each will respond in his own degree to the pressure of the facts of the case. And each will make his own appraisal of the weight to be given to the other considerations I have mentioned.[9]

Different judges will, therefore, reach different results, for their personal experiences and their worldviews differ. One judge may reach different results at different times, for with the passage of time, both his personal

8. Schaefer, *supra* note 94, ch. 2, at 23.
9. Ibid., at 22.

experience and his judicial worldview change.[10] Sometimes, the judge who is faced with a hard case may find himself in a difficult dilemma, for his personal experience and his judicial worldview do not lead him to choose a single possibility, but rather they pull him in different and conflicting directions. His personal experience may advise him to be cautious. His judicial worldview may prod him to be daring. He knows that he must balance the two, but what weight should he give to the various factors? In this field, objective standards do not help. The judge stands alone. A battle may rage within him, for sometimes the forces pulling in different directions are of equal strength. He will find himself hesitating and pondering.[11] Days and weeks may pass before he is able to decide. It will be the best decision the judge can make, yet it will also be one that bears the stamp of his personality.

In the hard cases, therefore, when the objective standards are of no help, the decision is made by the judge himself, as the product of his personal experience and his worldview as a judge. His judicial philosophy may be the compass that directs him in solving the difficult problem with which he is faced. Indeed, in the hard cases this is the most practical thing the judge has. Justice Cardozo spoke of this, saying,

> You think there is nothing practical in a theory that is concerned with ultimate conceptions. That is true perhaps while you are doing the journeyman's work of your profession. You may find in the end, when you pass to higher problems, that instead of its being true that the study of the ultimate is profitless, there is little that is profitable in the study of anything else.[12]

Thus, in the hard cases, the final decision depends to a large extent on the judge's judicial philosophy, on his approach to the judicial function, and on his judicial worldview.

THE ZONE OF REASONABLENESS AND JUDICIAL OBJECTIVITY

My goal is to formulate standards for determining the reasonableness of the exercise of judicial discretion. I hope to create objective tests,

10. See Friendly, *supra* note 123, ch. 1, at 229.
11. See Cardozo, *supra* note 125, ch. 1, at 80.
12. Cardozo, *supra* note 6, ch. 1, at 23; see also Freund, "Social Justice and the Law," in *Social Justice* 93, 110 (R. Brandt, ed., 1962): "It may therefore be said that the most important thing about a judge is his philosophy; and if it be dangerous for him to have one, it is at all events less dangerous than the self-deception of having none."

according to which judicial discretion can be examined. The question is, How must a reasonable judge exercise his discretion in the circumstances of the case? How would a reasonable judge balance the various values in formulating the judicial policy of norm X? or, How would the reasonable judge balance the various considerations in deviating from a precedent or distinguishing it? or, How would the reasonable judge fill a lacuna in the laws?

But who is this reasonable judge? Every judge seems to think that he himself is the reasonable judge. When a judge describes the reasonable person, in most cases he is thinking of himself. Yet nothing could be further from the truth. Just as not every person is a reasonable person, neither is every judge a reasonable judge. "The court" is the reasonable person. This transition from "the judge" to "the court" is the transition from the subjective to the objective. For reasonableness is an objective matter. It attempts to escape the subjectivity that surrounds each and every individual by searching for the general and the shared. In the words of Lord Justice Greene, M.R.,

> The judge's sense of justice must . . . be universalised. He, no less than the juryman, is the reasonable man, his sense of justice is that of the *bonus paterfamilias*. He must avoid idiosyncracies, his views of right and wrong must conform to a practical standard, they must not be governed by mere psychological or ethical theories, however attractive they may be. It is justice as it appears to the reasonable man, the good citizen, that he must administer.[13]

When the judge is required to identify the values of society, he looks for those values that are shared by the members of the society, even if they are not his own. He avoids imposing on the society his subjective values, to the extent that they are inconsistent with the articles of faith of the society in which he lives.[14] A judge with a religious worldview, for example, will not impose his religious worldview on the secular society in which he lives, and a judge with a secular worldview will not impose his secular worldview on the religious society in which he operates. Justice Landau discussed this:

> This does not mean that the court may decide according to a judge's private conception of what is good and beneficial in his eyes from these fundamental

13. Greene, *supra* note 42, ch. 1, at 7.
14. See Johnson, "In Defense of Judicial Activism," 28 *Emory L.J.* 901, 909 (1979).

perspectives; instead, he must be an interpreter faithful to the views accepted by the enlightened population in whose midst he sits.[15]

Justice Cardozo took a similar approach:

> A judge, I think, would err if he were to impose upon the community as a rule of life his own idiosyncracies of conduct or belief. Let us suppose, for illustration, a judge who looked upon theatre-going as a sin. Would he be doing right if, in a field where the rule of law was still unsettled, he permitted this conviction, though known to be in conflict with the dominant standard of right conduct, to govern his decision? My own notion is that he would be under a duty to conform to the accepted standards of the community, the *mores* of the times.[16]

When the judge must balance various values according to their weight, he should strive to do so according to what seems to him to be the society's fundamental conception. He should avoid doing so according to his own fundamental conception.[17] As President Agranat said, "For the principle of the rule of law means that the judge must distance himself, insofar as possible, from giving preference to his personal views over what justice demands."[18] In the words of Justice Cardozo, "Their standard must be an objective one. In such matters, the thing that counts is not what I believe to be right. It is what I may reasonably believe that some other man of normal intellect and conscience might reasonably look upon as right."[19]

Thus, this objectivity demands something from the judge. He must conduct his own mental accounting.[20] He must be aware that he may have values that not everyone shares and that his personal views may be exceptional and extraordinary. He might attach great importance to issues that the general public sees as trivial and meaningless. The judge must be aware of his characteristics, and he must make every possible

---

15. H.C. 58/68 *supra* note 51, ch. 2, at 520.

16. Cardozo, *supra* note 67, ch. 1, at 108.

17. See Friendly, *supra* note 123, ch. 1, at 231: "The Judge should try to make sure he is interpreting the long-term convictions of the community, rather than his own evanescent ones."

18. H.C. 58/68 *supra* note 51, ch. 2, at 600.

19. Cardozo, *supra* note 67, ch. 1, at 89.

20. See J. Frank, *Courts on Trial* 250 (1950).

effort not to exercise his discretion on the basis of these subjective traits. Justice Frankfurter spoke of this in the following words:

> We may not draw on our merely personal and private notions and disregard the limits that bind judges in their judicial function. . . . To practice the requisite detachment and to achieve sufficient objectivity no doubt demands of judges the habit of self-discipline and self-criticism, incertitude that one's own views are incontestable and alert tolerance toward views not shared.[21]

The judge must be capable of looking at himself from "the outside." He must put up a net for himself that catches and sifts out the anomalous and unusual and that feeds into his discretion the accepted and the general. The judge must be capable of analyzing, criticizing, and restraining himself. A judge who thinks that he knows everything and that his own views are the best and most appropriate will not be able to fulfill his function properly. He will not be able to distinguish between his private articles of faith and the articles of faith of the nation. As a judge, he must take into consideration the articles of faith of the nation, not his personal articles of faith. He must be aware of this difference, if it exists, and he must avoid giving expression in his discretion to his own articles of faith. A judge who is aware of his function and the responsibility that is imposed on him will be able to meet these demands. As Judge Roger Traynor said,

> Although the judges' predilections may play a part in setting the initial direction he takes towards the creative solution, there is little danger of their determining the solution itself however much it bears the stamp of his individual workmanship. Our great creative judges have been men of outstanding skill, adept at discounting their own predilections and careful to discount them with conscientious severity.[22]

The judge is the product of his period. He lives at a given time and in a given society. The goal of objectivity is not to cut him off from his surroundings, but the opposite: to enable him to formulate properly the fundamental principles of his period. The goal of objectivity is not to "liberate" the judge from his past, his education, his experience, his

---

21. *Rochin v. California*, 342 U.S. 165, 170, 172 (1952). See also F. Frankfurter, *Of Law and Life and Other Things That Matter* 188 (1965).

22. Traynor, "Comment on Courts and Lawmaking," in *Legal Institutions Today and Tomorrow* 52 (J. Paulsen, ed., 1950).

faith, and his values. On the contrary: its purpose is to stimulate him to make use of all of these in order to reflect as purely as possible the fundamental values of the nation.[23] A person who is appointed as a judge need not and cannot change his stripes, but he must develop a sensitivity to the weight of his office and to the constraints it imposes.[24] "You thought I was giving you power? It is slavery that I am giving you."[25] The judge must demonstrate a self-criticism and lack of arrogance that enable him not to identify himself with all that is good and beautiful.[26] He must demonstrate self-restraint that lets him separate his personal feelings from the inner feelings of the nation. He must demonstrate an intellectual modesty that permits him to say, "I erred, for I confused what I want with what I am entitled to." A judge who does not act accordingly and who imposes on the society all that is subjective in him will create tension between himself and his environment.[27] As long as he and others persist in this, the tension between the judicial branch and the other branches will mount. The result of this tension may be bad for the society, and above all it may be bad for the status of the court and for the confidence the public reposes in it.

In order to avoid tension between the judge and his surroundings, every legal system maintains institutions and processes that help the judge channel his discretion in objective paths. The judge enjoys independence, which enables him to be free of any subjective pressure that

23. See Tate, " 'Policy' in Judicial Decisions," 20 *La. L. Rev.* 62, 69 (1959): "They do so as representative voices of their generation. Individualistic and non-representative views of any participating judges as to what should constitute a fair legal disposition with relation to a given set of facts tend to be brought into conformity with the general social and moral feelings of the times by availability of appellate review."

24. See Frankfurter, *supra* note 7, ch. 1, at 40: "No, he does not change his character. He brings his whole experience, his training, his outlook, his social, intellectual and moral environment with him, when he takes a seat on the supreme bench. But a judge worth his salt is in the grip of his function. The intellectual habits of self-discipline which govern his mind are as much a part of him as the influence of the interest he may have represented at the bar, often much more so."

25. *Horaiot*, 10.

26. See Tate, "The 'New' Judicial Solution: Occasions for and Limits to Judicial Creativity," 54 *Tul. L. Rev.* 877, 914 (1980).

27. See Cox, "Judge Learned Hand and the Interpretation of Statutes," 60 *Harv. L. Rev.* 370, 373 (1947): "Society will not long tolerate the wisest judge who, knowing no master, decides cases only according to his individual sense of justice."

might have been his lot in the past. He does not belong to any sector or division. He is a judge of all the people. The adversary process is intended to place before the judge—without requiring his involvement—different possibilities of which he might not be aware. The attorneys uncover and present him with the various possibilities that are embedded in the given situation. Various rules ensure the integrity of the judicial process and the absence of internal and external influences. The publicity of the proceedings and the duty of reasoned judgments increase the objective element. The rules of judicial ethics guide the judge's conduct into objective paths.

In addition to these procedural factors that guide the objective choice, one must also point out social factors. Judges are influenced by one another. A fraternity is created, affecting objectivity. The judges are influenced by the tradition that exists in the court. This is the ember that passes from one generation of judges to another. It is not written in any book, yet it seeps bit by bit into the consciousness of the judge and produces the objectivization of his discretion. The judge is influenced by the intellectual factors and by the legal thought that exist in his generation. The judge is part of his nation. He may sometimes live in an ivory tower, but it is an ivory tower in the hills of Jerusalem, not on Olympus. He is aware of what is taking place in his nation. He knows the problems of the state, reads its literature, listens to its songs. All of these are absorbed by the judge and find expression in his discretion. The judge is part of his period. He is a creation of his era. He moves with history. All of these factors affect, to a certain extent, the emphasis of the objective and the rational in judicial discretion.

The Difficulties of Judicial Objectivity

This objectivization of discretion is far from simple. Indeed, it raises a number of problems. First, can the required objectivity be attained? Even when we regard ourselves from the outside, we do so only with our own eyes.[28] Are we capable of seeing ourselves as something other than what we are? Second, this objectivization may weaken the humane element in the decision. Do we not suppress the good in us when we try to cut ourselves off from the subjectivity within us? Moreover, does the objec-

28. See Cardozo, *supra* note 67, ch. 1, at 13: "We may try to see things as objectively as we please. Nonetheless, we can never see them with any eyes except our own."

tivization not weaken the personal responsibility of the judge for his discretion? Third, an objective approach raises difficulties when societal values are opposed to fundamental principles of justice and morality. Is the judge supposed to give expression to whatever his society accepts, even if this conflicts with what seems to him to be just and moral?

These are difficult questions. One cannot avoid grappling with them. They indicate the fragility of objectivity. However, as long as we do not find a better replacement, it is appropriate to continue using this terminology. The truth of the matter is that objectivity is not imposed on the judge—especially not the judge of the lowest court—from the outside, but rather he is required to struggle with it from within. His education and legal instruction help him. A judge is accustomed to looking for the objective in the "reasonable person." This sensitivity to the distinction between the subjective and the objective also surely helps him understand himself to the best of his ability. This understanding need not weaken the humane side of the judge, nor his responsibility for decisions. On the contrary, these may well increase if the judge is aware of the objective need to give appropriate weight to the humane side and to his personal responsibility. When the judge encounters the various social values, he must give expression to those fundamental values that reflect, in his view, the articles of faith of the democratic regime. The objective tests force the judge to give expression to the fundamental values of the society and not to its subjective values, to the extent the two are different. The objective element does not require the judge to give expression to the temporary and the fleeting. He must give expression to the central and the basic. Thus, when a given society is not faithful to itself, the objective test does not mean the judge must give expression to the mood of the hour. He must stand firm against this mood, while expressing the basic values of the society in which he lives. In doing so, the judge will raise the level of the society in which he lives. This "instructional" activity is compatible with his judicial function and with the objectivity required of him.[29] The judge need not demand of the members of society that they behave like lambs, but he must demand that they refrain from acting like wolves. Objectivity enables him to demand of them that they act like human beings. Objectivity forces the judge to plumb the

29. See J. Morris, *Law and Public Opinion* 22 (Holdsworth Club, Presidential Addresses, 1958).

depths of the national consciousness. He must draw inspiration from the "sources of the social consciousness of the nation in whose midst the judges sit."[30] He must understand that "one learns the law of a nation from the perspective of the complex of its national life."[31] He must give expression to "the fundamental ideas upon which our social regime is founded." In all of these the judge does not conduct a vote. He does not always seek out the majority view, unless it is expressed in a statute. He attempts to effectuate the fundamental values, those values and conceptions "that are accepted by the enlightened public in whose midst he sits."[32]

I do not know whether from a philosophical standpoint one may speak of absolute objectivity. It certainly does not exist in the field of judicial discretion. All judicial objectivity contains a large dose of subjectivity, in the sense of a certain subjectivization of the objective. The judge is only human, and with all his willingness to cut himself off from his personal predilections, he is unable to cut himself off from himself. The goal is not, therefore, to attain absolute objectivity, but rather to find an appropriate balance between objectivity and subjectivity. For this purpose, self-criticism, self-restraint, and an intellectual effort to look for the objective are required. In this search, it is only natural that different judges will sometimes find different things in a given system. Their personal composition, tendencies, conceptions, and education—everything that makes us what we are—may lead judges to reach different results. There is no escaping this. But the mental accounting that produces objectivization ensures that the general starting point will be the same. As Judge Kaufman said, "There are variations in judges' points of departure and processes of reasoning, but they are variations on a common theme."[33] When the general starting point is common, there is a good chance that the end points, too, will not be far apart.

"The Judge on His Own"

When the judge has to choose the solution that appears best to him, he is on his own. The full weight of responsibility is thrust upon him. No

---

30. Landau, *supra* note 17, ch. 1, at 306.
31. Justice Agranat in H.C. 73/53, *supra* note 56, ch. 2, at 884.
32. Justice Landau in H.C. 58/68, *supra* note 51, ch. 2, at 520.
33. Kaufman, "Chilling Judicial Independence," 88 *Yale L.J.* 681, 688 (1979).

external standard guides him. The judge must look inside himself. As
Justice Cardozo said,

> In all this, one must beware of an axiology that is merely personal and
> subjective. A judge is to give effect in general not to his own scale of values,
> but to the scale of values revealed to him in his readings of the social
> mind. . . . Many are the times, however, when there are no legislative
> pronouncements to give direction to a judge's reading of the book of life and
> manners. At those times, he must put himself as best he can within the heart
> and mind of others, and frame his estimate of values by the truth as thus
> revealed. Objective tests may fail him or may be so confused as to bewilder.
> He must then look within himself.[34]

But in this state of affairs, does the judge return to the subjective and to
his personal inclinations? Does the objective "purification" lose its
strength and is the judge referred to all that is special and unique within
himself? In my opinion, the answer is no. The judge must not return to
his unique personal inclinations or to his unique opinions. He must not
return to those particularistic values that are incompatible with the articles of faith of the society in which he lives. The path of subjectivity is
closed. There is no turning back to it. The judge must make the best
objective decision he can. In this situation, the circle does not close. The
judge does not go back to his starting point. He tries to march forward,
not backward. He tries with all his strength—against the background of
his experience, education, faith, and culture, all purified of subjective
inclination—to give the best solution he is capable of giving. He ignores
neither the articles of faith of the people nor the special problems of
adjudication. He takes all of these into account, and, on the basis of this
perfected set of factors, he arrives at his exercise of discretion. At this
stage, no longer subject to binding standards, he has discretion that
enables him to choose from among a number of possibilities. He has not
come down from the mountain that he climbed in order to find the
objective answer. He continues to climb that mountain until he reaches
the heights of the summit.

Justice Holmes wrote, "It is a misfortune if a judge reads his conscious or unconscious sympathy with one side or the other prematurely
into the law."[35] From this others concluded that the judge may consider,

34. Cardozo, *supra* note 125, ch. 1, at 55.
35. Holmes, *supra* note 122, ch. 1, at 295.

if only at a late stage, his "sympathies" for one side or the other. But such is not the case. The judge cannot return to his personal sympathy. When Justice Holmes speaks of the judge's "premature" consideration of his personal sympathy, he is referring to the societal values that have not yet crystallized as part of the fundamental values of the nation. The sympathy that Holmes calls upon the judge to consider at the later stage does not refer to his personal sympathy, but rather to his consideration of those values that emerged triumphant from the social struggle. Here are Justice Holmes's words:

> As law embodies beliefs that have triumphed in the battle of ideas and then have translated themselves into action, while there still is doubt, while opposite convictions still keep a battle front against each other, the time for law has not come; the notion destined to prevail is not yet entitled to the field. It is a misfortune if a judge reads his conscious or unconscious sympathy with one side or the other prematurely into the law, and forgets that what seem to him to be first principles are believed by half his fellow men to be wrong.[36]

Thus, each judge carries with him, as Justice Holmes noted, his own "can't help it." Yet this can't help it is not a return to the subjective, but rather an operation in the objective field. Whoever has made his personal mental accounting and succeeded in overcoming his personal inclinations must not fall back upon them. He must find the best solution within the framework of the objective factors among which he operates.

Intuition

In determining the best solution, the judge is sometimes aided by his intuition.[37] He operates according to that internal sense that creates a link between the problem and its solution. At times the judge senses the desired result even before he has given himself an accounting as to the appropriate path for getting to the appropriate result. In analyzing the various factors that affect judicial discretion in hard cases, in which the various values conflict, Justice Cardozo said, "It [judicial discretion] will be shaped by his experience of life; his understanding of the prevailing canons of justice and morality; his study of the social sciences; at

---

36. Ibid., at 294.
37. See Hutcheson, "The Judgment Intuitive: The Function of the 'Hunch' in Judicial Decision," 14 *Cornell L.Q.* 274 (1929); Hutcheson, "Lawyer's Law, and the Little Small Dice," 7 *Tul. L. Rev.* 1 (1932).

times, in the end, by his intuitions, his guesses, even his ignorance or prejudice."[38] Indeed, one must not overlook the role and importance of intuition in the judicial decision.[39] This is a reality that many judges have experienced. It arises primarily when the judge determines the facts and when he applies a given norm to a set of facts. Yet one also cannot ignore it in the determination of the scope of application of the norm itself. As we have seen, the building blocks are intertwined. Sometimes the judge arrives at the result intuitively, and, working backwards, he then formulates the principle according to which he will operate.[40]

Thus, intuition plays a role in judicial discretion. The judge is human, and intuition plays an important role in the activities of every person. But it does not follow that judicial discretion begins and ends with intuition. Intuition must be reviewed, must go through a process of rationalization. Judge Schaefer discussed this as follows: "And, if I have reached a decision by means of a hunch, it has been a hunch with a long-delayed fuse, for often I have started confidently toward one conclusion, only to be checked and turned about by further study."[41] Therefore, one must not impose on the society an intuition that draws its lifeblood from an anomalous personality or from values that are incompatible with the fundamental values of the system.[42] The intuition must be well founded, and it must be convincing. Thus, intuition may be a flash that lights the proper way. But it is not the way itself. Neither is intuition a substitute for intellect. It cannot, therefore, replace the proper standards for exercising judicial discretion, but it can be a spur to additional examination, deeper and more rational.[43]

A judge must find a balance between his rational thought and his intuition. Frequently, he will find that the two are compatible, but in certain cases he discovers a gap between the two. He must then explain to himself the source of the gap. He must not ignore his intuition, for it might be an indicator of incomplete thinking. If, after the judge conducts this examination and checks himself and his thought processes in light of

38. Cardozo, *supra* note 6, ch. 1, at 85. See also *Selected Writings of Benjamin Nathan Cardozo* 26 (M. Hall, ed., 1947).
39. See Pound, *supra* note 27, ch. 2, at 59.
40. See Frank, *supra* note 9, ch. 1, at 110.
41. Schaefer, *supra* note 94, ch. 2, at 23.
42. See G. White, *Patterns of American Legal Thought* 136, 159 (1978).
43. See Friendly, *supra* note 123, ch. 1, at 230.

the tests I have discussed, a gap remains between his rational conclusion and his intuition, he should give preference to his rational thought. At this point, there is a good chance that the intuition is simply the accumulation of those subjective factors from which the judge successfully sought to free himself. In the final analysis, judicial discretion must be expressed in rational thought, not in a subjective sense. This is the responsibility required of the judicial function.

AWARENESS OF JUDICIAL DISCRETION

Awareness and its Consequences

Judicial discretion means making a choice from among a number of lawful possibilities. A reasonable exercise of judicial discretion means making a choice based on appropriate considerations from among the various possibilities. The selection of an option by flipping a coin would yield a lawful choice, but the choosing itself would be unreasonable. From this one may conclude that the reasonable exercise of judicial discretion requires an awareness of the act of choice. A judge who exercises judicial discretion must be conscious of the fact that he is in the realm of the hard cases. He must be aware of the significance of the use of judicial discretion. A judge who is not conscious of all of these factors cannot make a proper selection among the possibilities open to him. His choice cannot be reasonable.

The reality is that the judge is sometimes unaware that he is exercising judicial discretion. This is the result of the incidentality of the use of judicial discretion. The judge has to decide in the dispute, and the exercise of judicial discretion is merely a by-product of this decision. At times, the judge assumes a certain normative situation and bases his decision in the case on it, without realizing that his assumption involves a type of choice of one among a number of possibilities. In reality, the judge is sometimes not aware that he is in the realm of the hard cases. He thinks he is faced with an easy case or an intermediate case. The judge thinks he is simply repeating an existing norm, when in fact he is creating a new norm. This is related also to the declarative theory, which certain judges accept and which holds that judges do not create law—thus, that they are not using judicial discretion in the sense in which I am using the term.

This reality of unawareness is undesirable. An appropriate exercise of judicial discretion must be done out of an awareness of the different foundations that comprise judicial discretion. An appropriate exercise of judicial discretion is an objective exercise of judicial discretion. Yet the judge must be aware that he is exercising objective discretion. A proper objective exercise of judicial discretion must be done out of subjective awareness that judicial discretion is being activated. This approach places a heavy burden upon the judge. The dispute does not come to him with a label announcing, "I am an easy case" or "I am a hard case." The judge must analyze for himself the case that is before him, by examining the type of difficulty facing him. He must ask himself whether he is applying a given norm or creating a norm that did not exist previously.

What if the judge exercises his discretion without being aware that he is doing so? Does the unwitting exercise of judicial discretion cause the voiding of the discretion? In Professor Raz's opinion, the unconscious exercise of judicial discretion does not impair the discretion:

> [T]he courts make law in unregulated disputes. They do so regardless of whether they are aware of the fact that they do. This makes for an important conceptual difference between legislative and judicial law-making. A legislative action is an action intentionally changing the law. Judicial law-making need not be intentional. A judge may make a new rule in a decision which he thinks is a purely law-applying decision. Nowadays judges are for the most part fully aware of their law-making powers. Yet this conceptual distinction has not lost its importance. Even though judges know that they often make law, they do not always judge correctly whether a particular point made in a judgment is innovative or applicative. It is naturally of crucial importance to the proper functioning of the administration of justice that judicial decisions are valid regardless of whether the court correctly identified their character as innovative or applicative.[44]

I agree with this approach. The distinction between the application of existing law (in the easy and intermediate cases) and the creation of new law (in the hard cases) is difficult and delicate. Sometimes it is also hard to know whether the judge was or was not aware of the exercise of discretion. The judge does not always write his consciousness into the judgment. For these reasons, I accept the conclusion that it is impossible to condition the lawfulness of a judge's ruling on the existence of

44. Raz, *supra* note 12, ch. 1, at 207.

awareness. The need for stability and security in the judicial system may require the result that even if judicial discretion is exercised without awareness of its exercise—or without being able to tell from the judgment whether there was awareness—this does not impair the lawfulness of the decision itself. However, this does not make the need for awareness superfluous. A proper and reasonable exercise of judicial discretion requires the judge to be aware of his exercise of discretion. Nonetheless, the lack of awareness and an unreasonable exercise of judicial discretion do not invalidate it.

Although I find this result acceptable, it does not set one's mind at ease. Thus, I understand that from the perspective of the decision in the particular case, lack of awareness does not invalidate the decision. But it seems to me that the lack of awareness must affect the status of the decision in the normative realm. The normative weight of a new judicial creation that was arrived at out of an awareness that it was a new creation differs from the weight of this same creation if it was produced without any awareness. One cannot establish hard and fast rules here either. In a legal system in which the legitimacy of the judicial creation is cast in doubt, one cannot expect that an unwitting exercise of judicial discretion will have any effect in the normative plane. This may explain why, in the English common law of the nineteenth century, the problem never arose. If the prevalent theory is that the judge simply declares the law, no great importance is attached to awareness of the existence of judicial discretion. It is otherwise in a legal system in which the legal community is quite aware of the judicial creation and distinguishes carefully between easy and intermediate cases, on the one hand, and hard cases, on the other hand. It seems to me that the latter type of legal system may have a rule according to which a judicial creation loses some of its normative force if it is made unknowingly.

Nonetheless, it appears to me that even before the legal community develops a sensitivity to the distinctions among the different cases, one may formulate a legal norm according to which a judgment that contains no normative discussion, and that is all facts and decision, will not constitute a rule for the future. The holding will serve as *stare decisis,* but not as a precedent. This would, I believe, give proper expression to the fact that for a normative creation, the judge's awareness of his creation is required. Furthermore, to advance the importance of awareness in judicial discretion, judges should give expression to their awareness in their opinions, so that one might know, simply by reading the judgment, whether the decision was reached out of an awareness that judicial discretion existed. If the judge knew that he was expected to give outward expression to his awareness, he would in practice be aware of his actions.

Types of Awareness

Awareness of judicial discretion includes a number of main types:

1. Awareness of the existence of judicial discretion;
2. Awareness of what it means to use judicial discretion;
3. Awareness of the need to formulate the purpose behind the legal norm.

Awareness of the Existence of Judicial Discretion

Awareness and Reasonableness A basic condition of the reasonable exercise of judicial discretion is awareness of the existence and exercise of judicial discretion. A judge cannot decide in a reasonable manner among the possibilities open to him if he is not aware that different possibilities exist. A judge who thinks that in every case he is simply the "mouth" of the legislature cannot decide reasonably among the normative possibilities arrayed before him; his eyes do not even see them. Professor Roscoe Pound wrote, "Socrates was not all wrong in holding that much which seems wrong-doing is but ignorant doing. Much will be gained when courts have perceived what it is that they are doing, and are thus enabled to address themselves consciously to doing it the best that they may."[45] A judge who thinks he is faced with an easy case or an intermediate case when in fact he is deciding in a hard case cannot grapple with the problems that judicial discretion places before him.

Awareness and Responsibility A judge who exercises judicial discretion without being aware of it does not sense the responsibility imposed on him. He exercises power without a sense of responsibility. This is an undesirable state of affairs. As Professor Julius Stone said,

> To exercise a discretion left by law, believing that one is only applying a precise directive of law, is to exercise power without a sense of responsibility

45. Pound, *supra* note 17, ch. 1, at 959.

for its exercise. This is so whether the belief proceeds from false ideas of logic or from false ideas of the scope of legal precepts, or from mere confusion.[46]

And later:

We still believe that where there is a judicial choice responsibility should match power and that this requires awareness of choice and attention to relevant facts and policies, as well as the legal precepts.[47]

Anyone who exercises power must sense the responsibility that is imposed on him. This feeling ensures that he will make every possible effort to exercise the power in a rational and reasonable manner. In my opinion, there is no danger that information about the existence of judicial discretion will lead to insensitivity to the need to exercise it rationally. On the contrary, awareness increases judicial sensitivity. In any event, even if such a danger exists, it must be confronted directly, not through the guise of a lack of power.

Awareness and Objectivity If the judge is not aware that judicial discretion exists, he will not make any conscious effort to distinguish between his own out-of-the-ordinary subjective feelings and the need to make an objective decision. As Professor Stone said, "With judges as with other men (we still believe) unconscious subjectivity limits objective performance."[48] Judge Edwards repeated this observation when he said, "The real threat that a judge's personal ideologies may affect his decisions in an inappropriate case arises when the judge is not even consciously aware of the potential threat."[49] Awareness of the exercise of discretion puts the judge on guard and makes it possible for him to cut himself off from those subjective factors that he should not take into account. I do not propose that judges should undergo psychoanalysis in order to make them aware of the subjective within them. Yet it seems to me that subjective awareness of the existence of judicial discretion is an essential condition of its objective exercise.

One cannot hide the fact that there are cases in which a judge exercises judicial discretion without being aware that he is doing so. Yet neither should one exaggerate the frequency of these cases: first, judicial discre-

46. Stone, *supra* note 40, ch. 1, at 678.
47. Ibid., at 686.
48. Ibid.
49. Edwards, *supra* note 2, ch. 1, at 410.

tion is sometimes granted by explicit language. In these cases, one must assume that the statutory language makes the judge aware that judicial discretion may exist. Second, even in the absence of an explicit rule granting judicial discretion, the reality today is that many judges are aware of the discretion placed in their hands. Empirical studies prove this thesis. In summarizing a series of interviews with judges of the House of Lords between 1957 and 1973, while quoting extensively from their written answers, Professor Paterson said the following about the judges' subjective feeling:

> Law Lords do exercise choices. Many cases do not have right answers which the Law Lords could derive if only they were sufficiently discerning. Their job is to make the best decision they can from the materials available—in the last analysis. Law Lords are craftsmen, not treasure hunters.[50]

I am convinced that this is also the situation in Israel, insofar as the judges of the Supreme Court are concerned. True, this awareness is not always expressed in the Court's judgment. At times, judges commit to writing only the result of their struggles, not the struggle itself. Yet as an empirical matter, based on experience, I believe that in most of the cases in which judges have discretion, most of them are in fact aware of it.

Awareness of What It Means to Use Judicial Discretion

Awareness of the Change in Law with the Change in Reality The use of judicial discretion means the creation of new law. This is lawmaking in its functional sense. Of course, the degree of discretion changes from one case to the next. The judicial discretion that exists in the interpretation of a vague statutory rule differs from the judicial discretion given in deviating from precedent or in drawing an analogy from a statutory rule. In all these cases, discretion is limited. Yet lawmaking always takes place. A reasonable exercise of judicial discretion means the judge is aware that he is involved in lawmaking, in other words, in changing the law. Justice Holmes said,

> But hitherto this process has been largely unconscious. It is important, on that account, to bring to mind what the actual course of events has been. If it were only to insist on a more conscious recognition of the legislative function of the courts, as just explained, it would be useful.[51]

50. Paterson, *supra* note 4, ch. 1, at 194.
51. O. Holmes, *The Common Law* 36 (1881).

A judge who believes that it is not his job to change the law does not exercise his discretion reasonably. Even if he believes that he is not changing the law, by applying the old law to the new reality he is in fact changing the law.[52] But the change is unwitting. The judge is not aware of the possibilities open to him, and thus he is acting unreasonably. The social changes necessarily produce changes in the law. The change in the law follows from the relation between the reality and the rule. The legal norm regulates given relations among people, and with a change in this system of relations, a change takes place in the legal norm itself, even if it is not changed formally. Justice Cardozo wrote,

> We live in a world of change. If a body of law were in existence adequate for the civilization of today, it could not meet the demands of the civilization of tomorrow. Society is inconstant. So long as it is inconstant, and to the extent of such inconstancy, there can be no constancy in law. The kinetic forces are too strong for us. We may think the law is the same if we refuse to change the formulas. The identity is verbal only. The formula has no longer the same correspondence with reality. Translated into conduct, it means something other than it did. Law defines a relation not always between fixed points, but often, indeed oftenest, between points of varying position. The acts and situations to be regulated have a motion of their own. There is change whether we will it or not.[53]

Thus, the law that negates or recognizes a duty of care where the foreseeable danger is harm resulting from carts and carriages and stones, is not the same law—even if it is not formally changed—where the foreseeable danger is from cars, trains, and atomic explosions. The social change has caused a change in the functioning, character, results, and actions of the legal norm. A river dam ceases to be a dam when the river becomes a lake. Even though no physical change occurs in the dam itself, its function changes, and the consequences of its action change. The judge must be aware of this reality. He must understand that in the hard cases, any decision he makes—even if it is a decision not to change the law—involves a change in the law. Only this kind of awareness can lead to a reasonable exercise of judicial discretion.

Awareness of the Need to Consciously Change the Law There are always changes in the law resulting from changes in the social reality. The

---

52. See Radcliffe, *supra* note 42, ch. 3, at 271.
53. Cardozo, *supra* note 125, ch. 1, at 10.

history of law is also the history of adapting the law to life's changing needs. Sometimes an informal change in the law is not enough; sometimes a formal, initiated change is needed. The life of the law is not always just logic or experience, but also renovation on the basis of experience and logic in order to adapt the law to the social reality. This task of renovation is imposed, first and foremost, upon the legislature. One of the principal functions of the legislative branch is to create new legal tools that can contain the new social realities and even determine its image and character. Yet this task is not the sole preserve of the legislature. Applying the law to the social reality is also the job of the judge.[54] As Justice Agranat said,

> Where a set of facts is revealed to the judge, that are based on new conditions of life, not those for which the existing rule was established, the judge is compelled to review again the logical premise underlying the rule that was created in a different general setting, with a view to adapting it to the new conditions, whether by broadening or by narrowing it, and also—when there is no alternative—with a view to abandoning altogether that logical premise, that serves as a support for the existing rule, and to use in its stead a different legal norm—even if this be a new legal norm that was theretofore unknown.[55]

Of course, there are many limitations on this legal path. For example, not every change that is possible is desirable. Not every power must be exploited. It is frequently preferable to leave the task to the legislature. But for the judge to be able to decide reasonably whether or not to initiate a change in the law, he must be aware that he is changing the law.[56]

Awareness of the Need to Formulate the Purpose Behind the Legal Norm

The Centrality of the Purpose of the Norm The legal norm is a purposeful norm. It is intended to attain a certain goal. The judge must give the legal norm that meaning which will realize its goal. To do so, the judge must be aware of the goal of the norm. One cannot achieve the purpose of the norm without being aware of it. Awareness of the goal of the norm does not raise any particular difficulty in the easy or intermediate cases, in

---

54. See *Packer v. Packer* [1953] 2 All E.R. 127.
55. CA 150/50 *Kaufman v. Margines,* 6 P.D. 1005, 1034.
56. See Hart and Sacks, *supra* note 26, ch. 1, at 316.

which it is for the most part relatively easy to clarify—from the legislative history (in the case of a statutory rule) and from the case law (for a case law rule)—what goals the legal norm sought to achieve. Not so in most of the hard cases. Frequently, what transforms a case into a hard case is precisely the fact that it is difficult to locate the goal of the legal norm. The sources that exist may not point clearly to the goal of the norm, or else the goal that emerges from them does not help solve the difficulty facing the judge. Yet the judge must overcome these difficulties and find the goal of the norm. He must formulate a conception of the goal of the norm and its purpose. The zone of reasonableness includes only those possibilities that put this purpose into effect. The final choice will be made only among these possibilities. Thus, if the legal norm is a purposeful norm and if the judge's function is to give the norm the meaning that realizes its purpose, then a reasonable decision among the possibilities cannot be made unless the judge is aware of the purpose of the norm.

Public Policy The goal and purpose of the legal norm are the public policy that lies at the foundation of the norm. The judge must formulate this policy. A reasonable exercise of judicial discretion is not possible until the judge is aware of the public policy at the basis of the legal norm. Sometimes one can expose the public policy from the legislative or case law history. Sometimes there is no alternative but to turn to the fundamental values of the system, either through an assumption that they lie at the basis of the public policy or as an independent source for formulating policy. Either way, the establishment and formulation of the public policy are among the judge's main tasks. He cannot exercise his discretion reasonably without being aware of the public policy at the basis of the legal norm.

And yet, many judges refrain from dealing with policy in the belief that setting public policy is a matter for the legislator, not for the judge.[57] Of course, the policy of the statutory rule is a matter for the legislature. By enacting the statute, the legislature gave expression to its policy. But the judge's task is to interpret the legislative rule, and for this he must uncover the public policy that the legislature established. As Justice

---

57. See Lord Morris in *Home Office v. Dorset Yacht Co. Ltd.* [1970] A.C. 1004, 1039; Lord Scarman in *McLaughlin v. O'Brien* [1983] A.C. 410.

Sussman said, "The legislator started with a thought or an idea and ended with words: we start with his words and attempt to retrace the legislator's footsteps from there in order to reveal his opinion. This is the task of the interpreter."[58] To the extent the legislature's policy emerges from the reliable sources, it should be given expression. The judge does not impose his own public policy. He exposes the policy of the legislature. But sometimes in the hard cases there is no reliable expression of the legislative policy, and the judge has no alternative but to determine the policy himself. Yet this determination is not arbitrary: he does not invent public policy. The judge consults the fundamental values of the system and attempts to learn the public policy from them. Sometimes he cannot escape channeling new values into the system in order to learn from them the policy behind the norm.

A "Wild Horse" Many judges flinch at weighing considerations of public policy. They see public policy as a "wild horse"—in the words of Judge Burrough in *Richardson v. Mellis* (1824)[59]—from which whoever values his life should distance himself. The approach that refuses to take considerations of public policy into account is itself an expression of a certain public policy. Since the wild horse image was first used, some one hundred and fifty years have passed, and our understanding of the law has grown. Today we are aware that every legal norm has a goal and purpose, which the judge must discover and expose so that he may give meaning to the norm. One may learn about the goal and purpose of the norm from the legislative history. Yet at times one cannot avoid turning to the general values of the system. In all these activities, the judge must be, in Justice Landau's words, "a faithful interpreter of the views accepted by the enlightened public, in whose midst he sits."[60] Every judge, upon his appointment, is placed astride that wild horse, and he has no choice but to ride it. As Professor Corbin noted,

> However unruly the horse may be, it is not possible for the courts to refuse to ride. Justice (whether described as "natural" or "artificial"), public policy, general welfare, the settled convictions of mankind, community ideals, are all modes of describing substantially the same thing. It is this that the courts are established to administer, and upon which in the last analysis their judgments are based.[61]

58. F.H. 3/62 *The Interior Minister v. Musa*, 16 P.D. 2467, 2474.
59. 130 E.R. 294.
60. C.A. 461/62 *Zim v. Maziar*, 17 P.D. 1319, 1335.
61. Corbin, *On Contracts*, 121n9 (1962).

Thus, every judge must take into account considerations of public policy when he chooses among the various options. Lord Reid spoke of this as follows:

> So long as the powers that be . . . can see to it that the new race of judges are not mere technicians but are men of the world as well, we can—indeed we must—trust them to acquaint themselves with public policy and apply it in a reasonable way to such new problems as will arise from time to time.[62]

In C.A. 207/79, *Raviv v. Beit Yules Ltd.* I observed,

> The judge must acknowledge the fact that in his judicial function he must weigh considerations of public policy, that are none other than considerations of justice and of balancing among conflicting interests. He must base himself on the past. He must recognize the present. He must prepare tools for solving problems in the future. Life is in constant flux. So too the law. The judge must balance between stability and movement. He does this with the help of public policy. This principle of public policy is what connects the specific rules of the legal system with the center of its spiritual life. It channels blood and life to these rules. The judge must recognize this state of affairs. He does not change it by closing his eyes to it. The question is only whether when he reaches a decision, the judge is aware of the freedom of choice given him and the responsibility placed upon him in the choice he makes, or whether he judges without awareness and therefore also irresponsibly.[63]

Justice Holmes referred to this, saying,

> I think that the judges themselves have failed adequately to recognize their duty of weighing considerations of social advantage. The duty is inevitable, and the result of the often proclaimed judicial aversion to deal with such considerations is simply to leave the very ground and foundation of judgments inarticulate, and often unconscious.[64]

I added in the *Beit Yules* case: "Every judge sits astride the 'wild horse.' . . . The question is only whether, in reaching this result, the judge was led by the 'wild horse', or whether it was the judge who led the horse to his destination. Thus, the better we learn to recognize the public policy, the better we will understand our judicial function."[65] If judges are not aware of public policy, they will not be able to carry out their task properly.

62. Reid, *supra* note 39, ch. 3, at 27.
63. 37 P.D. 1, 533, 556.
64. Holmes, *supra* note 17, ch 1, at 467.
65. C.A. 207/79, *supra* note 63, at 557.

The Values that Battle for Primacy The judge must be aware of the public policy that lies at the basis of each of the possibilities that make up the zone of reasonableness. He must be aware of the principles, lines of policy, and standards that lie at the basis of the legal norm. He must understand that the legal norm—whether he interprets it or creates it—is a purposeful norm. It must attain certain objectives. It usually represents a compromise among conflicting values. A reasonable exercise of judicial discretion requires that the judge be aware of this reality. Justice Holmes said,

> But I think it most important to remember whenever a doubtful case arises, with certain analogies on one side and other analogies on the other, that what really is before us is a conflict between two social desires, each of which seeks to extend its dominion over the case, and which cannot both have their way. The social question is which desire is stronger at the point of conflict.[66]

Professor Pound reiterated this idea: ''The body of the common law is made of adjustments or compromises of conflicting individual interests in which we turn to some social interest, frequently under the name of public policy, to determine the limits of a reasonable adjustment.''[67] Both Justice Holmes and Professor Pound speak of conflicting interests. This approach is too narrow. We are dealing with values that are competing for primacy and that reflect principles and lines of policy that contain various interests and standards. The judge cannot fulfill his task properly if he is not aware of this and if he does not properly identify these values, assign them suitable weight, and establish the appropriate balance among them.

Awareness of the Fundamental Problems

I discussed the judge's awareness of judicial discretion itself. Without this awareness, a reasonable exercise of judicial discretion is impossible. Needless to say, for a reasonable exercise of judicial discretion, the judge must be aware of the fundamental problems that lie at the basis of the exercise of judicial discretion. He must be aware of the fundamental normative problems. Thus, for example, he must understand that a reasonable exercise of judicial discretion requires consideration not only of the existing fundamental values, but also of new values. He must be

66. Holmes, *supra* note 122, ch. 1, at 239.
67. Pound, ''A Survey of Social Interests,'' 57 *Harv. L. Rev.* 1, 4 (1943).

conscious of the need for organic growth. He must be aware that he fills a dual role of deciding in the particular conflict before him and establishing a general norm, and that between these two tasks there is constant tension. He must recognize the need to ensure consistency and neutrality, while showing special understanding for the problem of retroactivity. At the same time, he must be aware of the institutional problems that lie at the foundation of judicial discretion and of the incidentality of the exercise thereof. He must understand that in the exercise of discretion he is limited in information and in means. He must realize that he must do justice and that justice must also appear to have been done. For this, he must act objectively. In addition to all these requirements, he must be aware of the place of the judge in the system of separation of powers. He must be cognizant of the problem of democracy and of the society's conception of the judicial role. He must also take into account the relations among the various governmental authorities.

Such broad awareness imposes a difficult burden upon the judge. Professor Dworkin was right when he called the ideal judge a Hercules.[68] Of course, one should not exaggerate. Judicial discretion arises in a given sector and according to a given set of facts. It does not raise the entire spectrum of problems in their full scope. Frequently, only a limited awareness is required. Undoubtedly, however, the choice is often difficult.

THE MOST REASONABLE POSSIBILITY AND THE DISTINCTION BETWEEN JUDICIAL ACTIVISM AND JUDICIAL SELF-RESTRAINT

Definition of Terms

Much has been written about the question of judicial activism or restraint.[69] These terms are usually not defined,[70] despite their multiple meanings. Any discussion of the question of judicial activism or self-

68. Dworkin, *supra* note 16, ch. 1, at 105.

69. See Edmund-Davies, "Judicial Activism," *supra* note 38, ch. 3; *Supreme Court Activism and Restraint* (S. Halpern and C. Lamb, eds., 1982); A. Miller, *Toward Increased Judicial Activism* (1982); Oakes, "Judicial Activism," 7 *Harv. J.L. and Pub. Pol'y.* 1 (1983); M. Wilkey, *Activism by the Branch of Last Resort: Of the Seizure of Abandoned Swords and Purses* (1984).

70. See Canon, "A Framework for the Analysis of Judicial Activism," in Halpern and Lamb (eds.), *supra* note 69, at 385.

restraint must assume that the judge acts within the bounds of the zone of reasonableness. When the judge has no judicial discretion, and only one possibility exists, the distinction between activism and self-restraint is meaningless. The judge must choose this possibility, whether the choice makes him an activist judge or a passive judge. Thus, the activism–self-restraint distinction has meaning only where there is judicial discretion, when the judge is free to choose from among a number of lawful possibilities open to him.

For my needs, I define an activist judge as a judge who chooses, from the group of possibilities open to him, the possibility that changes the existing law more than any other possibility, and I define a self-restrained judge as a judge who chooses from among all the possibilities the one that, more than any of the others, preserves the existing situation. The difference between the two, therefore, is only relative. At times it is easy to distinguish between activism and restraint. Thus, for example, when a precedent exists, the activist judge is the one who deviates from it, while the restrained judge is the one who preserves it. Sometimes it is difficult to distinguish between the two. For example, when we are dealing with a vague statutory rule that has not yet been interpreted and that is capable of being interpreted in several ways, or a new case law issue that has not yet been considered, it is sometimes hard to determine which interpretation and which rule change the rule more than the others.

"Activism–Self-Restraint" and the Adaptation to Life's Requirements and Stability

Sometimes one may identify an activist judge as a judge who seeks to adapt the law to the changing needs of life, and a restrained judge as a judge who seeks to maintain stability and security in the law. Indeed, the law is changed not just for the sake of change, and the activist judge sometimes seeks to make the change because of his desire to create greater harmony between life and the law. Similarly, preservation of what exists is not done for its own sake, and sometimes the passive judge seeks to do so in order to maintain stability and security in the life of the law. But this conjunction is not always present. Sometimes the activist judge causes a change in the law that produces a mismatch between life and law. On the other hand, the restrained judge may preserve the existing law, which contains within it potential for change. Take a case in which the law was changed in the past to adapt it to the requirements of life. The restrained judge preserves this rule and is not prepared to change it. On the other hand, his colleague, the activist judge, is not satisfied with the change and wants to amend it. In this example, it is the passive judge who adapts the rule to the needs of life, while the activist judge acts in the opposite direction. Also, one should not equate activism with the pursuit of justice and self-restraint with indifference to considerations of justice. The existing law might be the just law, which the restrained judge wishes to preserve. The activist judge, on the other hand, wants to change that just law. Of course, one can also imagine the opposite situation.

"Activism–Self-Restraint" and the Fundamental Problems of Judicial Discretion

The activist judge and the self-restrained judge—each from his own perspective—encounter the fundamental problems of judicial discretion. The existing limitations on judicial discretion cut across this distinction and affect both the activist judge and the restrained judge.[71] Take, for example, the fundamental problems of the normative system. Organic growth is a problem for the activist judge. The judge who desires change may encounter the need to preserve organic growth. Yet the passive judge also encounters this problem, since organic growth may in fact point to a need for change. Or, take the fundamental problems of the institutional system. Both the judge who wants to change the existing law and the judge who wants to preserve it encounter these institutional problems. The same is true for the relations among the institutional systems. Thus, for example, the activist judge may collide with the democratic question from the perspective of majority rule, while the restrained judge may collide with the democratic question from the perspective of the fundamental values of the society. The public's faith in the judiciary also may be harmed both by excessive activism and by excessive restraint.[72]

At the same time, it appears that the activist judge is in greater danger than his restrained colleague of colliding with the limitations imposed on judicial discretion. One who preserves what exists is tied to a legal norm

71. See Wright, "The Role of the Supreme Court in a Democratic Society—Judicial Activism or Restraint?" 54 *Cornell L. Rev.* 1 (1968).

72. See Hazard, "The Supreme Court as A Legislature," 64 *Cornell L. Rev.* 1 (1978).

that has already passed through the melting pot of the limitations on judicial discretion. The risk that in the wake of the changes that took place in the meantime, the judge will again encounter these limitations is smaller than the risk facing someone who seeks to introduce change.[73] Thus, the activist judge may come up against the fundamental normative problems, because the demands of coherence and organic growth sometimes pose an obstacle to excessive change. Needless to say, only he collides with the problem of retroactivity. Similarly, the fundamental institutional problems will weigh particularly heavy on the activist judge. For example, the question of judicial objectivity will arise mainly with respect to him. The same is true for the relations among the branches. These will arise primarily in the matter of a change that may intrude upon the spheres of the other branches and harm the public's confidence in the judiciary. Thus, both the activist judge and the restrained judge must be aware of their activity, but it would appear that the activist judge must be especially careful.[74]

"Activism–Self-Restraint" and the Most Reasonable Possibility

From my analysis, it emerges that there is no a priori connection between the most reasonable possibility within the zone of reasonableness and the activity or self-restraint of the judge. One cannot say in advance that the most reasonable possibility is that which is selected by the activist judge, just as one cannot say ahead of time that the most reasonable possibility is the one the restrained judge chooses. Thus, neither activism nor self-restraint is what establishes the most reasonable possibility; rather, it is the most reasonable possibility that calls for activism or self-restraint. Consequently, it is meaningless to say that an activist judge is a "good" judge or that a self-restrained judge is a "good" judge. A good judge is a judge who chooses the best possibility, which may either produce change or preserve what exists.[75] It also follows that it is meaningless to say that an activist judge is by definition a liberal judge and that a self-restrained judge is a conservative judge.[76] Whatever meaning one ascribes to the

73. See Wallace, "The Jurisprudence of Judicial Restraint: A Return to the Moorings," 50 *Geo. Wash. L. Rev.* 1 (1981).

74. See Traynor, "The Limits of Judicial Creativity," 29 *Hastings L.J.* 1025, 1039 (1978).

75. See J. Agresto, *The Supreme Court and Constitutional Democracy* 31 (1984).

76. See Shetreet, "On Assessing the Role of Courts in Society," 10 *Manitoba L.J.* 357 (1980).

terms *liberal* and *conservative,* an activist judge might be conservative, when the change he makes produces new conservative positions. Similarly, a restrained judge might be liberal, if in preserving what exists he preserves the liberal values embedded in the existing rule.

Thus, in my opinion the distinction between activism and self-restraint, as we have defined them, is of no help. It contains no value element and it is incapable of answering the key question: when to be an activist and when to exercise self-restraint.[77] As for myself, I would avoid this distinction.[78] By its nature it must indicate the final result of the legal analysis. In fact, it generates independent force for itself and it occasionally becomes a primary factor that determines the ultimate result, though it contains no standard for doing so. Thus, not infrequently we find someone who is dissatisfied with a given rule preaching the virtues of judicial activism as an independent reason to change it, while anyone who is pleased with that rule preaches judicial restraint as an independent reason to preserve it.[79] Yet these are barren reasons.[80] If activism is by itself a reason—and not merely a result—then it will be applied also as a means of changing a rule that no one wants to change, and if self-restraint by itself is a reason—and not just a result—it will be activated in order to preserve a rule no one wants. Thus, we often find people preaching activism as a reason for changing a rule they dislike, and once the change has been achieved, they begin to preach judicial restraint as a reason for keeping it. These double standards are unfortunate. They jar the public's confidence in the judicial system. Activism and self-restraint are not independent considerations, and they are incapable of leading the judge to the most reasonable possibility. Activism and self-restraint are results that are reached by exercising judicial discretion, which is guided by other considerations.[81]

77. See Kurland, "Toward A Political Supreme Court," 37 *U. Chi. L. Rev.* 19, 21 (1969).

78. See Traynor, *supra* note 74, at 1030: "The misbegotten catch phrase: judicial activism."

79. See Greenawalt, "The Growth of Judicial Power: A Comment," *The Judiciary in a Democratic Society* 89 (L. Theberge, ed., 1979).

80. See Deutsch, "Neutrality, Legitimacy and the Supreme Court: Some Intersections between Law and Political Science," 20 *Stan. L. Rev.* 169, 171 (1968).

81. See Cappelletti, "The Law Making Power of the Judge and Its Limits: A Comparative Analysis," 8 *Monash U. L. Rev.* 15, 51 (1981).

Chapter 5
Fundamental Problems in the Normative System

THE COHERENCE OF THE SYSTEM AND JUDICIAL DISCRETION

What is a normative structure, and what does such a structure do to a legal system—these are the fundamental queries of a legal philosophy.[1] As I noted, I do not intend to deal with these questions. For our purposes, it is enough to say that from the fact that judicial discretion is limited, and not absolute, it follows that the judge is not free to give the legal norm whatever content he desires. The institutionalized normative system[2] limits the scope of the considerations he may take into account. For example, a judge in such a legal system is not entitled to say, ''I don't like precedent X because the best solution is different, and so I am deviating from it.'' In order to deviate from a precedent—even if the judge is not bound by the earlier precedent and is free to deviate—the judge who is operating in an institutionalized normative legal system such as the Israeli one, for example, must base himself on special reasons that allow him this deviation. As Professor Raz said,

> But the courts in Common Law jurisdictions do not have this power with respect to the binding Common Law rules. They cannot change them whenever they consider that on the balance of reasons it would be better to do so.

1. See J. Raz, *The Concept of a Legal System* (1970); J. Raz, *Practical Reason and Norms* (1975).
2. What Professor Raz calls an ''institutional system,'' as opposed to a ''system of absolute discretion'': see Raz, *Practical Reason and Norms* 133 (1975).

They may change them only for certain kinds of reasons. They may change them, for example, for being unjust, for iniquitous discrimination, for being out of step with the court's conception of the body of laws to which they belong. But even if the court finds that they are not the best rules for some other reason not included in the permissible list, it is nevertheless bound to follow the rules.[3]

These factors, which either permit or negate deviation, obviously change from one system to the next. Legal system X might establish certain conditions that have nothing in common with the rest of the rules of the system. Thus, for example, one may determine that the standard for deviating from existing norms is inherent in a particular doctrine. But in general a legal system will not operate like this. In any event, where the standard for exercising judicial discretion is a reasonableness standard, one must strive to ensure that the legal system will not stray from itself and will not make itself hostage to a standard that is foreign to it. Thus, in my opinion, the test of reasonableness requires that a deviation from an existing arrangement (as in the case of deviation from an earlier precedent), or a progression from it (such as a new case law creation), or a balancing of values in its framework (regarding the interpretation of a vague rule) be done in a manner that preserves the system's normative coherence. Professor Lon Fuller discussed this as follows:

> Those responsible for creating and administering a body of legal rules will always be confronted by a *problem of system*. The rules applied to the decision of individual controversies cannot simply be isolated exercises of judicial wisdom. They must be brought into, and maintained in, some systematic interrelationship; they must display some coherent internal structure.[4]

The very existence of a certain legal system creates a reality that affects—in the framework of the test of reasonableness—the nature of the options open to the judge and the nature of the options that are closed to him. Thus, for example, a statutory rule may stipulate that where a judge encounters a legal problem to which his system provides no solution, he must turn to a foreign legal system in order to derive the solution. But a similar result cannot be reached by means of judicial discretion.

The principle of reasonableness requires, in my view, internal coherence and internal links among the various norms. It is not reasonable

3. Ibid., at 140.
4. Fuller, *supra* note 81, ch. 2, at 94.

to come up with a solution to a new problem that is completely divorced from the solutions that were given to similar problems within the system. The degree of coherence may change from one system to the next. A given legal system may contain no rules on this issue, and the matter will then be left to judicial discretion. Yet it seems that in every existing system one finds the fundamental rule that a minimal degree of coherence must exist.

THE FUNDAMENTAL VALUES OF THE SYSTEM

The Importance of the Fundamental Values

The fundamental values of the state fulfill an important function in the law of that state.[5] Sometimes they constitute part of the constitutional or statutory text itself. This is the case, for example, when the statute establishes that a right or duty must be carried out "in customary manner and in good faith." This is also the case when the statute refers to "negation of the democratic character of the State." Even when the text itself does not adopt the language of values, these always serve as standards for interpreting the text. They also constitute a standard for changing the existing case law rule, whether by distinguishing or by deviation. A judge who operates in the confines of a given system at a given time has before him a given set of fundamental values. Rare is the case in which a judge is faced with a novel situation. However, even a judge who operates within the boundaries of an existing system, that is based upon an accepted value system, may be faced with hard questions concerning the values of the system. Thus, for example, he may find himself confronted with competing values and be forced to balance them. Sometimes he must decide the question whether he is entitled to add a new value, which had not been previously recognized, to the existing values.

How is he to exercise his discretion in these circumstances? What does the reasonableness standard demand of him? It seems to me that it raises before him the need to decide these questions rationally. In the present context, this means that his decision must be adapted to the existing structure of the system. He must choose the option that preserves a certain degree of coherence in the system. He is not free to issue

5. See Wellington, *supra* note 20, ch. 1; Raz, *supra* note 21, ch. 1, at 841.

a solution that appears to him, subjectively, to be the best. He must provide a solution that will create a certain degree of coherence in the existing system. The situation is different, of course, from the legislature's perspective. It may give whatever solution it thinks best, without having to satisfy this requirement of internal structure.

Balance among Competing Values

Competing values must be balanced on the basis of the standard of reasonableness. It is not enough for the judge to believe, from his subjective viewpoint, that one value is preferable to the next. He must justify this preference on the basis of rational explanations. The coherence of the system as a whole is a point of reference that permits such rational explanation. For example, the need to preserve the system itself from destruction is a rational consideration, and it is reasonable to give preference to the value of the existence of the state over other values, such as the right to elect and to be elected. "The interest of the existence of the State and the interest of the right to vote are not equivalent interests. The first clearly takes priority over the second, for the first is a condition of the existence of the second."[6] The same is true of the decisive importance of the value of the democratic character of the state.

Sometimes the system gives priority to value X over value Y, in a certain context. This preference must be used as an appropriate standard if a similar question of preference comes before the judge. The need to ensure overall coherence in the system requires this result. Thus, for example, the Supreme Court determined that the principle of equality takes priority over the need to protect a public employee from tort liability.[7] It seems to me that a coherent approach requires the judge to adopt a similar standard when he must interpret a rule of immunity in the field of criminal law,[8] such as the immunity of a member of Knesset from criminal responsibility. Similarly, the Court established the priority of the principle of the fair trial over that of freedom of the press, through the determination of an appropriate standard for balancing.[9] This same standard may also serve the court when it is forced to decide between the

6. See E.A. 2/84 *Naiman v. Chairman of the Central Election Committee,* 39 P.D.(2) 225.
   7. See C.A. 507/79 *Roundnoff v. Hacim,* 36 P.D.(2) 757.
   8. See C.H. 507/81 *Abu Hazera v. Attorney General,* 35 P.D.(4) 561.
   9. See Cr. App. 126/62 *Disenchik v. Attorney General,* 17 P.D. 169.

principle of the fair trial and freedom of demonstration. The two examples are similar, and coherence demands similar solutions.

The need to balance among conflicting values arises in many areas of the law. When a judge is faced with a problem of balancing, he must inquire how the balance was reached in similar cases. The need to guarantee the unity of the system requires taking this past practice into account. Thus, for example, the Court decided on a certain "balancing formula" between freedom of the press and the security of the state[10]— "the probability test." When another court is faced with the need to determine the balancing formula between freedom of demonstration and public welfare, it must take this formula into account.[11] The two problems are similar from the structural perspective and involve similar values competing for primacy. The need to ensure coherence in the framework of the system demands application of similar balancing formulas.

Frequently, of course, the new case does not resemble the old one. The values competing for supremacy are not identical, and this must be taken into account. This is a rational reason for not adopting the old solution, yet it requires explanation. The old case must be referred to. Despite the differences, the old case must constitute a starting point for the new direction. The judge in the second case is not writing on a blank slate. The law does not begin with him. He stands before an entire system of rules, which may offer possible analogies. If certain solutions that were given in the past do not seem to him sufficiently similar to the present case, he must refrain from applying them, yet he cannot avoid taking them into account. Furthermore, sometimes a judge thinks a solution given in the past in a similar case is not an appropriate solution and that it must be abandoned. This is possible in a legal system in which the judge is not bound by the earlier precedent. Yet the deviation, too, must be based on tests of reasonableness. Therefore, in a developed legal system that has a certain normative structure and solutions and balancing formulas for conflicts among values, the judge must take into account the existing structure before he contributes his own particular judicial brick.

These considerations are important, for example, when a judge has to

10. See H.C. 73/53 *supra* note 56, ch. 2.
11. See H.C. 153/83 *Levi v. Commander of the Southern District of the Israel Police,* 38 P.D. (2) 393.

decide whether to recognize a new "duty of care" in the framework of the tort of negligence. To answer this question, the judge must balance among competing values. These values conflict, not only with respect to the new duty of care, but also with respect to notional duties that were recognized or rejected in the past. The judge must take all of these into account. He must consider the solutions and balances that were reached in the past and, unless there is a new reason for deviating from them, apply them in the future. This follows from the need to maintain the coherence of the system. Similarly, when the judge seeks the point of balance in the confrontation between freedom of movement and security of the state, he must consider the point of balance that his system established in the conflict between freedom of expression and security of the state. The issues are similar. Both freedom of expression and freedom of movement stem from a democratic-liberal conception. If the court arrives at different balancing formulas, it must explain the difference, or else it will damage the internal coherence of the system.

Locating the Values

The fundamental values of the system are extremely important for its operation. But what are these values? The judge is not free to invent values, no matter how appropriate they seem to him. He must uncover the values that are already hidden in the framework of the system or take into account the values that have not yet infiltrated it. In neither case does he have absolute discretion. He must operate reasonably and he must consider the overall structure of his system.

It is clear that this consideration of the system is required insofar as locating the existing values is concerned. They are inside the system, and therefore the judge must consider his system in order to discover its values. This is not difficult, especially when the values are recognized explicitly in a constitutional or statutory enactment. In Israel this is the case with respect to the values mentioned in the Declaration of Independence. Yet what of values for which one does not find such explicit expression? These also may be among the system's values, although they are not explicitly mentioned in it. It is sufficient that they are implicit in the very structure and nature of the system.[12] The Israeli Supreme Court, in the early days of the state, said as much about certain fundamental

12. See Friedmann, *supra* note 17, ch. 1, at 843.

values, such as freedom of expression and freedom of occupation.
Justice Agranat wrote,

> The set of statutes, according to which the Israeli political institutions were
> founded and operate, bear witness that this is a State whose foundations are
> democratic. So, too, the words that were pronounced in the Declaration of
> Independence—and especially with respect to basing the State ''on the
> fundamentals of freedom'' and guaranteeing freedom of conscience—mean
> that Israel is a freedom-seeking State.[13]

From these detailed principles Justice Agranat concluded the value of
freedom of expression. From it, freedom of procession was derived.[14]
Similarly, from the foundations of the legal system, Justice Shneor
Heshin learned that the individual's natural right to seek out sources of
livelihood and income was recognized.[15] The principles in the matter of
separation of powers, rule of law, and dignity of man were also derived
from these foundations. Basic rights ''that are not written in any book''
come to us from the system itself, without being expressly declared in it;
rather, they are implicit in its very nature.

Surrounding the core of fundamental values that are expressly recognized in the system, there is a penumbra that contains a core of other
fundamental values that are not explicitly recognized but that follow
from them. Around the core of these additional fundamental values,
there is a penumbra that contains cores of still other principles.[16] Thus
the values are intertwined, one supporting the other, all of them maintaining the legal system as a whole.

Sometimes the judge must depart the confines of his legal system in
order to channel into it fundamental values that are not yet found in it.
This is permitted. The list of fundamental values is not closed, and a
judge is entitled to enrich his legal system with fundamental values that
have not yet been accorded judicial recognition. Yet in so doing, he is not
free to operate according to his unbridled discretion. He is not entitled to
introduce any fundamental value he likes. His discretion is limited in that
the new values must be compatible with those that already exist in the
system. Thus, for example, if the legal system is based on values of
sexual equality, a judge who believes in inequality is not entitled to

13. H.C. 73/53 *supra* note 56, ch. 2, at 884.
14. H.C. 153/83, *supra* note 11.
15. H.C. 1/49 *Bezerano v. Minister of Police,* 2 P.D. 80.
16. See *Griswold v. Connecticut,* 381 U.S. 479 (1964) (Douglas).

channel into the system values that are based on this inequality. Thus, the judge is not a crusader for new values that have no mention or memory in the system. He is entitled to introduce values that are consistent with those that exist or that represent their natural and consecutive development.

The judge may cross the borders of his system and find, in the society in which he lives, certain fundamental values that the public accepts. As we have seen, if these values are compatible with the values of the legal system, he is entitled to channel them into his system. To the extent a contradiction exists, the judge must contend with it, deciding whether the new values are sufficiently strong to replace the old ones. A judge may not ignore new values simply because they are new and not yet recognized in his legal system. A rational and reasonable examination must compare the new values with the old ones. Just as old values are not to be discarded on account of their age, neither must one prevent the infiltration of new values simply because of their novelty. But new values will not replace old ones where the new values are not founded upon a solid societal base. The judge must examine those values that are rooted in the consciousness of the public, or at least in a significant part of it.[17] The judge must not feed into his system values that have not yet matured[18] nor values that are the subject of bitter controversy. In this way one can ensure that the values of the legal system faithfully reflect the values of the society, and that only a mature change of the values of the society produces a change in the legal values. Thereby the coherence of the legal system will also be guaranteed, for new values that are channeled into the legal system have a way of being formulated slowly, through reciprocal relations and strong connections with the values that already exist in the system. President Agranat discussed this, saying,

> [T]he conception and the birth of these truths are the product of social thinking, their coming into being and evolution are the result of the discussions and elucidations that take place through a variety of social organs (political parties, newspapers, different associations and professional organizations and the like). Only after they have passed this process of initial crystallization, does the State—the laws of the legislature, the regulations and orders of the executive and the judgments of the courts—appear on the scene to remould them, translate them into the language of the law and impress upon them the seal of binding positive law. The explanation for this

17. See L. Hand, *The Spirit of Liberty* 15 (3d ed., 1960).
18. See Holmes, *supra* note 122, ch. 1, at 295.

matter lies in the fact that the function of the State, so democratic theory teaches, is to fulfill the will of the people and give effect to those norms and standards which it prizes. It follows from this that the common conviction must first form among enlightened members of society that these norms and standards are true and just, before we can say that a general will has been created to give them binding force, to stamp them as positive law and attach its sanctions. The essence of this conviction, it is to be noted, is not that the norms and standards need still to emerge, but that they already exist and are true, though they lack the official impress of the law. Thus the consensus of society as to the truth and justice of a particular norm precedes its meriting legal recognition by the State. Clearly also, the creation of such social consensus is not a process which commences and ceases within a day; the process is one of gradual evolution, protracted in time and ever renewing itself.[19]

Thus, just as the judge must not fail to express fundamental principles that have matured in his system simply because they do not appeal to him, he also must not give expression to principles he likes, if they have not yet matured. Consequently, the judge may find himself not infrequently in a situation in which those fundamental principles from which the law may be derived do not exist, or do not yet exist. In this state of affairs, the judge must acknowledge that the source of his sustenance has dried up, and he must not channel immature principles into the legal system. Referring to the question, Who is a Jew? Justice Landau said,

> As I have explained, the views common among the enlightened public are also a proper source of adjudication when no other source is available to us. The court has more than once drawn upon this source in decisions which have become sign-posts in the development of our case law and there will certainly be further opportunities for doing so in the future. But on the present occasion this source, too, fails us, in view of genuine differences of opinion which prevail among the public.[20]

ORGANIC GROWTH

A Living Organism

When a judge exercises judicial discretion, he does not perform a one-time act isolated from an existing normative order. Judicial discretion is used in the framework of a system and must fit into it. The legal system,

19. H.C. 58/68 *supra* note 51, ch. 2, at 602.
20. Ibid., at 530.

into which the judicial decision is inserted, is not a frozen body. It is a living organism, and judicial discretion is one of the forces that fertilize its cells. There must be harmony between the exercise of judicial discretion that develops the cells, on the one hand, and the development of the living organism that is the legal system, on the other; otherwise, cancerous cells are admitted. In the words of Justice Holmes,

> I recognize without hesitation that judges do and must legislate, but they can do so only interstitially; they are confined from molar to molecular motions. A common-law judge could not say, ''I think the doctrine of consideration a bit of historical nonsense and shall not enforce it in my court.''[21]

In general, organic growth of the legal system necessitates gradual development. The need to ensure the existence of the system demands evolution, not revolution. Usually, continuity, rather than a series of jumps, is involved. Of course, sometimes one cannot avoid sharp turns and dangerous leaps, but these occur in exceptional situations, and at times they can be explained only by the need to ensure gradual development. Normally, the proper functioning of a legal system requires slow and gradual movement. Judicial discretion must fit into these frameworks. Its movement must also be slow and gradual. Judge Traynor described this well: ''The greatest judges of the common law have proceeded in this way, moving not by fits and starts, but at the pace of the tortoise that steadily advances though it carries the past on its back.''[22] From this requirement that judicial discretion fit into the legal order flow a number of conclusions that are relevant to the exercise of judicial discretion.

Natural Development

Judicial discretion must ensure natural and organic growth and development. As Justice Landau wrote,

> The judge-made law, whose paths are not infrequently paths of twisting and meandering while cautiously groping from case to case toward more general solutions, and through organic development that leads to a weakening of the frail limbs and a strengthening of those that have life in them—this case law is a convenient practice range for gaining experience for the enactment of a statutory law.[23]

21. *Southern Pacific Company v. Jensen*, 244 U.S. 205, 221 (1917).
22. Traynor, *supra* note 74, ch. 4, at 1031.
23. Landau, *supra* note 17, ch. 1, at 297.

The slow process, from case to case, permits caution, security, and, if the need arises, a retracing of one's steps. The Israeli Supreme Court discussed this when it imposed a duty of care on the prosecution toward the person indicted. I said,

> If it turns out that we erred, we can change our approach in the future. Justice Jackson wrote that "we are not final because we are infallible, but we are infallible only because we are final" (*Brown v. Allen,* 344 U.S. 446, 540 (1953), whereas I believe that the honorable judge erred. The finality of our decisions is based upon our strength to admit our mistakes, and upon our willingness to do so in the appropriate case.[24]

The judicial ship does not normally sail into the stormy sea, but rather navigates its way cautiously and slowly along the length of the safe seashore,[25] occasionally attempting to conquer the raging waves and, if it discovers that this is impossible, it returns to its usual path. The characteristics of judicial law-making were accurately described by Lord Reid, who said,

> I am tempted to take as an analogue the difference between old-fashioned, hand-made, expensive quality goods and the brash products of modern technology. If you think in months, want an instant solution for your problems and don't mind that it won't wear well, then go for legislation. If you think in decades, prefer orderly growth and believe in the old proverb more haste less speed then stick to the common law.[26]

Professor Pound offered a similar approach:

> Judicial finding of law has a real advantage in competition with legislation in that it works with concrete cases and generalizes only after a long course of trial and error in the effort to work out a practicable principle. Legislation, when more than declaratory, when it does more than restate authoritatively what judicial experience had indicated, involves the difficulties and the perils of prophecy.[27]

Thus, the legal system's development is from one concrete case to another concrete case, through an abstraction that must fit into the framework of the system as a whole.[28]

24. C.A. 243/83 *supra* note 25, ch. 2, at 136.

25. See Wright, "The Study of Law," 54 *Law Q. Rev.* 185, 186 (1938).

26. Reid, *supra* note 39, ch. 3, at 28.

27. R. Pound, *The Formative Era of American Law* 45 (1938).

28. See Wasserstrom, *supra* note 89, ch. 2, at 172; E. Levi, *An Introduction to Legal Reasoning* 8 (1949); Stoljar, "The Logical Status of a Legal Principle," 20 *U. Chi. L. Rev.* 181 (1953).

The Triangular Link: Past-Present-Future

The requirement of meshing judicial discretion with the framework of the legal system means that the exercise of judicial discretion in the present, for the purpose of the specific controversy facing the judge, must connect itself to the past. However, today's present is tomorrow's past. Therefore, judicial discretion must look to the future. In arriving at the decision of today, the judge also establishes the norm for tomorrow. Thus, the judge is tied to yesterday and draws sustenance from it. He decides the particular dispute today. Thereby, he creates a general legal norm for tomorrow. The exercise of judicial discretion in the present must pass this triangular test. Justice Landau described the triangle nicely:

> [T]his process of the formation of law through case law requires that the discretion be exercised not only in order to find an answer that is just, and satisfactory, in the concrete case. Yet this is the primary requirement—I would even say the primitive requirement—like the judging of the city elders sitting at the gate. But the judge must always remember that "hard cases make bad law," and he must direct his glance backward and forward; his judgments must fit into the web of previously existing case law and at the same time must constitute a basis for making law in similar cases that will arise in the future. A judgment that does not pass this triangular test of consistency—justice in the concrete case, integration into the prior case law and basis for future judgments—is simply arbitrariness and its destiny is intolerable instability.[29]

The judge must decide in the controversy before him. It is only natural for him to strive to reach a just solution, yet he cannot ignore the fact that his solution must fit into the existing normative web. Nor can he ignore the fact that his solution must be just not only for the parties before him, but also for similar parties in the future. An ideal exercise of judicial discretion meets the triangular test of integration with the past, justice in the present, and an appropriate solution for the future. Yet such an achievement is not always attainable. In my opinion, an exercise of judicial discretion that takes into account only the present and only the parties whose issue is up for decision is an unreasonable exercise of judicial discretion. The judge must consider the entire normative order. A just solution in an extraordinary case may produce an unjust solution in similar cases that cannot be distinguished from this exceptional case.

29. Landau, *supra* note 17, ch. 1, at 293.

Thus, constant tension exists between the particular and the general, between the specific case and the general rule. A judge cannot ignore this tension. He operates unreasonably if he neglects the general and focuses only on the unique case before him. This kind of development may produce injustice for the entire system. A just solution to a certain concrete case may create an unjust norm for other cases. Yet by the same token, the judge acts unreasonably if he ignores the concrete case and focuses only on the general norm. One must not forget that the general norm exists only in order to solve specific cases. A possible way of reducing the tension is to examine whether the specific case suggests that the general norm should be changed or that an exception should be created for a certain category of case. This examination takes into account the specific case for it is this case that led to a rethinking of the entire issue. Yet the examination cannot end with the facts of the specific case. It must examine its influence on events that took place in the past and think about the situations that might arise in the future. A reasonable exercise of judicial discretion must weigh the basic advantages and disadvantages of undertaking a normative change. Only if the advantages outweigh the disadvantages should the change be made; thereby two (past and future) of the three ideal components of the appropriate solution are attained. If the general advantages do not outweigh the general disadvantages—even though the advantages outweigh the disadvantages in the concrete case—the existing rule should be left in place. The requirements of the past and of the future may be more important than the needs of the present.

Continuity

The requirement that judicial discretion fit into the past and the future produces continuity in the judicial enterprise. The judicial creation is a book written by a number of authors,[30] with each writer contributing one chapter to the joint creation. The author of one chapter cannot ignore the preceding chapters. They established the general framework, and his chapter must fit in with them. His chapter will be unprofessional if

---

30. This is an analogy from an image used by Professor Dworkin: see Dworkin, *supra* note 86, ch. 1 at 168; Dworkin, *supra* note 89, ch. 1. This image has been criticized. See Fish, "Working on the Chain Gang: Interpretation in Law and Literature" 60 *Tex. L. Rev.* 551 (1982). This criticism drew a response: see Dworkin, "My Reply To Stanley Fish (and Walter Ben Michaels): Please Don't Talk About Objectivity Any More," in *The Politics of Interpretation* 287 (W. Mitchell, ed., 1982).

suddenly it is composed entirely of new heroes and a new plot. There must be continuity. At the same time, however, the writer of a given chapter cannot merely repeat the previous chapters. Such behavior, too, would be unprofessional. He must develop the plot. Some characters may grow old and die, new characters may enter the plot. Sometimes it is even justified to introduce a turning point in the plot, in order to exploit the potential that was concealed in it. And when that chapter is concluded, it becomes an integral part of the old plot, and new authors will write new chapters based on it.

Judicial creativity, like the writing of a book in serial installments, is a continuous activity. Judges who are no longer on the bench wrote the early chapters. Sitting judges write the continuation, but they do so by basing themselves on the past. It is all written in a continuous process. And the chapters being written, as they are written, become part of the past, and new chapters, the fruits of new judges' labors, are written. Thus is achieved the judicial creation, which has no beginning and no end and is all continuity.

The comparison of exercising judicial discretion to writing a chapter in a literary work contains an important moral. On the one hand, it indicates the degree of judicial freedom. The judge does not blindly follow what was written in earlier chapters. He is entitled—indeed required—to develop the plot. But on the other hand, the comparison points to the limitations on judicial discretion. The judge cannot act as he likes. He acts within the confines of a system into which he must fit. He must preserve coherence.

Continuity affects judicial rhetoric. The judgments that judges write are for the most part the continuation of case law that began in years past and that continues until the time of the writing of the opinion. It seems to me that in important cases, the judicial continuity should be noted in the opinion. This is important not only for underscoring the historical truth that not everything began today, but also to make the public aware of the existence of that continuity. It also increases the public's confidence in the judicial system. Therefore, the judge should base his opinion not only on the most recent judgments, but also on the earliest ones and thus give proper expression to judicial continuity.

Judicial Discretion Based on Fundamental Values

I discussed the importance of fundamental values. Once these have been established, a judge who acts according to them guarantees the organic growth of the system. The new ruling will be natural to the judicial process. This is, in the words of Judge Dixon, "an enlightened application of modes of reassuring the traditional respect in the courts. It is a process by the repeated use of which the law is developed, is adapted to new conditions, and is improved in content."[31] Judicial discretion, in its natural operation, relies upon fundamental principles. The transition from one concrete case rule to another concrete case rule is not made only at the "level" of the concrete law. The transition from case law to case law is made by means of the common fundamental principle. The physiology of the judicial process contains a concrete case law that does not stand alone, but rather follows from a fundamental principle. This principle itself serves as a workshop for a new concrete case law, according to life's changing demands. This is the "genius" of the case law process.[32] It is not a collection of isolated decisions exhibiting the exercise of judicial discretion, but a normative system, in which the different norms are connected by means of the fundamental principles. New norms follow from existing fundamental principles. Thus the system develops organically and naturally and ensures the continuity of the judicial creation. The individual judge makes his own contribution, but the law is the result of the fundamental principles of the entire system, which reflect values with which the public identifies.[33] It is not the subjective feeling of the judge regarding right and wrong that activates his discretion, but rather the fundamental values of the system.[34] As a result, it is possible to develop the law in a methodical, balanced manner by integrating the new norms into the existing fabric of the system, while maintaining public faith in the objectivity of judging.

Consistency

To be reasonable, judicial discretion must be consistent.[35] Only thus will discretion fit into the legal system as a whole and become an integral part

31. Dixon, "Concerning Judicial Method," 29 *Aus. L. Rep. J.* 468, 472 (1956).

32. See Viscount Simonds in *Scruttons v. Midland Silicones* [1962] 1 All E.R. 1, 7; "The law is developed by the application of old principles to new circumstances. Therein lies its genius."

33. See Chafee, "Do Judges Make or Discover Law?" 9 *Proc. Am. Phil. Soc'y* 405, 409 (1947).

34. See Barwick, "Precedent in the Southern Hemisphere," 5 *Isr. L. Rev.* 1, 8 (1970).

35. See Hart and Sacks, *supra* note 26, ch. 1, at 161.

of it. A judge is not entitled to exercise his discretion in a certain way in one case and in another way in another case, if the two cases are similar. A reasonable exercise of judicial discretion requires that in similar cases discretion be exercised in a similar manner.[36] This is a fundamental requirement of justice, and it marks the limit of the reasonableness of the judicial discretion. Consequently, a consistent exercise of judicial discretion also means a neutral exercise of judicial discretion.[37] Thus, for example, when a judge decides that the test for authorizing a demonstration is the test of "probability" of harm to public safety, he must apply this test in every case, without giving any weight to the identity of the demonstrator or of those he may harm. Similarly, when a judge adopts a certain interpretive method (such as literal interpretation), he must employ this method in every case and cannot switch over to another interpretive method (such as purposive interpretation), merely in order to attain a result that he finds desirable in a particular case.

Of course, a judge might exercise his discretion in such a way as to cause a deviation from the previous law. Consistency does not require abstention from all change. Yet even here the judge must be consistent and neutral. He must apply the new rule in every similar case, and he must be prepared to deviate similarly from the prior law when like circumstances arise. Herein lies one of the differences between the discretion of the judiciary and the discretion of the legislature. No legal obligation is imposed on the latter to be consistent. It need not act neutrally. Not so the judge: his discretion must be reasonable and must fit into the legal fabric. As a result, he must be consistent and neutral.

JUDICIAL DISCRETION AND THE PROBLEM OF RETROACTIVITY

The coherence of the legal system and its organic growth requires that a person's activities be examined according to the law in effect at the time he undertakes them. A retroactive change in the law copies the law of the present onto the past and thus retroactively produces a drastic change in the law, without its having been preceded by the natural growth and organic development of the legal system. Therefore, the approach ac-

36. See Wasserstrom, *supra* note 89, ch. 2.

37. Wechsler, "Toward Neutral Principles of Constitutional Law," 73 *Harv. L. Rev.* 1 (1959).

cepted in every enlightened society is that generally, its legal rules shall not be applied retroactively. This is part of the principle of the rule of law. It is not fair or just to impose on a person the sanction of the organized society for acts that were not prohibited when they were done. Proper societal life requires that people act according to rules that are known in advance. On the basis of these one can plan one's behavior. Their retroactive application affects expectations and thereby muddles the fabric of proper social life. Retroactive application of legal norms harms the very nature of the judicial process. This process was meant to decide in a conflict that took place in the past. Its perspective is from the present to the past, and the question is whether or not, when the events took place, they were legal. A retroactive application of laws involves in effect—although not technically—a copying of the controversy from the past onto the present, and the question the court must decide is whether in light of the new norm the acts were or were not lawful. This changes the entire nature of the judicial function.

The problem of retroactivity does not arise at all, or arises only in weakened form, when a judge decides an easy case or an intermediate case. In these cases, a norm exists from the outset that directs the parties to only one permissible act. The judge who decides the conflict determines the only correct solution that exists. However, even in these cases the problem of retroactivity may arise. For example, the court may deviate from an earlier rule, and its new rule will apply retroactively. As we saw, such a deviation may fall within the borders of the intermediate cases, whenever the legal community is united in the view that the prior rule was fundamentally flawed. In this example, the new judicial rule will apply retroactively. Yet it causes minimal harm, because by definition the legal community thought the first rule was basically flawed, so the arguments against retroactive application of the laws in this situation are greatly blunted.

On the other hand, the problem of retroactivity arises in full force in the hard cases. By definition, these cases do not have just one correct solution. The judge makes the law by exercising his discretion. If this exercise is retroactive, a conflict is created between the exercise of judicial discretion and the need to apply the law prospectively. The declaratory theory attempts to cover the bare spots of this conflict by emphasizing that the new rule that emerges from the exercise of discretion does not retroactively cancel the old law, but simply announces that the latter was never the law. But it is plain to everyone that this "king" has no clothes. Whether the old law is voided retroactively or whether it is declared that it never had been law, a conflict that occurred in the past is being decided on the basis of a law that was not in effect when the conflict took place, and all the arguments about retroactivity apply. Bentham stressed this issue in his writings. He sought to note the advantages of statutory law over the judicial rule. One of the main drawbacks he found in the common law was its retroactive character. Here is how he described the problem:

> It is the judges (as we have seen) that make the common law. Do you know how they make it? Just as a man makes laws for his dog. When your dog does anything you want to break him of, you wait till he does it, and then beat him for it. This is the way you make laws for your dog; and this is the way the judges make law for you and me. They won't tell a man beforehand what it is he should not do—they won't so much as allow of his being told; they lie by till he has done something which they say he should not have done, and then they hang him for it.[38]

Thus, judicial discretion raises a complex problem of retroactivity.[39] Consequently, one of the major justifications Professor Dworkin offers for his theory, which denies the existence of judicial discretion, is based on the injustice in the existence of judicial discretion, all due to its retroactive nature.[40] Others think that Professor Dworkin's system itself contains strong elements of retroactivity.[41]

Considerations in Solving the Problem: Is the Exercise of Judicial Discretion Necessarily Retroactive?

The starting point for the whole problem is that the judicial rule that emerges from the exercise of judicial discretion is retroactive.[42] Is this an inviolable rule? As we have seen, the declaratory theory assumes this

38. *The Works of Jeremy Bentham,* vol. 5, 233, 235 (Bowring, ed., 1843).

39. As to prospective overruling, see *infra* note 47.

40. See R. Dworkin, supra note 16, ch. 1, at 84.

41. See Kress, "Legal Reasoning and Coherence Theories: Dworkin's Rights Thesis, Retroactivity, and the Linear Order of Decisions," 72 *Calif. L. Rev.* 369 (1984).

42. See Justice Holmes in *Kuhn v. Fairmont Coal Co.* 215 U.S. 349, 372 (1910): "I know of no authority in this court to say that in general state decisions shall make law only for the future. Judicial decisions have had retrospective operation for near a thousand years."

result and explains it. With the increase in criticism of the declaratory theory, the recognition that the judicial ruling is not inevitably retroactive has also increased. The approach accepted today is that the question of the application in time of the judicial rule is a question of positive order in each system, and that there is nothing in the nature of the judicial rule itself[43] or of the constitutional structure of the separation of powers[44] that demands retroactivity. Therefore, in a common law system this question is left to the courts themselves to decide on the basis of considerations of public policy.[45] Lord Diplock discussed this, saying,

> And yet the rule that a new precedent applies to acts done before it was laid down is not an essential feature of the judicial process. It is a consequence of a legal fiction that the Courts merely expound the law as it has always been. The time has come, I suggest, to reflect whether we should discard this fiction.[46]

Indeed, in the United States various methods of "prospective overruling"[47] are known, and the issue has been dealt with in a number of other countries, such as England, Germany, and France.[48] The matter has not yet been decided in Israel, neither from the standpoint of jurisdiction nor from the standpoint of policy.[49] For present purposes it is important to emphasize that in a legal system which leaves the question of the application of the common law from the standpoint of time to judicial discretion, the judge must include it among the totality of considerations he weighs. This question is one of the elements that make up the reasonableness of the use of discretion.

43. See J. Salmond, *On Jurisprudence* 127 (12th ed., 1966).

44. See *Great Northern Ry v. Sunburst Oil and Refining Company,* 287 U.S. 358 (1932).

45. See *Jones v. Secretary of State for Social Services* [1972] 1 All E.R. 145, 189 (Lord Simon).

46. Diplock, *supra* note 3, ch. 3, at 17.

47. See Currier, "Time and Change in Judge-Made Law: Prospective Overruling," 51 *Va. L. Rev.* 201 (1965); Schaefer, "The Control of 'Sunburst': Techniques of Prospective Overruling," 42 *N.Y.U.L. Rev.* 631 (1967); Traynor, "Quo Vadis, Prospective Overruling: A Question of Judicial Responsibility," 28 *Hastings L.J.* 533 (1977).

48. See Tedeschi, "Prospective Revision of Precedent," 8 *Isr. L. Rev.* 173 (1973); Tur, "Varieties of Overruling and Judicial Law-Making: Prospective Overruling in a Comparative Perspective," 23 *Jurid. Rev.* 33 (1978).

49. See Tedeschi, *supra* note 48; Kaplan, "Prospective Overruling for the Supreme Court's Precedents," 9 *Mishpatim* 221 (1979); Nicol, "Prospective Overruling: A New Device for English Courts," 39 *Mod. L. Rev.* 542 (1976).

Considerations in Solving the Problem:
Judicial Discretion and Retroactivity

The question of retroactivity is particularly important in a legal system in which the common law does not recognize prospective overruling, and thus all judicial rulings operate retroactively. In a system such as this, the judge must take this factor into account when exercising discretion. As a result, it may be reasonable not to adopt a certain possibility among those open to the court, simply because choosing this possibility would produce unwanted consequences related to the retroactive character of the common law.[50] Thus, the judge must always bear in mind the question of retroactivity. He must always examine how his rule operates in the dimension of time. In this context, there may be a significant difference between a case in which a judge-made law exists, from which the court deviates or which it distinguishes, and a case in which the retroactive ruling of the court neither deviates from an existing rule nor distinguishes it, but rather gives an initial interpretation to a statutory rule or fills a void in the system. It is only natural that the damage to the public's expectations is much greater in the first case (deviation from a previously existing rule) than in the second case (a new rule).[51] Even where there is a prior rule, from which the court deviates or which it distinguishes, the scope of the damage caused by retroactivity can be mitigated. Thus, for example, a case in which the legal community is aware of the problems of the earlier rule and expects it to be changed is not the same as a case in which the change is unexpected. In this connection, the court may use different methods—such as employing dicta—to raise the consciousness of the legal community to prepare them for the change that is going to come and that will apply retroactively.

---

50. See Jackson, "Decisional Law and Stare Decisis," 30 *A.B.A.J.* (1944); Sprecher, *supra* note 94, ch. 2; *United States v. Southeastern Underwriters Ass.* 322 U.S. 533, 573 (1944) (Stone, J.); *Florida Department of Health v. Florida Nursing Home Ass.* 450 U.S. 147.

51. On reliance interest and the overruling of precedent, see *Washington v. W.C. Dawson & Co.* 269 U.S. 219, 238 (1924); Cardozo, *supra* note 6, ch. 1, at 122; Currier *supra* note 47; Schwartz, "New Products, Old Products, Evolving Law, Retroactive Law," 58 *N.Y.U.L. Rev.* 796 (1983).

Chapter 6
Fundamental Problems in the Institutional System

LIMITED JUDICIAL DISCRETION AND INSTITUTIONAL PROBLEMS

The Institution in which Judicial Discretion Is Exercised

We saw that in the hard cases, the judge is faced with an "open" terminology. He must decide from among a number of possibilities open to him. These are connected, among other things, to values and to ideology. The judge must determine the values and strike a balance among them. The standard that directs judicial discretion, in its limited form, is that of reasonableness. The judge must exercise his discretion and choose among the various possibilities in a reasonable manner. Reasonableness requires the examination of "environmental" factors, one of which, namely, the overall normative system (law), I have already discussed. Now I turn to a second environmental factor, which is none other than the institution in which the exercise of judicial discretion takes place (the court).

The Anatomy of a Judicial Decision

From an institutional viewpoint,[1] one may describe the judicial process, in which judicial discretion is exercised, as follows:[2] it begins when one

---

1. On this issue, see Fuller, "The Forms and Limits of Adjudication," 92 *Harv. L. Rev.* 353 (1978); Freeman, "Standards of Adjudication, Judicial Law Making and Prospective Overruling," 26 *Curr. Legal Probs.* 166 (1973); Laskin, "The Institutional Character of the Judge," 7 *Isr. L. Rev.* 329 (1972).
2. My description characterizes generally the "private law" controversy. A change in

side approaches the court and the other side responds. The parties, through their respective positions, establish the factual base, in whose framework the judicial decision in the controversy will be made. The rules of evidence (in the realms of admissibility and relevancy) determine the type of evidence that will be brought before the judge or the panel of judges. The proceeding itself must satisfy the rules of natural justice. Each side must have the right to hear and to be heard. The judge must demonstrate objectivity and impartiality, which are ensured by his independence. Each party—whether alone or with the help of attorneys—presents the legal arguments that support its approach. At the conclusion of the arguments the judicial decision is given, whether unanimously or by majority opinion. It must be reasoned. It establishes the facts and applies the law. The prevailing party obtains relief, for whose execution the judge is not responsible. From the judicial decision emerges the holding, which by virtue of the principle of binding precedent is imposed on the entire public.

The Fundamental Problems

This summary description of the institutional framework within which judicial discretion is exercised suggests a number of fundamental problems tied to the exercise of judicial discretion.[3] I have already discussed one of them—the problem of retroactivity. In the next chapter I will discuss two other problems—the problem of democracy and the problem of the separation of powers. Here I focus on two institutional problems: the incidentality of judicial discretion in relation to the decision in the dispute and the problem of judicial objectivity.

THE INCIDENTALITY OF JUDICIAL DISCRETION

Judicial Discretion for the Purpose of Deciding in the Conflict

A study of the structural aspect of the judicial process reveals its most important basic characteristic. The court is an institution for adjudication. This is its primary function. The exercise of judicial discretion, which chooses from among various possibilities concerning the legal

---

it occurs when one of the parties is the state or a public body: see Chayes, ''The Role of the Judge in Public Law Litigation,'' 89 *Harv. L. Rev.* 1281 (1976). See also Dan-Cohen, ''Bureaucratic Organizations and the Theory of Adjudication,'' 85 *Colum. L. Rev.* (1985).

3. Kurland, ''Toward a Political Supreme Court,'' 37 *U. Chi. L. Rev.* 19 (1969).

norm—its existence, its scope of application—is simply a means to adjudication. Discretion is not the goal of the process, but merely a by-product. It is not an independent activity, but rather is incidental to a decision in the dispute. Justice Landau said, "The function of the court is to hand down the law in the matter brought before it, and its judicial rule must emerge naturally from the judgment in the concrete case."[4] The same idea appears in the writings of Salmond:

> We must distinguish Law-Making by legislatures from law-making by the courts. Legislatures can lay down rules purely for the future and without reference to any actual dispute; the courts, in so far as they create law, can do so only in application to cases before them and only so far as is necessary for their solution. Judicial law-making is incidental to the solving of legal disputes; legislative law-making is the central function of the legislature.[5]

This view finds clear expression in the words of Hart and Sacks:

> The development of a body of decisional law is only a by-product of the judicial process. The basic function of courts is the function of adjudication— or more accurately, the function of settling disputes by the method of adjudication.[6]

Professor Tedeschi expressed this well, when he said,

> In the doctrine of precedent, rulemaking is simply a by-product of adjudication. This is the difference between a statute (or custom) and a precedent: the former has effect even if not applied in legal proceedings, while the latter exists only if it is activated as the "ratio decidendi" of the judgment.[7]

The court is required to decide in the dispute. For this, it must determine the facts before it and the law according to which it is to decide the case. It cannot determine the facts or decide in the conflict until it has formu-

4. Landau, "Trends in the Decisions of the Supreme Court," 8 *Tel-Aviv U. L. Rev.* 500, 503 (1982).

5. Salmond, *supra* note 43, ch. 5, at 155.

6. Hart and Sacks, *supra* note 26, ch. 1, at 367.

7. Tedeschi, *supra* note 27, ch. 1, at 31. Professor Tedeschi notes that the separation between the judge's law-making and his adjudication "is possible only if the judge's rulemaking takes place outside the framework of the judicial decision and therefore outside the framework of the precedent. This is the case for example, of the *arrets de reglement* of French parliament of the past, which had only the form of the judicial arrest, and which were normally not even issued incidentally to a judicial process."

lated the legal norm by which the conflict is to be decided. For this, it must sometimes make use of its discretion and choose in the hard cases from among various solutions, each of them lawful within the framework of the system. As long as the choice has not been made, there is no law according to which one can adjudicate. Making the choice makes the decision possible. But the choice is not capable of standing alone. It is made for the purpose of deciding in the conflict, and incidentally to a decision in the conflict.

The incidentality of the exercise of judicial discretion is especially striking in the court that establishes the facts. It is less striking in the highest court,[8] which, by the principle of precedent, turns the product of its discretion into a general and binding rule. However, one must not blur the borderline between legislation and adjudication. Even the highest court is involved in creating law only incidentally, and as a by-product of its decision in the conflict. In truth, judicial lawmaking becomes a central function of the Supreme Court. However, even this central function is incidental to a decision in the controversy. Even the Supreme Court is a court that rules in the dispute between the parties. In this it differs from the legislature, for whom creating law is an independent, central function. At times the legislature is handed a political dispute and solves it by enacting a statute that decides the fate of the parties to the conflict. One might say that this act of lawmaking by the legislature was done incidentally to a decision in the conflict and as a by-product of this decision. Nevertheless, there is a wide gulf between the ''incidentality'' and ''by-product'' of the legislature's lawmaking, and the ''incidentality'' and ''by-product'' of the lawmaking of the judiciary. In the case of the legislature, the incidentality is historical-environmental, in other words, the question one asks about it is, What caused there to be lawmaking? For the judge, on the other hand, the incidentality is functional. The lawmaking grows out of the act of adjudication, and it has no existence without the act of adjudication. It also follows from this that the legislature is always involved in creating the law as an independent matter. On the other hand, the judge always deals with creating law incidentally to a decision in a case. The court can never carry out its function by merely creating law. Its lawmaking grows out of its ad-

8. See Hofstedler, ''New Blocks for Old Pyramids: Reshaping the Judicial System,'' 44 *S. Cal. L. Rev.* 901 (1971).

judication. This situation reflects reality, and there is no one who argues
that it should be changed. The court was, and must remain, an institution
for adjudication. The Supreme Court must not be turned into an Upper
House in the framework of the legislative body. The court is not a
"second House," and this distinction must be maintained. The Court's
contribution to the creation of law is made only within the bounds of its
adjudication. Professor H. Hart discussed this:

> The courts can make their distinctive contribution as lawmakers only when
> they are acting as agencies for the settlement of controversies—either of
> controversies between individuals or of controversies between an individual
> and the government. This fact marks the outer limits of the potential area of
> competition between courts and other lawmaking institutions.[9]

Of course, this difference between the court and every other body that
is involved in lawmaking affects the organizational structure of the court.
This has additional consequences, with implications for the choice of the
most reasonable of the various solutions. Thus, Professor Greenawalt
was right when he said, "Part of any defensible theory of the judicial
decision must include consideration of what judges are able to do better
than legislators and bureaucrats and what they cannot do as well."[10] The
incidentality of the judicial decision affects the totality of the court's
institutional structure. It imbues it with advantages and disadvantages in
its lawmaking role. Reasonable discretion is discretion that takes these
factors into account.

The Need for the Existence of a Controversy

Judicial discretion is not exercised whenever the court thinks it should
be. The court does not create opportunities for the exercise of judicial
discretion. Judicial discretion is exercised only when a plaintiff or an
accuser decides to approach the court with a conflict needing decision. In
the absence of a plaintiff there is no case, and without a case there is no
judicial discretion. Unlike a member of the legislature, the judge cannot
initiate lawmaking. He is tied to the initiative of a party. As a result,
judicial discretion is exercised sporadically and unmethodically.[11]

9. Hart, "The Courts and Lawmaking: A Comment," in Paulsen (ed.), *supra* note 22,
ch. 4, at 41.

10. Greenawalt, *supra* note 79, ch. 4, at 90.

11. See Traynor, "Transatlantic Reflections on Leeways and Limits of Appellate
Courts," *Utah L. Rev.* 255, 261 (1980).

There is an entirely random selection of what matters are brought before the court. A problem that is troubling the public may lie submerged for decades before being brought for decision, while another problem might arise in a number of varied and balanced contexts within a short period of time, without any coordination.[12] The court does not control the issues that plaintiffs or accusers choose to bring for its decision. The court's control begins only once the case is already before it. And when a problem comes to the court, it cannot, generally speaking, refuse to decide it simply because the decision will not be to the court's liking.[13] As a result, it is generally impossible to plan judicial lawmaking in advance, and if one wants to cover an entire area by judicial lawmaking, one sometimes has to wait many years.

The Information at the Court's Disposal

The incidentality of judicial lawmaking to the decision in the case is closely linked to the factual base the court has before it. This base comprises the factual events tied to the occurrence that is the subject of the controversy. The laws of evidence that have been developed, whether in the field of admissibility or in the field of relevancy, weed out any fact that is not linked to the occurrence at issue. As a result, the court is usually prevented from examining and establishing facts that are not connected to the factual side of the case, but that are linked to considerations of public policy that fashion the content of the rule. These so-called legislative or social facts are not, for the most part, presented to the court, for they do not constitute part of the history of the case itself.[14] Such a state of affairs is the natural consequence of the institutional

12. See Friendly, "The Courts and Social Policy: Substance and Procedure," 33 *U. Miami L. Rev.* 21, 22 (1978).

13. See Eckhof, *supra* note 70, ch. 1, at 42: "Nor can they refuse to decide a case for reasons of judicial policy like a newspaper editor who rejects articles that do not fit into the policy of his paper."

14. For the distinction between adjudicative facts and legislative facts, see Hart and Sacks, *supra* note 26, ch. 1, at 384. Professor Horowitz draws a distinction between social facts and historical facts: see D. Horowitz, *The Courts and Social Policy* 45 (1977). See also Lamb, "Judicial Policy-Making and Information Flow to the Supreme Court," 29 *Vand. L. Rev.* 45 (1976); Baade, "Social Science Evidence and the Federal Constitutional Court of West Germany," 23 *J. of Pol.* 421 (1961); Daynard, "The Use of Social Policy in Judicial Decision-Making," 56 *Cornell L. Rev.* 919 (1971); Miller and Barron, "The Supreme Court, the Adversary System and the Flow of Information to the Justices: A Preliminary Inquiry," 61 *Va. L. Rev.* 1187 (1975).

structure of the court, whose purpose is to decide the controversy. Nonetheless, this situation hinders a rational choice among various possibilities in the framework of judicial discretion. The choice is related not only to the facts of the dispute, but also to the social and legislative facts, and these, generally, are not before the court. As Justice Frankfurter said, "Courts are not equipped to pursue the paths for discovering wise policy. A court is confined within the bounds of a particular record and it cannot even shape the record. Only fragments of a social problem are seen through the narrow windows of a litigation."[15]

Even if the rules of evidence permit a broadening of the factual framework, they are not always fully utilized. The factual base depends on the parties, their abilities, and their talents. There are facts that the parties do not bring before the court, even if they are entitled to do so. Sometimes the parties may refrain from laying a suitable base for the exercise of judicial discretion because they are not interested in the solution that may emerge from it. In the adversary process, it is the parties who determine the scope of the conflict, and it is they who lay the evidentiary base for solving it. As a result, the court may obtain only a partial picture, which does not sufficiently take into account the interests either of third parties or of the public as a whole.

And even if the broadest possible factual base is laid, the judge is not always possessed of the intellectual tools to contend with them. One must keep in mind that the judge who sits in the "regular" courts does not necessarily have any special expertise. His legal education and judicial experience do not always qualify him to deal with complex questions of social or economic policy. As Judge Henry Friendly put it, "Save in a few specialized courts, judges are generalists, and although much of their virtue has been thought to lie in that very fact, it seriously handicaps them in lifting masses of technical, social and economic data."[16] It is only natural that this reality will affect the judge who exercises judicial discretion when he prepares to choose from among the various options open to him. This explains the inclination of judges in the regular courts not to intervene in and to defer to the decisions of courts that specialize in a certain issue, such as labor or military law, or in the

15. In *Sherrer v. Sherrer*, 334 U.S. 343, 365 (1948).
16. Friendly, *supra* note 12, at 23.

decisions of specialized agencies when the problem has more than one lawful solution.[17]

The Means at the Judge's Disposal

The centrality of the decision in the particular controversy naturally affects the relief and the remedies that the court awards. These are primarily forms of relief that bring the problem of the plaintiff or accuser to its solution. They are not forms of relief that aim to solve the problem in its entirety. A prisoner who complains about poor prison conditions may be satisfied with an improvement in his own conditions, without this resulting in a fundamental change in the prison conditions of all prisoners. The court gives relief to the plaintiff before it, and not all the prisoners were before it. One may find partial solutions to this problem[18]—such as the class action—but the fundamental problem remains. The court deals with problems from the point of view of specific people. It does not deal with problems in the abstract, and it awards relief only in order to solve the problem of the plaintiff who comes to it.

The means at the court's disposal are limited. Judge Friendly said, "Unlike legislators, courts are generally confined to prohibiting or enforcing conduct whether by the award of damages or . . . by injunction or declaratory judgment. Legislatures, however, have many further options available to them, including taxation and subsidies."[19] Thus, the court may impose an obligation or establish a prohibition, but it is not entitled, in general, to fix upper or lower limits of liability. The court is entitled to broaden or to narrow tort liability. Yet it is not entitled, in general, to set up a fund for payment of damages. It is not entitled to impose a licensing system or the payment of taxes. The court is limited in the legal material with which it can legislate, although these limitations are sometimes not stringent. There is some leeway in the creation of new

17. Deference to the interpretation of special tribunals or agencies—as distinct from fact-finding and law application—should be made only in hard cases. Furthermore, it should be done only after weighing all of the relevant considerations—including the special position of the tribunal or agency: see L. Jaffe, *supra* note 54, ch. 1; K. Davis, *Administrative Law Treatise* 400 (2d ed., 1984). Compare, Woodward and Levin, "In Defense of Deference: Judicial Review of Agency Action," 31 *Ad. L. Rev.* 329 (1979).

18. See O. Fiss, *The Civil Right Injunction* (1978).

19. Friendly, *supra* note 12, at 23.

forms of relief, especially in the framework of using conditions to apply the existing forms of relief. Thus, for example, the court might have trouble formulating a detailed plan for living conditions for prisoners, but it can say that if such a plan is not implemented, it will exercise its authority to issue an injunction.[20] The court cannot administer public agencies, yet it may issue an order to close it unless it is run a certain way.[21] The court uses this system in the field of private law, in the framework of the conditions for giving an injunction in a case of breach of contract. The court may also use this method in the field of public law. However, the flexibility given the court is minimal.[22] A court acting responsibly will not usually order a hospital or a prison closed. Ultimately, the responsibility for running the health agencies, prisons, and other institutions is in the hands of the other branches. The court lacks information about them.[23] It also lacks means. It does not control the budget, which is limited and which has an order of priorities established by the parliament. Hamilton's words are well known: "The judiciary . . . has no influence over either the sword or the purse."[24] Yet even so, if a public authority breaks the law, it is the court's obligation to order it to follow the law, even if this involves financial expenditure. But the rate of expenditure, its sum, and the practical ways of effecting the matter are not in the court's field of expertise.[25] By intruding into the details of the execution, the court would enter a field in which it lacks knowledge, means, and expertise.

Furthermore, whatever means the court applies in its judgment, it

20. See Johnson, "The Constitution and the Federal District Judge," 54 *Tex. L. Rev.* 903 (1976); Baude, "The Federal Courts and Prison Reform," 52 *Ind. L. J.* 761 (1977); Johnson, "In Defense of Judicial Activism," 28 *Emory L. Rev.* 901 (1979).

21. See Note, "Implementation Problems in Institutional Reform Litigation," 91 *Harv. L. Rev.* 428 (1977); Special Project, "The Remedial Process in Institutional Reform Litigation," 78 *Colum. L. Rev.* 784 (1978); Eisenberg and Yeazell, "The Ordinary and the Extraordinary in Institutional Litigation," 93 *Harv. L. Rev.* 465 (1980).

22. See Chayes, *supra* note 2. See also Cavanagh and Sarat, "Thinking about Courts: Toward and Beyond Jurisprudence of Judicial Competence," 14 *Law and Soc'y* 371 (1980).

23. See Glazer, "The Judiciary and Social Policy," in *The Judiciary in a Democratic Society* 67 (Theberge, ed., 1979); Glazer, "Should Judges Administer Social Services?" 50 *The Pub. Interest* 64 (1978).

24. *The Federalist,* at 480 (B. Wright, ed., 1961).

25. See Frug, "The Judicial Power of the Purse," 126 *U. Pa. L. Rev.* 715 (1978).

does not have the means to maintain ongoing, effective supervision and review of what takes place outside the courthouse walls. In this, as in other issues, the court is limited to what the parties themselves bring before it. Even in this issue it seems there is some flexibility that permits the court to know about what is happening (beyond the information that the parties bring to the court) and to supervise it. But this flexibility is limited. Thus the reluctance to issue injunctions that would entail continuing supervision. One also must not forget that the enforcing of the judgment is not the judge's concern, but rather lies in the hands of the executive branch. The court's function ceases with the decision in the conflict. Thus, the court's activity is limited, and its means are limited. This reality has implications for the use of judicial discretion.

The Scope of the Required Reform

I emphasized that judicial discretion is exercised only when there is a conflict and that the court generally does not control the bringing of the conflict before it. This factor has important implications for the reasonableness of the use of judicial discretion and judicial law-making. When we are dealing with limited and compact reform,[26] it is appropriate for this reform to be accomplished through the use of judicial discretion. On the other hand, the institutional limitations of adjudication make comprehensive reform of an entire legal field difficult. Thus, for example, even if the requirement of consideration originated in case law and not statute law, it is doubtful whether it would be appropriate for the court— in a legal system in which consideration is essential for the creation of a contractual obligation—to repeal this requirement by means of judicial law-making.[27] Repealing the requirement of consideration involves a deep dissection of the entire contractual fabric. It has implications for an entire set of laws. All this leads to the conclusion that it is proper for this change to be made by the legislative branch. Judicial law-making in this field would, by the nature of things, take a long time. It would be done unmethodically. Insecurity would increase. The institutional limitations of the judicial branch are conspicuous in their severity.

26. In the House of Lords, opinions were divided over whether it was appropriate for the House to introduce a comprehensive reform in the laws of hearsay: see *Myers v. Director of Public Prosecutions* [1964] 2 All. E.R. 881. The majority decided to leave this matter to the legislature. For a critique of this approach, see Freeman, *supra* note 1.

27. See Justice Holmes in *Southern Pacific Co. v. Jensens*, 244 U.S. 205, 221 (1917).

Inflation and Valuation An interesting case occurred in Israel in the matter of valuation of debts as a result of the increase in inflation. Theoretically, the question of valuation is a broad topic, covering various areas of law, and it seems that reform in this field should be carried out by statute. The legislature, having before it the overall picture of the state's economy, can weigh the short- and long-term effects of the valuation of debts. The legislative branch can also make distinctions among types of debts and can even establish different methods of valuation. On the other hand, the economic picture presented to the court— because of the institutional limitations I discussed—is one-sided and often very narrow. I wrote many judgments on the issue of inflation and valuation, and I can attest that I was never presented with the complete picture of the economy and the effect of inflation upon it. Not once was I given information about whether indexing debts was not itself an inflationary factor, and whether this consideration of public policy should not tip the scales. Judicial reform was always partial and was always brought about in the absence of a complete legal picture. First in torts,[28] then in contracts,[29] quasi-contracts,[30] and statutory obligations.[31] To be sure, the legal work has not been completed. It seems to me that legislative intervention is most desirable. However (and in spite of that) I believe that the court had no alternative but to intervene in this field. It is one thing to refer the parties to the legislature—as Justice Yitzhak Kahan did in FH 39/75, *The Ports Authority v. Ararat*[32]—when inflation is double digit. It is another matter to do so when inflation is triple digit. Thus, it seems to me that the judicial experience in this matter is not negative.[33] This was aided by the fact that the significant increase in inflation multiplied the appeals to the court in matters of valuation, and in a relatively short period of time it was possible to cover most of the areas requiring solution.

28. F.H. 39/75 *Port Authority v. Ararat,* 31 P.D. 533; C.A. 467/77 *Horowitz Port Authority,* 33 P.D.(1) 256.
    29. C.A. 158/77 *Rabinai v. Man Shaked,* 33 P.D. (2) 281.
    30. C.A. 741/79 *Kalanit Hasharon v. Horowitz,* 35 P.D. (3) 533.
    31. C.A. 91/78 *Megda v. The Minister of Finance,* 33 P.D. (2) 393.
    32. F.H. 39/75, *supra* note 28.
    33. See A. Yoran, *The Effect of Inflation on Civil and Tax Liability* (1983). On the general effects of inflation on legal obligations, see also K. Rosenne, *Law and Inflation* (1982).

Close Cases Naturally, the distinction between limited, compact reform (in which judicial law-making is reasonable) and comprehensive, open reform (in which judicial law-making is not reasonable) is not clear, and there are many borderline cases. An example of these cases is the rule prohibiting hearsay testimony. Is the creation of additional exceptions—to the point of depleting the rule of any meaning—a limited reform that it is appropriate for the case law to undertake, or is it rather a comprehensive reform that should be left to the legislature?[34]

The Nature of the Public Policy Considerations

I indicated the factual base that lies before the judge. I noted that this base is rich in historical information and poor in social data. I also directed the reader's attention to the fact that sometimes the judge does not have adequate intellectual tools to grapple with information about social policy. All of these factors directly influence judicial discretion. When the policy at the base of the new norm is of a type that the judge, with the tools at his disposal, is capable of learning and applying in a reasonable manner, then these considerations may be taken into account in fashioning judicial discretion and judicial law-making. On the other hand, when the policy that lies at the base of the new norm is of a type that causes the judge difficulty in formulating a position, given his institutional limitations, then it is preferable not to create that new norm, but rather to leave the task to the legislature.

It seems to me that considerations of policy in the matter of individual and civil rights—such as freedom of expression, freedom of demonstration, human dignity, freedom of occupation, freedom of association, freedom to vote, and other fundamental human rights—are considerations that the judge possesses the necessary tools to weigh. Similarly, the court has no difficulty taking into account considerations of policy that may be derived from logic or from the articles of faith of the society or from existing statute law, such as protection of third parties to a contract, protection of common-law spouses, release from the requirement of consideration, and other considerations, at various levels of abstraction, that may be gleaned from the body of legislation.

On the other hand, the judge should beware of applying complex considerations of economic or social policy, which frequently are the

34. See *Myers v. Director of Public Prosecution* [1964] 2 All E.R. 881.

subject of controversy, require expertise and information, and may necessitate the making of assumptions and hypotheses that in turn require additional assumptions.[35] The safe and reasonable way usually will be[36] to leave the matter to the legislature, which can obtain all the relevant information from experts and which can formulate a public policy that suits the issue in its entirety.

This distinction between policy considerations that the judge is qualified to deal with (because of the information at his disposal and his legal education) and policy considerations that the judge is not qualified to deal with is, naturally, imprecise. Broad judicial discretion exists in determining where the border lies. Furthermore, it often happens that the two types of considerations are mixed together in a single issue. Questions of contracts or torts, for example, raise not only considerations of policy that the judge can contend with, but also socioeconomic problems that demand data that generally are beyond the reach of the judge. The same is true for considerations of state security and public welfare. It is not even always possible to know in the courtroom about problems of the court's workload. For this reason, I am highly skeptical about the validity of a claim that a certain rule will lead to an inundation of the courts (the "flood argument"). I always suspect that this argument requires social research, which the court usually does not have before it.

Another class of policy considerations are those in which the court may have an institutional ability of comprehension and scrutiny, yet whose nature makes it appropriate for the court to stay its hand. This is the issue of nonjusticiability, or the doctrine of the "political question," and requires separate treatment.

The Nature of the Required Solutions

The means at the judge's disposal are limited. It follows that the nature of the solutions he is called upon to give affects the reasonableness of judicial discretion. When the proposed solution is to narrow or broaden

35. See Fuller, *supra* note 1. Professor Fuller develops the concept of polycentric discretion, which is not appropriate for adjudication.

36. One must, however, examine whether the other branches are more suitable for collecting data, understanding it, and deriving conclusions from it. See R. Neely, *How Courts Govern America* (1981). Often the legislator does not make use of his advantages. It is advisable not to idealize nonjudicial legislation. Some of the limitations on the judicial branch exist in effect also with respect to the other branches.

liability, to repeal an immunity or defense, or to establish a standard of conduct (for the individual or for the government) judicial law-making may be an appropriate framework for this activity. The reason for this is that the judicial branch has the necessary means for giving a proper solution to those problems. It should also be noted that these areas are by their nature based on a cumulative life experience of individual cases, through movement from one to the next on the basis of considerations of logic and experience. Therefore, recognizing new duties of care and establishing the proper standard of care are acts of law-making appropriate for the judge. The same is true for laying down rules for exercising administrative discretion according to standards of reasonableness and fairness. On the other hand, when the proposed solution is to erect institutional structures, the judicial branch is not an appropriate framework for this type of law-making.

Torts By virtue of these considerations, the accepted approach is that torts, and especially negligence, is an appropriate field for the exercise of judicial discretion aimed at changing liability and the extent of damages.[37] But here, too, one must point out the institutional limitations of the judiciary. These limitations involve not only the potential social ramifications of tort liability and considerations of the coherence of the case law and its natural development, but also the question of the remedies that the court is entitled to use. For example, a judge may not set up a fund or an institution to compensate victims. Therefore, even if the court were entitled to determine that a certain tort liability is an absolute liability and not liability based on fault, the court would not be able to produce the arrangement established in the Law for Compensation of Road Accident Victims (1975). This law established—in addition to absolute liability—compensation ceilings and a special fund to cover hit-and-run and other situations.

A New Status? A special case of setting up institutional structures is that of recognizing a special legal status. In principle, it is appropriate for this to be done by way of legislation by the legislative branch, for a legal

---

37. See R. Keeton, *Venturing to Do Justice* (1969); Keeton, "Creative Continuity in the Law of Torts," 75 *Harv. L. Rev.* 463; Peck, "The Role of the Courts and Legislatures in the Reform of Tort Law," 48 *Minn. L. Rev.* 265 (1963); Peck, "Comment of Judicial Creativity," 69 *Iowa L. Rev.* 1 (1983).

status has implications in all branches of law, and a common law development through judicial law-making is not desirable. Consequently, some think that the possibility of adoption should not be created by case law but by statute only.[38] Yet it seems that in this matter, too, one should not lay down hard and fast rules. For example, the status of common-law spouse has developed in Israel through the common efforts of the judicial branch and the legislative branch. This experience seems to have been positive.

Spousal Property An interesting case is that of spouses' shared resources. Here, too, from the theoretical perspective, the appropriate framework is the legislature, for the reason that the sharing of property has many implications for different fields of law (property, inheritance, bankruptcy). It has effects on third parties.[39] Considerations of normative coherence and the institutional limitations make case law development in this field extremely problematic, especially because in a given society there might be disagreements about the entire subject. And yet, despite these considerations, this matter has developed in Israel primarily through case law, and it appears that the overall balance of the experience is positive; on the other hand, legislative intervention was not very successful. Any common law development of the issue of common property must, however, take into account the measure of suitability of the judicial branch for creativity in this field. It seems that in the future there will be no alternative but to set a limit to the possibilities of case law development, at the degree of the court's institutional suitability for developing this unique issue. Thus, in the matter of mutual relations between spouses, the common law field is wide open. Not so in the area of the impact of common property on third parties. Here judicial caution, based on the court's limitations, is called for.

The Judge's Discretion as a Member of a Panel

My focus to this point has been on the individual judge. The question was how he should select the most reasonable possibility. But when the decision is made by the highest judicial instance, it is usually made by a panel of several judges. Does this reality necessarily change the exercise

38. See Friedmann, *supra* note 17, ch. 1.
39. See Weisman, "Can a Spouse Confer a Better Title Than He Possesses?" 7 *Isr. L. Rev.* 302 (1972).

of judicial discretion? At first glance, the answer is no. The judge formulates his position concerning the most reasonable possibility and puts it in writing. It may be the majority opinion or the minority opinion. Indeed, this is often also the situation in practice. But not always. It is natural that in a panel of several judges, efforts will sometimes be made to reach unanimity.[40] This has advantages from the perspective of the system as a whole.[41] If unanimity on the bench is not possible, it is natural that an effort will be made to achieve a common position for a majority of the panel. Such an attempt naturally requires a certain concession from the point of view of the individual judge. Sometimes the concession is only in the style of the words. Sometimes it is in the margins of the ruling or in its scope and sometimes in the sharpness of the reasoning. In this situation, a judge may write an opinion, or join in an opinion written by a colleague, that reflects the most reasonable possibility attainable at that time. Of course, a judge will not concede an issue that appears to him fundamental and essential. He will not go along with a possibility that does not appear to him to be reasonable. Yet within the bounds of the most reasonable possibility, he may join in a ruling even though, if he were deciding the case as an individual judge, he would have established its borders and reasoning in a slightly different manner. Again, the difference between the possible and the desirable, from the point of view of the individual judge, will always be marginal. Nonetheless, what appears marginal in one factual setting may be decisive in another.

The Most Reasonable Possibility and Judicial Time

Our theoretical examination of the most reasonable possibility has assumed until now that the judicial branch has unlimited time at its disposal. Sometimes, this assumption is a far cry from reality. Not infrequently, the judge is under time pressure that prevents him from devoting the time needed to examine all aspects of the problem. Often, the real question is, What is the most reasonable possibility that can be reached in the period of time at the judge's disposal? Time constraints plague many courts in the modern age, especially a Supreme Court such as that of

40. See the experience in England: Paterson, *supra* note 4, ch. 1, at 109.
41. See Cross, "The *Ratio Decidendi* and a Plurality of Speeches in the House of the Lords," 93 *Law Q. Rev.* 378 (1977).

Israel, which does not control the number of issues with which it deals. In this situation, the judge not infrequently is pressured because he does not have enough time to devote to certain matters. Of course, he will not render his decision until he is convinced that he has arrived at the appropriate solution. Yet sometimes he is hurried into joining in a colleague's opinion that may not be acceptable to him in all its details, and he does so without writing anything himself—other than "I concur"—simply because of the lack of time. At other times he may content himself with the parties' arguments and not conduct his own research. Under these time limitations the judge does not always reach the best possible decision.

The degree of negotiations among a panel of judges differs from one state to the next. The degree of convincing that takes place in the United States Supreme Court[42] is not the same as that one finds in the British House of Lords.[43] And both of these differ from the degree of convincing done among the judges of the Supreme Court of Israel. Much depends on the judicial tradition that is customary in that court. However, traditions change over the years. Changes of judges frequently produce changes in traditions in matters of negotiation. Sometimes one judge—usually the president—plays a key role in this issue.[44] A full analysis of judicial negotiating is outside the framework of this study. It is sufficient to note that the model of judicial discretion that is based on the individual judge must take into account the fact that the judge is frequently a member of a panel, whose judgment may contain a majority opinion, a concurring opinion, a dissenting opinion,[45] or simple agreement without explanation. One should also take into account strategies of negotiation between judges,[46] without, however, overplaying this factor. It seems to me that it deals with a marginal issue. The main point was and continues to be the internal conviction of the judge that his choice is the correct one. He may

42. Murphy, "Marshaling the Court: Leadership, Bargaining and the Judicial Process," 29 *U. Chi. L. Rev.* 640 (1962).

43. See Paterson, *supra* note 4, ch. 1, at 109.

44. See Danelski, "The Influence of the Chief Justice in the Decisional Process," in *Courts, Judges and Politics* 695 (W. Murphy and C. Pritchett, eds., 3d ed., 1986).

45. See Simpson, "Dissenting Opinions," 71 *U. Pa. L. Rev.* 205 (1923); Stephens, "The Function of Concurring and Dissenting Opinions in Courts of Last Resort," 5 *U. Fla. L. Rev.* 394 (1952); Traynor, "Some Open Questions on the Work of State Appellate Courts," 24 *U. Chi. L. Rev.* 211 (1957); Fuld, "The Voices of Dissent," 62 *Colum. L. Rev.* 923 (1962); Brennan, "In Defense of Dissents," 37 *Hastings L.J.* 427 (1986).

46. See W. Murphy, *Elements of Judicial Strategy* (1964).

become convinced during negotiation that he erred. But negotiation cannot bring a judge who believes in the correctness of his position to join an opposing view. At most, this mutual convincing can produce compromise in marginal issues. As important as they are, they remain marginal nevertheless. Consequently, it seems to me that if the effort to convince causes tension in the personal plane, it is better to give it up than to achieve that marginal advantage. The justices of the Supreme Court live in close proximity many hours a day, many days a year, and many years of their professional lives. Maintaining good, friendly personal relations is usually preferable to the tension involved in making repeated attempts to persuade a colleague to change his position. Of course people hold a variety of positions on the matter, and my opinion on the subject, too, has changed and is changing continually.[47]

JUDICIAL DISCRETION AND JUDICIAL PARTIALITY

A fundamental characteristic of every proper judicial process is that the judge who decides the controversy acts impartially. It is essential that the parties to the proceeding and the public as a whole be convinced that the judge does not prefer one party or the other because of that party's characteristics or because he belongs to one or another group of people. What determines the law is not the character of the claimants, but the strength of their claims. Impartiality means that the judge relates to the parties before him equally, providing them with an equal opportunity and an equal relation. That he has no personal stake in the outcome. That he arrives at his judgment not through his inclination toward one side or the other, but because of his submission to the law. Absence of bias is essential to the judicial process. Without it, the public's confidence in the judicial branch will wane. And without public faith, adjudication cannot carry out its function.[48] As Justice Frankfurter noted, "The Court's

47. See Schaefer, *supra* note 94, ch. 2, at 10: "On a multijudge court no man can or should have every opinion expressed in words which he chooses. Of course every judge can and should make suggestions to his colleagues. But the relationship among the judges is a personal one and a continuing one and effectiveness can be blunted by excessive suggestions. The balance between complacent acquiescence and over assertiveness is delicate indeed."

48. See Kurland, *supra* note 3, at 42: "The Court's capacity to express whatever will it has is entirely dependent upon the support of public opinion. Without it, as Tocqueville told us long ago, the Justices are impotent."

authority—possessed of neither the purse nor the sword—ultimately rests on sustained public confidence in its moral sanction.''[49] From this follows the image of the blindfolded judge. From this follows the rhetoric that it is ''the court'' that decides, and not ''the judge.''[50]

Many laws are based on the desire to ensure this impartiality that is so dear to the law. Thus, for example, one of the explanations offered for the adversary system, in which the task of preparing the factual base is left to the parties and not to the court, is that it guarantees the judge's objectivity in the eyes of the parties. According to this argument, the inquisitorial system, which imposes the task of investigation and demand on the judge himself, damages this notion. Similarly, system-binding precedent itself is explained, in part, by the desire to ensure the concept of the impartial judge, who decides on the basis of a lag that is imposed upon him by the rule of precedent.[51] Indeed, the declaratory theory itself, according to which the judge declares the existing law rather than create new law, is based in part on the need to ensure this notion in the eyes of the parties. So, too, the duty of giving reasons in the judgment—which is among the foundations of the judicial proceeding—draws its logic in part from the need to convince the parties and the public of the lack of partiality of the adjudication.

This elementary need for impartiality is fully satisfied in the easy cases and the intermediate cases, in which the judge acts on the basis of a given law, and his decisions follow clearly from this law. From the very definition of these cases as cases in which the legal community fully supports the result, one concludes that judicial impartiality exists, for no reasonable judge would decide on any other basis. Even when the judge deviates from a precedent, in the belief that it was clearly erroneous, impartiality is not affected, for a reasonable lawyer would justify this result.

The picture changes when the judge decides in hard cases. In these, the judge has freedom of choice. He is not obliged to decide one way or another. He chooses option X and rejects option Y, according to his

49. *Baker v. Carr*, 369 U.S. 186, 267 (1962).

50. See J. Noonan, *Persons and Masks of the Law* (1976).

51. See Lucke, ''The Common Law: Judicial Impartiality and Judge-Made Law,'' 98 *Law. Q. Rev.* 29, 75 (1982); Hart and Sacks, *supra* note 26, ch. 1, at 588; Christie, ''A Model of Judicial Review of Legislation,'' 48 *S. Cal. L. Rev.* 1306, 1316 (1975); Stevens, ''The Life Span of a Judge-Made Rule,'' 58 *N.Y.U.L. Rev.* 1 (1983).

discretion. This may cast doubt on his impartiality in the eyes of the parties or the public. It is natural that they will ask why he decided against one side, if he was free to decide in that party's favor. The judge must consider this reality when he exercises his discretion in the hard cases. The judge does not solve this problem by ignoring it; instead, he merely draws on the credit that the judicial branch enjoys. But this credit is not unlimited. Therefore, the judge must exercise his discretion in a manner that takes this impartiality factor into account, for it can affect the formulation of what constitutes reasonable discretion. For example, it demands that the judge be aware of his choice and its appropriate explanation. It demands that he convince the parties of the neutral application of his ruling, namely, that the rule will be applied even if the parties change. It demands special sensitivity when the judge considers whether or not to deviate from a precedent. The judge must take these and other considerations into account in exercising his discretion.

Chapter 7
Interrelations among Institutional Systems

FUNDAMENTAL PROBLEMS IN THE RELATIONS AMONG GOVERNMENTAL SYSTEMS

The judge exercises his discretion and decides in the case before him, but the significance of his decision does not end there. Incidentally to his adjudication, he establishes a general norm, which must be integrated into the overall normative system. It must be consistent with the institutional system within whose framework the decision was rendered. Yet beyond this, the judicial discretion must fit into the general structure of the institutional-governmental systems. The judge who exercises discretion does so as part of the judicial branch. His judicial decision must match the fundamental conceptions of the relations between this branch and the other authorities of the state. These fundamental conceptions stem from the society's view of democracy and of the separation of powers. They are affected by the society's view of the judicial function. Thus, judicial lawmaking is not the only form of lawmaking or even the main form. The other branches also create law. From the universal point of view, judicial lawmaking must mesh with this overall lawmaking. The judge is only one musician in the entire legal orchestra, and his playing must harmonize with the rest of the concert.

JUDICIAL DISCRETION AND THE DEMOCRATIC PROBLEM

The fundamental characteristics of judging are independence and impartiality. In order to ensure these fundamental principles, various arrangements were established. These require that the judge not be accountable to the public or to its representatives.[1] He is not subject to a vote of no-confidence. These arrangements do not raise difficulties in the democratic sphere in the easy cases and the intermediate cases. The situation is different when the judge exercises his discretion in the hard cases. In these cases, he must decide among a number of possibilities. This decision is reached mainly by taking a position with respect to different values, which battle for supremacy. For this, the judge must give priority to policy X over policy Y. Whatever the judge's decision may be, he establishes the society's policy. He places behind this policy the power of the organized society. This policy determination by the judge appears at first glance to contradict the basic democratic principle according to which policy in a democratic regime is determined by the people through their representatives, not by the judge.[2] Therefore, the argument goes, judicial discretion in the hard cases contains an undemocratic element.[3] The "democratic" argument is not that adjudication is undemocratic because the judge is not representative and is not responsible to the public. The democratic argument is that adjudication in the hard cases is undemocratic because policy is determined by the judge and not by the people, as required in an enlightened democracy.

Considerations in Solving the Problem: In the Absence of Judicial Review of the Constitutionality of a Statute

In a legal regime such as the United Kingdom or Israel, where there is no judicial review of the constitutionality of statutes, the formal answer to

1. See Justice Frankfurter in *American Federation of Labor v. American Sash and Door Co.*, 335 U.S. 538, 555 (1948): "Because the powers exercised by this Court are inherently oligarchic, Jefferson all his life thought of the Court as 'an irresponsible body' and 'independent of the nation itself.' The Court is not saved from being oligarchic because it professes to act in the service of human ends." See also Levontin, "On Law and Other Things," 9 *Mishpatim* 175, 179 (1979). Speaking of judges, Levontin says, "The latter do not present a platform to the public, do not identify with it and do not undertake to advance and defend it. The public has no opportunity to prefer or reject them on the basis of ideas and programs they proposed in public."

2. See McClesky, "Judicial Review in a Democracy: A Dissenting Opinion," 3 *Hous. L. Rev.* 354, 356 (1966).

3. For the "democratic" argument, see Rostow, "The Democratic Character of Judicial Review," 66 *Harv. L. Rev.* 193 (1952); Dahl, "Decisionmaking in a Democracy: The Supreme Court as a National Policy-Maker," 6 *J. Pub. L.* 279 (1957); Choper, "The Supreme Court and the Political Branches: Democratic Theory and Practice," 122 *U. Pa. L. Rev.* 810 (1974); Bishin, "Judicial Review in Democratic Theory," 50 *S. Cal. L. Rev.* 1099 (1977).

the democratic argument is twofold. First, the legislature itself agrees (explicitly or implicitly) to judicial establishment of policy by establishing open rules—or by establishing procedures for filling gaps in the system—thereby giving the judge authority to determine the legal norm on the basis of policy considerations; second, the legislature has the power to change the policy established by the judge, for it can change the judicial rule by means of statute.[4] It is appropriate for the legislative branch to use this power of repeal, and its use does not indicate disrespect for the judicial branch. This formal argument has great force. It enables the nation, through its representatives, to put the determination of policy where it sees fit. However, this argument does not solve the problem in all its aspects, for the claim is that the court should not determine policy in the first place and thereby impose on the legislature the obligation to change the court's determination (an obligation it may sometimes have trouble meeting, for a variety of reasons). The argument is, therefore, that in a democratic regime, policy is established by an elected body, not by the court.[5]

If, in fact, there is tension between judicial discretion and the democracy it would appear to be possible to eliminate it in either of two ways: first, by eliminating the hard cases. In the absence of hard cases, the court does not establish policy and the conflict is avoided. Second, by transforming the court into a representative body accountable to the public. But both ways are out of the question. As for the first, we have already seen that discretion may be narrowed but not eliminated altogether. As for the second option, certain aspects of it are common practice in a number of states in the United States, which choose judges in regular elections. As is well known, this system is controversial. It

4. See Agresto, *supra* note 75, ch. 4. From this argument, Justice Sussman gleaned an authorization for judicial activism: see Sussman, *supra* note 44, ch. 1, at 216: "This superiority of the Israeli legislature, which is not constrained by a formal written constitution, justifies, in my view, this conclusion regarding the work of the courts: the judicial restraint in favor of which Justices of the United States Supreme Court preached, lest the national patterns be determined by people whom the public did not choose, and the Congress be powerless, this restraint is unnecessary in Israel, whose legislature is all-powerful."

5. On the dangers in the determination of policy by the courts, see P. Devlin, *The Judge* 17 (1979): "It is a great temptation to cast the judiciary as an elite which will bypass the traffic-laden ways of the democratic process. But it would only apparently be a bypass. In truth it would be a road that would never rejoin the highway but would lead inevitably, however long and winding the path, to the totalitarian state."

seems that the accepted view is that the disadvantages of this system are so numerous that the alternative is not practical in the least. In any event, to the extent one seeks completely to eliminate the tension between the existence of judicial discretion and the democratic regime, one cannot stop with the election of judges, but rather one must allow them to act like all other representatives of the public. Such a pure "political" model of adjudication leads to its destruction, for it eliminates the independence, neutrality, and impartiality of adjudication. Thus, the basic starting point must be that the judiciary is not a representative body and that the judge is not accountable to the public (neither directly nor to the public's representatives, such as the legislature). This is the judge's main strength as an adjudicator, and it must be vigilantly guarded, for the judge's main function is to adjudicate. As Professor Philip Kurland wrote of the judiciary, "It is politically irresponsible and must remain so, if it would perform its primary function in today's harried society."[6] Yet it is equally accepted that in the hard cases the judge makes policy, and according to the democratic argument this is inconsistent with a proper democracy.

In this form, the argument sharpens the question about the nature of democracy. Is democracy merely the rule of the people and their determination of policy through their elected representatives? Or is democracy also certain fundamental values to which the regime must be faithful? My argument is[7] that democracy is not one-dimensional. It is not simply majority rule. Democracy is multidimensional. It is the realization of certain fundamental values, such as basic human rights. Thus, the Israeli Declaration of Independence, which announces the founding of the state and the establishment of its institutions based on majority rule, further decrees that Israel

> will foster the development of the country for the benefit of all its inhabitants; it will be based on freedom, justice and peace, as envisaged by the prophets of Israel; it will ensure complete equality of social and political rights to all its inhabitants irrespective of religion, race or sex; it will guarantee freedom of religion, conscience, language, education and culture.

A regime in which the majority denies the basic rights of the minority is a regime of majority rule. Yet it is not a democratic regime.[8] Democracy

6. See Kurland, *supra* note 77, ch. 4, at 44.
7. See Bishin, *supra* note 3.
8. See Rostow, *supra* note 3, at 199; Bishin, *supra* note 3, at 1131.

cannot be maintained without human rights. Majority rule is democratic
as long as it ensures human rights. Majority rule without human rights is
not democracy. Democracy, therefore, is a delicate balance between
majority rule and certain fundamental values, such as human rights.
When there is a formal constitution, the constitution itself determines the
balance between the two. In the absence of a formal constitution, the
majority determines the balance. In a regime such as this, the counter-
weight to majority rule is the majority's self-restraint.

Against this background, one must examine again the claim that
determination of policy by the judge is incompatible with a democratic
regime. As the argument goes, a democratic regime demands that policy
be made by the people, through their elected representatives, not by the
judges, who do not represent the nation and who are not accountable to
it. It seems that this claim must now be seen in a different light. When a
judge makes policy in the context of the fundamental values of the
democracy, he does not act against the democracy but rather according to
it. If democracy is a balance between majority rule and certain fundamental values, then the judge who makes policy on the basis of the
fundamental values puts into effect those values that the democracy
seeks to protect. A judge who adopts policy on the basis of the democracy's fundamental values makes the democracy faithful to itself. As
Professor Atiyah noted,

> An independent and not politically accountable judiciary, is surely just as
> essential to modern democratic government as elected and politically ac-
> countable legislatures and executives. A cynic might indeed argue that it is
> the independence and non-accountability of the judiciary which makes de-
> mocracy tolerable and workable.[9]

Of course, the assumption is that the judge acts lawfully within the
frontiers of the zone of legitimacy. One also assumes that the legislature
can at any time establish the balance that appeals to it. Yet as long as the
legislature does not act and the judge operates within the limits of the
zone of formal legitimacy, a determination of policy that is based on the
fundamental values of the democratic regime should not be perceived as
an undemocratic act. All the judge is doing is determining the borderline,
as he sees it, between the power of the majority and its self-restraint. If
the legislature, representing the majority, does not approve of this bor-

9. Atiyah, "Judges and Policy," 15 *Isr. L. Rev.* 346, 363 (1980).

derline, it has the authority to move it into the zone it believes is appropriate.

This analysis sharpens the various sides of the problem, but it does not solve them. We are left with the questions, What are those fundamental values that the democracy seeks to attain? and how is policy to be determined according to them? The problem of judicial discretion arises with full force when the fundamental values are not sufficiently anchored in legislation, but rather must be fashioned. The problem of judicial discretion is difficult when the fundamental principles are not incompatible with one another. The difficult problem is, for example, whether privacy is accepted as a fundamental principle of democracy. The difficulty arises when the principle of freedom of political expression, elections, demonstrations, or freedom of the press collides with the freedom of movement (in the matter of demonstrations) or with the individual's right to dignity (in the matter of libel) or with the fair trial (in the matter of the *sub judice* rules). How is the judge supposed to fashion policy in the context of these principles, which need internal balancing?

My approach is that in setting policy against the background of the fundamental values of the society, the judge must consider the fact that he is not operating in outer space. He must be aware that he is working in the framework of an equation whose one side is majority rule and whose other side is the society's fundamental values. When he determines policy within the context of the fundamental values, he must take into account the factor of majority rule. Thus, for example, a policy based on a national consensus is preferable to a policy that does not enjoy consensus. Thereby, one side of the equation acknowledges the existence of the other side. The judge does not have to concede fundamental values for the sake of majority rule, because in this he would be operating against the democratic principles. But where the fundamental values contradict one another, and the judge must decide and must balance between them according to their weight and their force, he should consider the fact that democracy is not simply fundamental values, but also majority rule. One must not forget that majority rule is a principle component of democracy and not an antidemocratic matter. Thus, the democratic principle affects the exercise of judicial discretion in the solution of the hard cases. It is one important factor, among others, that the judge must take into account if he seeks to exercise his discretion reasonably.

Considerations in Solving the Problem: When There Is
Judicial Review of the Constitutionality of a Statute

The democratic problem intensifies in a legal system such as that of the
United States, which has a formal written constitution that guarantees
judicial review of the constitutionality of statutes. In this regime the
legislature, which represents the people, may find itself in a situation in
which it is not authorized—through regular legislation—to change the
policy of the judicial branch, as the latter was expressed through the
judge's discretion in interpreting the constitution. Here, too, one can
give a formal answer, according to which the people, when they adopted
the constitution, gave the judge the power to determine policy and even
to strike down policies of the other branches when they conflict with the
constitution. In this state of affairs, not only is the judge not acting
against the wishes of the people, but the opposite is true: he effectuates
the national will, as it was expressed in the constitution.

This is a strictly formal answer, for the question is, Who decides the
national will from the substantive standpoint? Policy is established by the
judge of today and not by the nation of today (through its lawful representatives). The substantive answer, as we have seen, is found in determining the nature of the democratic regime itself. This regime, as we
saw, is not only the rule of the majority, which decides policy through its
representatives. A democratic regime also defends certain fundamental
values. A constitution contains both of these elements; it is not a document that only ensures a representative regime. A constitutional document also seeks to limit the majority and to restrain its power. A constitutional regime is a regime that balances between the power of the majority
to decide the society's policy and certain values that the majority cannot
injure. When the court gives expression to this quality of the constitution
by establishing policy opposed to that of the representative majority, it is
protecting the values of the constitution itself. De Tocqueville wrote that
the formal written constitution and judicial review defend against "the
tyranny of political assemblies."[10] It follows that the claim that judicial
policy-making is an antidemocratic act is like the claim that the constitution is an antidemocratic document.[11] Thus, the democratic character of
the state is not determined by the representative nature of each of its
organs, but rather by the democratic quality of the entire regime.

10. See A. de Tocqueville, *Democracy in America* 83 (Oxford U. Press, 1946).
11. See Raz, *supra* note 12, ch. 1, at 198.

This fundamental conception of the democratic regime did not solve the problem, although it adjusted its center of gravity. The question before us now is, What are those fundamental values that the constitution seeks to protect? Constitutional rules, because of their generality, are sometimes defined in broad, open-textured terms.[12] Many fundamental rules do not establish clear anchors for agreed-upon basic values. Therefore, the question becomes one of defining the nature of the fundamental values. This may generate significant controversy—as the American experience has shown—within the population of lawyers, among the general public, and among judges themselves. Everyone agrees that in a constitutional government that recognizes judicial review of the constitutionality of a statute, the final decision about the fundamental values is in the hands of the court. But there is disagreement regarding the standards by which the court determines these fundamental values.

Thus, in a constitutional regime that recognizes judicial review, there is constant tension between judicial discretion and majority rule. The majority, in its law-making, thinks it is maintaining the fundamental principles of the system. The court, in striking down the statute, determines that the majority's approach was wrong. This tension may be reduced by initially drafting the constitution in precise terms, thereby giving both legislator and judge a certain direction. Yet this solution is problematic, in light of the desire to avoid freezing the constitution in a particular reality and the desire to give the constitution a comprehensive meaning that can withstand the test of time. And even a cautious drafting, one that is conscious of the tension between legislator and judge, cannot prevent it altogether. In the final analysis, reduction of this tension depends upon the various organs themselves, that is, on the legislative and executive branches, which must attempt to legislate and to execute within the core of accepted values and to avoid adventures in the margins. Yet it also depends on the judicial branch, which must restrain itself in determining the protected values. It, too, must operate within the framework of the core of accepted values, and it, too, must avoid adventures in the margins. Thus, here too we have arrived at a policy that the judicial branch must formulate for itself when it exercises discretion in the determination of policy on the basis of the system's fundamental values in a constitutional regime.

12. See Carter, "Constitutional Adjudication and the Indeterminate Text: A Preliminary Defense of an Imperfect Muddle," 94 *Yale L.J.* 821 (1985).

The Situation in Israel

In Israel, the constitutionality of most statutes is not subject to judicial review.[13] A minority of statutes (only those that contradict an entrenched rule of a Basic Law) are subject to this kind of review.[14] Even in this case, a majority, or a special majority, of the Knesset can always "entrench" the statute and thereby protect it from judicial review. This legal reality is due to the fact that no formal constitution was established when the state was founded; the matter was left—by the "Harari decision"—to evolve in a slow, piecemeal process of the enacting of Basic Laws. A majority of Knesset Members participating in the vote decides the policy, and it has the power to change policy made by the court. In a minority of cases, a majority of the Members of Knesset, or a special majority, is authorized to achieve this result. Of course, as long as the legislature has not voiced its opinion, the policy is established—to the extent required for interpreting the legal norm (whether statutory or common law) or for filling voids in the system—by the court, operating within the framework of the accepted values of the society.

It is, of course, questionable whether this situation is desirable. Would it not be preferable to lay down a formal, written constitution, judicial review of the constitutionality of statutes, and a limited ability to amend the constitution? To be sure, opinion is divided on this issue. Extensive analysis of the question is outside the scope of this book. Therefore, I will discuss it only from the perspective of the problem of judicial discretion. On the one hand, there are those who argue that we have no need whatsoever for a formal, written constitution and for judicial review of the constitutionality of statutes, or at least that there is no need for such a constitution in the matter of human rights. Here is the view of President Landau, who said,

> I had thought that the constitutional structure that was acceptable to all of us was parliamentary democracy, in which the people, through their elected representatives, express their will as the final arbiter in issues of policy. If the

13. See Nimmer, "The Uses of Judicial Review in Israel's Quest for A Constitution," 70 *Colum. L. Rev.* 1217 (1970); Klein, "A New Era in Israel's Constitutional Law," 6 *Isr. L. Rev.* 376 (1971).

14. H.C. 98/69 *Bergman v. Minister of Finance,* 23 P.D.(1) 693; H.C. 246/81 *Derech Eretz Association v. Broadcasting Authority,* 35 P.D.(4) 1; H.C. 141/82 *Rubinstein v. Chairman of the Knesset,* 37 P.D. (3) 141.

elected parliament does not fulfill its function properly, the remedy will not be found in establishing an oligarchical regime of a group of people—no matter how smart and wise and honest they may be—who will be authorized to strike down words of the public representatives in matters of law-making, without being brought to account to the public from time to time in elections.[15]

On the other side of the debate, some claim that a written constitution is desirable and that the court must guard the borders it establishes through the instrument of judicial review of the constitutionality of statutes.

It seems to me that the answer to this dilemma depends on two factors: the degree of confidence one can repose in the legislative branch that it will be able to restrain itself; and the degree of confidence one can repose in the judicial branch that it will be able to restrain itself. In the absence of a written constitution and judicial review, the balance between majority rule and the fundamental values of the democracy is determined by the majority itself, in other words, by its self-restraint. Thus, when one has confidence that the majority will restrain itself, there is less of a need for a written constitution and for judicial review. The parliamentary majority, in its self-restraint, will ensure an appropriate balance between majority rule and the fundamental values of the democratic regime. On the other hand, when one does not have faith that the majority will restrain itself and suspects that it will harm the fundamental values of the democracy, a written constitution and judicial review of the constitutionality of statutes are required. The decision in this question, of course, varies from one state to the next. William Bishin discussed this:

> The way to achieve democracy—if by that we mean a proper balance of majority rule and majority constraint—will vary from nation to nation. It will depend upon the traditions, institutions and education of the people. In a given society, it is conceivable that the majoritarian agencies could safely be granted much of the power to decide constitutional questions. But in another society, this may not be the best way of achieving the proper mix of majority power and constitutional rights essential to democracy.[16]

Thus, for example, it seems that in the United Kingdom, sufficient balance exists in the self-restraint of the legislature, and thus the trend

15. Landau, "The Court's Power and its Limitations," 10 *Mishpatim* 196, 200 (1980).
16. Bishin, *supra* note 3, at 1120.

there appears to be against a written constitution and judicial review of the constitutionality of statutes.[17] On the other hand, most new states founded after the Second World War, and most of the states that had a difficult experience in that war—such as Germany, Italy, and Japan—established formal constitutions and judicial review of the constitutionality of statutes.[18]

The situation in Israel depends, of course, on one's point of view. To me it appears that our historical experience indicates that it is desirable for us to have a formal constitution and judicial review. One has a strong suspicion—based on reality—that in its haste to attain short-term political goals, the legislature will harm fundamental democratic values. We are an ancient nation but a young state, without parliamentary experience and without the self-restraints that are imprinted deep in the spirit of the British nation, for example. However, we are in the midst of a historic process of building our state. Therefore, some flexibility is required. I would recommend enacting a written constitution and instituting judicial review, while enabling, under certain conditions that are not too burdensome, amendments in the constitution and in court decisions that interpret the constitution.

A written constitution and judicial review are also related to one's degree of confidence in the judicial branch. If the absence of a written constitution and judicial review means self-restraint by the legislature, then the existence of a written constitution and judicial review mean self-restraint by the judge.[19] Will the judge be able to restrain himself by finding an appropriate balance between majority rule and the fundamental values of the democracy? The answer to this question also depends on one's perspective. It seems to me that the cumulative experience since the establishment of the State of Israel is positive. Whenever it established policy on the basis of the fundamental values of the regime, the

17. See L. Scarmann, *English Law, the New Dimension* (1974); M. Zander, *A Bill of Rights?* (1975); Fritz, "An Entrenched Bill of Rights for the United Kingdom: The Constitutional Dilemma," 10 *Anglo-Am. L. Rev.* 105 (1981); Abernathy, "Should the United Kingdom Adopt a Bill of Rights?" 31 *Am. J. Comp. L.* 431 (1983).

18. M. Cappelletti, *Judicial Review in the Contemporary World* (1971).

19. See Justice Stone in *United States v. Butler*, 297 U.S. 1, 79 (1936): "While unconstitutional exercise of power by the executive and legislative branches of government is subject to judicial restraint, the only check upon our own exercise of power is our sense of self-restraint."

court always was able to restrain itself, and there have been very few cases indeed in which the legislature was forced to intervene and change our judgments in a fundamental issue; and some of them came at the court's urging. One must hope that this experience will also prove itself in the framework of a written constitution and judicial review.

JUDICIAL DISCRETION AND THE SEPARATION OF POWERS

The Problem

According to the pure, theoretical model, separation of powers means "that legislation in its functional sense is identical to legislation in its organizational sense, that adjudication by its functional test is identical to adjudication by its organizational test, and that administration in its functional sense is identical to administration in its organizational sense."[20] According to this model, the legislative branch must deal with legislation, and only with legislation. The executive branch must deal with execution, and only with execution. The judicial branch must deal with adjudication, and only with adjudication. The model leaves no room for judicial lawmaking and no room for judicial discretion, in the sense that I am using the term.

The pure, theoretical model of the separation of powers does not exist in any modern-day system. Montesquieu himself did not believe in this model, for his approach recognized that the legislature would deal with a number of matters of adjudication, such as judging the nobility, and that the executive branch would deal with a number of matters of lawmaking, such as exercising the right to veto legislation.[21] The judicial branch, according to Montesquieu, enjoys no personal independence. In our day, important exceptions to the theoretical model of the separation of powers are recognized. It is sufficient to recall that in Israel the Knesset is involved in adjudication, such as election appeals, lifting immunity, and suspension of a Member of Knesset. Similarly, the administration also is involved in adjudication and in lawmaking, namely, the secondary legislation of the administration, which is increasing in scope. The judicial branch deals not only with adjudication, but also with lawmaking—that is, judicial lawmaking—and with execution.

20. Klinghoffer, *supra* note 1, ch. 3, at 23.
21. See Montesquieu, *supra* note 13, ch. 1.

The pure, theoretical model of separation of powers, in which each governmental authority is separate, is not only not accepted, but also is not desirable. In a democratic regime, one must strike a balance between majority rule and fundamental democratic values. This balance cannot exist if each branch stands alone, without interacting with the other branches, and without balancing and supervision. This situation will ultimately lead to an accumulation of strength and power in the hands of one of the branches, with the result that the democracy's fundamental values may be harmed. This will frustrate the very goal of the separation of powers, which is not to create an independent, theoretical structure, but to guarantee the fundamental values of the democracy. Thus, the modern conception does not embrace a pure model of the separation of powers, but rather a more flexible model, one that is prepared to recognize that each organ will undertake a number of functions, provided there are mutual checks and balances among the various organs. President Shamgar spoke of this as follows:

> Separation of the powers does not necessarily mean the creation of a barrier that absolutely prevents any link among the branches, but rather it is expressed mainly in the maintenance of a balance among the powers of the branches, in theory and in practice, permitting independence through defined mutual supervision.[22]

Justice Witkon rightly noted that

> A proper democratic regime—notwithstanding the notion of separation of powers—does not mean parliamentary absolutism. There is plenty of room in this regime for checks and balances, and for this purpose we have bodies, foremost among them the judicial branch, that are not founded on popular election.[23]

Therefore, I concluded that "an enlightened democratic regime is a regime of separation of powers. This separation does not mean that each branch is on its own, without taking into consideration the other authorities. Such a conception would strike deeply at the foundations of democracy itself, for it would mean a dictatorship of each branch within its own confines. To the contrary: separation of powers means mutual balance and control among the various branches. The branches are not separated

22. H.C. 306/81 *supra* note 14, ch. 3, at 141.
23. A. Witkon, *Politics and Law* 71 (1965).

by walls, but by bridges that balance and supervise."[24] The aim of this approach is not increased efficiency—which it does not achieve—but the avoidance of arbitrariness,[25] whether this be arbitrariness of the legislative body, of the executive body, or of the judicial body.

"Bridges that Balance and Supervise"

The point of departure is that within the framework of the principle of separation of powers, the judge must adjudicate. This is the essence of his function. In order to adjudicate, he must fashion for himself, within the bounds of the zone of formal legitimacy, the legal norm according to which he is to decide the conflict. No problem arises in the easy cases or in the intermediate cases, in which the given norm and its scope of application are not problematic. Not so in the hard cases. In these, judicial discretion exists as to the actual fashioning of the norm. There is judicial discretion as to the interpretation of the norm (whether the norm is statutory or common law). There is judicial discretion as to the filling of the gap that exists in the absence of a norm. Does the principle of separation of powers not require that in this situation the judge turn to the legislature and request guidance as to the interpretation or creation of the norm? As odd as it may appear today, such arrangements existed in Europe in the seventeenth and eighteenth centuries. Nowadays, we are not in the habit of conducting this kind of dialogue with the legislature. Our basic conception of the separation of powers is that the authority to decide in a dispute includes also—explicitly or implicitly—the power and the duty to fashion the norm according to which the case is decided.[26] To judge means to interpret. Thus, the responsibility for interpreting the norm (whether statutory or common law) is placed on the judge and on him alone. Any other approach would produce unwanted intervention by the other branches in the judicial process and might harm the independence of the judicial act.

24. H.C. 73/85 *"Kach" Party Faction v. Chairman of the Knesset*, 39 P.D. (3) 141.

25. See Justice Brandeis in *Myers v. United States* 272 U.S. 52, 293 (1926): "The purpose was not to avoid friction, but by means of the inevitable friction incident to the distribution of governmental powers among three departments, to save the people from autocracy."

26. See *Marbury v. Madison* 5 U.S. (1 Cranch) 137, 177 (1803); *Powell v. McCormack* 395 U.S. 486 (1969); *United States v. Nixon,* 418 U.S. 683 (1974); H.C. 306/81 *supra* note 14, ch. 3; H.C. 73/85, *supra* note 24.

We saw, therefore, that judicial discretion and judicial lawmaking do not contradict the principle of separation of powers in its modern meaning. Yet the principle of separation of powers can still affect the choice among the various options that stand before the judge when he exercises his discretion. One must not forget that even though lawmaking is not the sole preserve of the legislative branch, it is its main function. One should also not forget that although execution is not the sole preserve of the executive branch, it is the essence of its role. Therefore, in the exercise of judicial discretion, it is appropriate for the judge to take these factors into account.[27] Thus, for example, if the possibility of leaving an act of lawmaking in the hands of the legislative branch is practical, that possibility should be chosen, for it will be more consistent with the principle of separation of powers than the alternative—judicial lawmaking. Similarly, if the possibility of leaving an act of execution in the hands of the executive authority is feasible, it is to be preferred, for it is more compatible with separation of powers than is an act of execution by the judicial branch. Of course, this approach should not be undertaken where the fundamental values of the democracy must be protected. But where there are several ways of guarding these values, the judge should choose the way that is consistent with the basic tendency that leaves most lawmaking to the legislative branch, whose task and expertise that is, and most execution to the executive branch, whose function and expertise that is.

JUDICIAL DISCRETION AND THE SOCIETY'S CONCEPTION OF THE JUDICIAL FUNCTION

Judicial discretion, as we have seen, raises difficult problems concerning its democratic character and its place in the separation of powers. An inappropriate exercise of judicial discretion might harm the society's conception of the place of judicial discretion in the institutional arrangement that comprises the governmental authorities. Here lies the importance of this conception of the judicial function for the exercise of judicial discretion. As Professor Freeman said, "Every institution embodies some degree of consensus about how it is to operate. To understand the judicial role and apprise the legitimacy of judicial creativity one

27. See Stone, *supra* note 40, ch. 1, at 667.

must explore the shared expectations which define the role of judge.''[28] Judicial discretion is exercised differently in a society whose basic conception of the judicial process is that the judge is the mouth of the legislature, than it is exercised in a society that gives substantive legitimacy to comprehensive judicial creativity. Each society has its own agreement as to the proper balance in the degree of judicial lawmaking— the product of judicial discretion—in comparison to the lawmaking done by the other branches. The judge must take this agreement into account. The exercise of judicial discretion outside the agreement, and its nonexercise inside the bounds of the agreement, may shake the public's confidence in the judicial system. The public's fundamental conception of the appropriate separation of powers and of the proper scope of judicial lawmaking should be before the judge when he exercises his discretion in the hard cases.

The Society's Conception—Reality in Flux

The society's conception of the judicial function is not static and may change. The persistence of the exercise of judicial discretion in a certain way, and public knowledge of it, may, in the long run, change the agreement as to the legitimacy of the exercise of judicial discretion. Consequently, judicial discretion must be exercised cautiously, while clearing a path for itself in the borders of the public agreement and thereby influencing the agreement itself. Therefore, judicial discretion must be exercised in such a way as not to harm the public's basic sense of the proper field in which judicial lawmaking should operate.

Special Elements in the Society

In the framework of the society's conception of judicial discretion, special account must be taken of the conceptions of several elements in the society:

(a) one must consider the members of the legislative branch and the executive branch. Their conception as to the proper exercise of judicial discretion is of particular interest because the three branches constitute the government of the state, and together they oversee the rule of law. Moreover, in a legal system that lacks a formal constitution, it is doubtful

28. Freeman, "Standards of Adjudication, Judicial Law Making and Prospective Overruling," 26 *Curr. Legal Probs.* 166, 181 (1973).

whether the judicial branch can exercise, over the long term, its discretion outside of the consensus as it is reflected in the legislative branch and the executive branch. There is always a danger that these authorities will use their lawmaking powers to "return" the judicial discretion to the parameters of the consensus;

(b) one must consider the group of judges themselves. It is desirable that there be an understanding among them as to the nature of the function and as to the nature of judicial discretion. Of course, one cannot expect full agreement, but it seems desirable that there be shared fundamental conceptions. True, there are always judges who travel ahead of the pack or behind it, and this phenomenon has its own advantages. Yet it seems advisable that most of the judges should have a common intellectual base regarding the nature of the judicial function;

(c) one must consider the lawyers and advocates who connect the judicial branch with the public. It is they who translate the language of the judge into the language of the people. They translate the judgments to the public. They influence to a large extent the creation of the public's expectations of the judicial branch. They give their opinion as to whether or not the exercise of judicial discretion was "legitimate." In doing so they create public opinion concerning the appropriate exercise of judicial discretion. It would be an unhealthy situation if the judicial branch and the lawyers held substantially different fundamental conceptions of how the discretion should be exercised. Furthermore, both attorneys and judges play a role in the exercise of judicial discretion: the attorney prepares the ground and sometimes plants the seed, while the judge harvests. Without real help from advocacy, the right ploughing will not be done, the necessary factual base will not be presented, and the proper alternatives will not be exposed. The attorney's function is decisive in the exercise of judicial discretion;

(d) one must consider the legal scholars, who deal with the theory of law and who in their research lay the foundation for legal science and the doctrine of judicial discretion and judicial lawmaking. Their opinion and their fundamental conceptions of the manner of the exercise of judicial discretion are particularly important in determining the manner of the exercise, in practice, of judicial discretion;

(e) finally, one must consider the enlightened public. The judge has special interest in the position of the enlightened public, which—while it does not have a formal role in the branches of government and is not expert in law—reflects the wisdom and the restraint required of the judge in his exercise of judicial discretion. This enlightened public—of which the judge generally sees himself a part—greatly influences the society's fundamental conception of judicial discretion.[29]

The Society's Conception of the Judicial Function and "Prospective Overruling"

A good example of the reciprocal relations between the society's conception of the judicial function and the exercise of judicial discretion can be found in the issue of "prospective overruling."[30] This subject revolves around the question whether it is advisable for the court's new rule not to operate retroactively, but rather in the future only. This approach is established to some extent in the United States.[31] In England it is the subject of debate.[32] Within the framework of this dispute, the society's conception of the judicial role is a major reason against adopting the rule of prospective overruling. The opponents of the "prospective rule" note that the English society's conception of the judicial function is incompatible with the prospective rule;[33] indeed, that the rule involves a complete distortion of the society's conception of the judicial function[34] and of the society's expectations of it.[35] Professor Freeman wrote of this, "It is my thesis that prospective overruling is not a judicial technique which is compatible with standards of adjudication expected by the legal profession or with values in the legal order which the layman looks to the judiciary to uphold."[36] And he continues: "The main argument against

29. See Landau J. in C.A. 461/62, *supra* note 60, ch. 4; H.C. 58/68 *supra* note 51, ch. 2, at 420, citing W. Friedmann, *Legal Theory* 403 (4th ed., 1960); W. Friedmann, *Law in Changing Society* 45 (abridged ed., 1964).

30. See Tedeschi, *supra* note 27, ch. 1.

31. See *supra* note 47, ch. 5.

32. See D. Lloyd, *supra* note 88, ch. 2.

33. See *Birmingham City Corporation v. West Midland Baptist (Trust) Association (Incorporated)* [1969] 3 All E.R. 172, 180: "We cannot say that the law was one thing yesterday but is to be something different tomorrow. If we decide that the rule as to the date of the notice to tread is wrong we must decide that it always has been wrong" (per Lord Reid).

34. Scarman, "Law Reform by Legislative Techniques," 32 *Sask. L. Rev.* 217, 219 (1967).

35. See D. Lloyd, *supra* note 88, ch. 2, at 858.

36. Freeman, *supra* note 28, at 202.

prospective overruling is that it distorts the public's expectations of the judicial role."[37] Lord Devlin expressed the opposition to the prospective rule well:

> I do not like it. It crosses the Rubicon that divides the judicial and the legislative powers. It turns judges into undisguised legislators. It is facile to think that it is always better to throw off disguises. The need for disguise hampers activity and so restricts the power. Paddling across the Rubicon by individuals in disguise who will be sent back if they proclaim themselves is very different from the bridging of the river by an army in uniform and with bands playing.[38]

To the argument that this system is accepted in the United States, one may answer that the society's conception of the judicial function in the United States differs from that in England. Of course, this consideration is not the only factor. Thus, for example, there are those who argue that the injustice of applying a rule retroactively damages the judicial branch more than recognition of the rule for the future. This is a complex subject, in which the society's conception of the judicial function occupies a central role.

JUDICIAL DISCRETION AND THE RELATIONS AMONG THE BRANCHES OF GOVERNMENT

Consideration of the Legislative Activities of the Other Branches

In exercising judicial discretion, it is appropriate for the judge to take into account this complex system of the branches of government, and their legitimacy in the eyes of the public in a democratic state that is based on the separation of powers. As we have seen, the exercise of judicial discretion and judicial lawmaking that follows from it are not done in a vacuum, and they are not the only nor the most important act of lawmaking. Alongside judicial lawmaking is the lawmaking of the legislative branch and that of the executive branch. The judge must look at the overall legislative picture and take this lawmaking into account.[39] He must consider the legislative activity of the other branches. Does the

---

37. Ibid., at 204.
38. Devlin, *supra* note 5, at 12.
39. See Koopman, *supra* note 45, ch. 3.

legislature—whether the primary legislature or the secondary legislature—react with due haste when a legislative[40] or judicial[41] mishap is revealed? Does the legislature have its own policy, according to which certain fields are appropriate for judicial lawmaking?[42] Was the question brought to the legislature in the past, and if it was—what was its reaction?[43] Is there a chance that the subject will come before the legislature in the near future? Perhaps the legal question is already on its agenda? What might its reaction be if judicial discretion is exercised in a certain way? Will a particular exercise of judicial discretion stimulate the legislature to undertake its own lawmaking activity?

These and other questions are relevant to the reasonable exercise of judicial discretion. The judge must consider the other branches, just as he expects them to take him into consideration. If it is appropriate for a certain question to be arranged through legislation, and it is already on the legislature's agenda, the judge should not choose a possibility that arranges this subject. A reasonable exercise of judicial discretion will leave the matter to the legislature itself. It is inadvisable to create competition among the branches. On the other hand, if the subject is not on the legislature's agenda, and it has no chance of being placed on the agenda unless unforeseeable events occur, there is no reason not to adopt a possibility that arranges the matter. In these circumstances, there is no reason to wait for legislative activity that probably will not take place. Between the extremes there are, of course, many cases in which the judge has discretion about whether to deal with them or leave them to the legislature.

40. See Friendly, "The Gap of Lawmaking—Judges Who Can't and Legislators Who Won't," 63 *Colum. L. Rev.* 787 (1963).

41. See Sussman, *supra* note 44, ch. 1, at 218: "The loyalty the court owes the legislature and its relation of subordination are not a one-way street. For the court to be able to fulfill its function as required, certain obligations are imposed on the legislature, and here I come to complain that the legislature does not always do its job properly. My first complaint against the legislature is that it does not keep track as necessary of the court's decisions, and when a break in the law becomes evident, the legislature does not plug it with due haste." See also Calabresi, *supra* note 11, ch. 1.

42. See Friedmann, *supra* note 17, ch. 1. Professor Friedmann distinguishes between "lawyers' law" and "political law." The former may be appropriately regulated through judicial lawmaking while the latter demands that the legislature regulate it.

43. See Lord Reid in *Shaw v. Director of Public Prosecution* [1962] A.C. 220, 275: "Where Parliament fears to tread, it is not for the Court to rush in."

The "Political Question"

The question of judicial discretion and the reciprocal relations among the branches of government arises with full force when the judge is required to decide the legality of an activity of the legislative branch in the area of its internal affairs.[44] Should the judge exercise his discretion in such a way as to take a position regarding this "internal management" of the legislature, or should he let the matter be? This is not an easy question, for two considerations collide in it. The Supreme Court discussed these two factors in H.C. 652/81, *Sarid v. The Speaker of the Knesset*,[45] where I said,

> On the one hand is the principle of the rule of law, which in its formal aspect means that all the actors in the state must respect the law. The principle of the rule of law is directed both to individuals and to the governmental agencies, and it applies also to the house of representatives itself,—this is "the rule of law over the law-maker." . . . For without a judge there is no law, and where the court does not get involved, the principle of the rule of law suffers. On the other hand is the principle that the rules of procedure of the house of representatives are its own internal affair, belonging from the perspective of separation of powers to the legislative branch itself, which also has the tools to examine itself and to check its own decisions. Therefore, it is appropriate that the judicial branch respect the internal affairs of the legislative body and not intervene in them. Moreover, the Knesset's decisions regarding the reciprocal relations between it and the government usually are saddled with heavy political baggage. It is appropriate for the judicial branch to stay its hand, in order to avoid insofar as possible the "politicization of adjudication." In solving this dilemma, it is possible to opt for one of the extreme solutions[46] or to search for the golden mean between judicial activism and restraint. The Israeli Supreme Court decided to seek the golden mean. Consequently, it established the principle that the court will not intervene in the internal proceedings of the Knesset, unless there is a fear of injury to the structural foundations of our constitutional regime.[47] Therefore, the Court established a standard "that takes into account the level of the alleged harm to

44. Zemach, "The Problem of Unjusticiability of Parliamentary Procedures," 3 *Tel-Aviv U. L. Rev.* 752 (1973).

45. 36 P.D. (2) 197.

46. In England parliamentary proceedings are immune from judicial intervention: see R. Heuston, *Essays in Constitutional Law* 92 (2d ed., 1964).

47. H.C. 652/81, *supra* note 45, H.C. 73/85 *supra* note 24.

the fabric of parliamentary life and the level of the impact of the injury on the structural foundations of our constitutional regime."[48]

This standard was applied with respect to the level of the court's intervention in the internal procedures of the Knesset. A similar dilemma exists in other matters in which similar questions about the reciprocal relations among the governmental branches arise.[49] These questions are outside the scope of this book. However, it is conceivable that an approach similar to the one adopted in the matter of intraparliamentary procedures may be applicable also to other situations. On the one hand, this would express the judge's awareness of the need to protect the appropriate reciprocal relations among the various branches, and on the other hand, it would express the court's role in determining what the law is and in protecting its rule in the sphere of matters that come before the court.

Judicial Discretion and the Question of Consensus

The Problem I have discussed the question of consensus in the matter of the infiltration of new fundamental values across the border of the legal system. The question I am asking now is related in that it deals with the level of societal agreement that must exist regarding the legal norm that the judge derives from the fundamental values. Must the judge exercise his discretion in such a way that the legal norm that follows from the exercise of discretion (whether through statutory or common law interpretation, or by other means) will enjoy societal agreement? This question is very important from the perspective of the reciprocal relations among the various branches and from the perspective of the public's confidence in the judiciary.

Taking Societal Agreement into Account My view is that the judge must take into account the level of the society's approval or disapproval of the social values and the legal norms that are derived from them.[50] The judge must aspire to a solution that is compatible with the societal agreement or

48. H.C. 652/81 ibid., at 204.

49. P. Strum, *The Supreme Court and Political Questions* (1974); Y. Zemach, *Political Questions in the Courts* (1976).

50. Lord Devlin distinguishes between activist discretion and dynamic discretion. The former operates in the framework of the social consensus. The latter seeks to change the consensus. A judge should be activist but not dynamic: see Devlin, *supra* note 5, at 5.

that at least does not contradict it.[51] I think it is advisable to avoid choosing an option that sharply contradicts the public's fundamental conception. Thus, for example, judicial restraint is justified in Israel in the entire area of "civil marriage," for this matter is the subject of bitter public controversy.[52] The reason for this approach is inherent in democratic considerations, in considerations of separation of powers and in the need to ensure the public's confidence. In my opinion, a judge should not see himself as a standard-bearer of a new societal agreement.[53] In general, the house of representatives is the appropriate institution for creating drastic changes in this matter. Activity that contradicts the societal agreement will, in the long run, damage the public's faith in the court system and in its ability to function properly.

To be sure, the question of consensus is complicated. Often there is no information about the consensus. Sometimes there is no consensus, in the sense that the question does not trouble the public one way or the other. Sometimes there is an honest dispute about whether a consensus exists. Sometimes the judge believes that the case is so exceptional in its severity and that the values of the hour so acutely contradict the fundamental values that there is no alternative but to lead the pack. In none of these situations can one establish hard and fast rules. Judicial discretion in this issue is substantial. Thus, if there is no consensus, or if it is difficult to identify it, the consideration of societal agreement need not influence judicial discretion, and the judge must take other considerations into account. I do not think judicial discretion may be exercised

51. See Diplock L. J. in *Greelong Harbor Trust Co. v. Gibbs Birght and Co.* [1974] 2 W.L.R. 507.

52. See C.A. 373/72, *Tefer v. The State of Israel*, 28 (2) P.D. 7, 15. Justice Etzioni writes: "This is not the case when one is dealing with initiating a new legal institution, such as civil marriage, in Israel. Here the legislature consciously omitted this institution from the statute books. It is obvious to anyone who follows the Knesset's work and the ideas of the various parties, that this issue is a major point of bitter conflict among the Israeli public, and that there has not yet been a decision to introduce civil marriage, a decision that will have the proper legal form. And should we judges, who are ordered to distance ourselves from any political debate and argument, take the place of the legislature and decide in a question that divides the public? And if we did so, would we not be asked, and rightly so, 'who put you here and who authorized you to cross the legislature's borders,' for the rule of law in which we live and which we are ordered to protect as the apple of our eyes—is based on the separation of powers and protecting the spheres among them so that none will cross the other's borders."

53. See Traynor, *supra* note 74, ch. 4, at 1030: "The very responsibilities of a judge as an arbiter disqualify him as a crusader."

only if there is a consensus, only within the parameters of the consensus. All I am trying to establish is the judge's consideration of the existence of the consensus, if indeed it exists. Here, too, I cannot offer a short and sweet formula. Perhaps the most one can say is that it is often inadvisable to act against the societal consensus and that it is desirable that activity in opposition to the consensus not become a routine matter. Furthermore, the societal agreement, within whose borders the judge must act, is an agreement that is anchored in the fundamental values of the system. The judge cannot act within the framework of a societal agreement that reflects fleeting moods of the hour. Rather, he must act within the framework of the central and the basic, not of the temporary and the fleeting. When the society is not faithful to itself, the judge does not have to give expression to the moods of the hour. He must stand firm against them, while giving expression to the societal consensus that reflects the basic principles and the articles of faith of the enlightened public of the society in which he lives.

"The Lawyers' Laws"

On the basis of these considerations, the judge has discretion in fields such as civil procedure and the laws of evidence. The same holds true for those other areas of law that are considered to be "lawyers' laws," such as contracts and torts. On the other hand, there are areas of law that carry heavy ideological baggage (such as some parts of family law in Israel), in which the judge must weigh his steps carefully in light of the considerations of consensus. Thus, for example, I believe that judicial restraint is desirable in all matters that involve the question Who is a Jew? for the purpose of statutes that use the expression *Jew*.[54] On the other hand, significant judicial activism may be developed regarding the question What is good faith? for the purpose of statutes that employ the expression *good faith*.

JUDICIAL DISCRETION AND THE PUBLIC'S CONFIDENCE IN THE JUDICIAL BRANCH

The Centrality of Public Confidence

I have discussed the interrelations among the various branches and the necessity of maintaining balance and review among them. I noted the

54. H.C. 58/68 *supra* note 51, ch. 2.

need to be aware of the society's conception of the judicial function. The basis of these considerations is my recognition that the most important asset the judge possesses is the public's confidence in him, that is, the public's sense that he renders justice according to law. If the public does not have this confidence, the judge cannot judge. The judge has neither sword nor purse. All he has is the public's confidence in him.[55] This is an asset that the judge must jealously protect. In one case, I discussed this in the following terms:

> An essential condition of the existence of an independent judicial authority is public confidence that the judicial branch pursues justice on the basis of laws; confidence that the judging is done fairly, neutrally, treating each side equally, and without any hint of personal stake in the outcome; confidence in the high moral level of judging. Without this public confidence, the judicial authority will not be able to function. . . . The public's confidence in the judicial authority is the most precious asset that this branch possesses. It is also among the most precious assets of the nation. De Balzac's expression is well known: "lack of confidence in the judiciary is the beginning of the end of the society." The need for the public's confidence does not mean a need for popularity. The need to ensure confidence means the need to sustain the public's sense that the judicial decision is made in a fair, objective, neutral, and unbiased manner. Not the identity of the claimants, but the strengths of the claims is what determines the result. This means the perception that the judge is not a party to the legal conflict, and that he is fighting not for his own power, but for the rule of law.[56]

Public confidence is not a given. Its existence cannot be taken for granted. The public's confidence is a fluid matter. It must be nurtured. It is easier to damage it than to guard it. Years of effort may be lost forever because of one unfortunate decision. Therefore, in exercising his discretion, the judge must bear this need in mind. If all the legal doctrines do not help and the judge is left with nothing but his conscience, he must ask himself what impact his decision will have on the public's confidence in the judicial system, in other words, on the public's sense that the judge is rendering justice according to the law. This confidence can be damaged by an inappropriate exercise of judicial discretion. From this stems the great importance of the rules of judicial ethics. A careless utterance in the courtroom or in the judgment is capable of undoing confidence that was

55. See Justice Frankfurter, *supra* note 49, ch. 6.
56. H.C. 732/84 *Tsaban v. Minister for Religious Affairs.*

acquired over the course of years. Therefore, every judge must see himself as though the public's confidence in the entire judicial system depended on him and on his conduct (outside the walls of the courthouse as well as inside them) and on the exercise of his discretion. Of course, there is not much one can do with just the public's confidence in adjudication. Yet without it one cannot do anything. The need to ensure confidence does not mean the need to guarantee popularity but rather the need to preserve the public's sense that judicial discretion is being exercised objectively, through a neutral application of the laws and of the fundamental values of the nation; that the judicial discretion is exercised in order to maintain the articles of faith of the people and not the articles of faith of the judge; that the judge is not a party to the power struggles in the state and that he is fighting not for his own power, but for the rule of law. These ideas were expressed eloquently in the following words of Chief Justice Marshall:

> Judicial power, as contradistinguished from the power of the laws, has no existence. Courts are the mere instruments of the law, and can will nothing. When they are said to exercise a discretion, it is a mere legal discretion, a discretion to be exercised in discerning the course prescribed by law; and when that is discerned, it is the duty of the court to follow it. Judicial power is never exercised for the purpose of giving effect to the will of the judge; always for the purpose of giving effect to the will of the legislature; or, in other words, to the will of the law.[57]

Justice Marshall here does not deny judicial discretion. He himself was among the great American judges who exercised judicial discretion in key cases in the constitutional life of the United States. Judicial review of the constitutionality of statutes itself comes from his judgment in *Marbury v. Madison* (1803).[58] In the above-quoted words, Chief Justice Marshall emphasized the basic truth that the judge creates law within the framework of the law and not outside it. In this he sought to ensure the public's confidence in the judicial branch. Thus, the judge is not the mouth through which the legislature speaks, but neither is the legislature the mouth of the judge. The judge is faithful to the legal norm, to the legal system, and to the supremacy of law. It is this loyalty of the judge to the law and its institutions that inspires public confidence in the judge.

57. *Osborn v. The Bank of the United States* 22 U.S. (9 Wheat) 738, 866 (1824).
58. 5 U.S. (1 Cranch) 137 (1803).

Public Confidence and Public Awareness

I have emphasized the essential nature of maintaining public confidence in the courts system. An important question is, What is the relation between the need to ensure this confidence and the public's awareness of the existence of judicial discretion and judicial lawmaking? I noted that the judge must be aware of the existence of judicial discretion. Does the public also have to be aware of it? Opinion is divided over this issue.[59] One view—held mainly by judges—maintains that it is not advisable to raise public consciousness about the existence of judicial discretion and judicial lawmaking.[60] The words of Lord Radcliffe are representative of this approach:

> Personally, I think that judges will serve the public interest better if they keep quiet about their legislative function. No doubt they will discreetly contribute to change in the law, because they cannot do otherwise, even if they would. The judge who shows his hand, who advertises what he is about, may indeed show that he is a strong spirit, unfettered by the past, but I doubt very much whether he is not doing more harm to general confidence in the law as a constant, safe in the hands of the judges, than he is doing good to the law's credit as a set of rules nicely attuned to the sentiments of the day.[61]

The reasons for this approach are complex. In part, they are connected to the desire to maintain a certain level of mystery about the judicial process. They rely on the belief that the public's confidence in the law will be shaken if it realizes that not only the legislature but also the judge creates the law.[62] They draw sustenance from the approach that the public's confidence in the judicial branch and the independence of the

---

59. See Atiyah, *supra* note 9.
60. See Edmund-Davies, *supra* note 38, ch. 3; Devlin, *supra* note 5, at 12.
61. Radcliffe, *supra* note 42, ch. 3, at 265.
62. See C. Radcliffe, *The Law and Its Compass* 39 (1960): "We know all this, it is commonplace among lawyers. It recognizes, of course, the judge's law-making capacity, a capacity which only judges themselves, and that for excellent reasons, are likely to dispute. It is to me a matter of surprise that so much pen and ink has been employed by commentators in demonstrating this fairly obvious conclusion. If judges prefer to adopt the formula— for that is what it is—that they merely declare the law and do not make it, they do no more than show themselves wise men in practice. Their analysis may be weak, but their perception of the nature of the law is sound. Men's respect for it will be greater, the more imperceptible its development."

judicial branch will be tainted if the public learns that judges not only declare existing law, but also create new law.[63]

I cannot accept this approach. It confuses two questions that should be kept separate: What is the desirable scope of judicial lawmaking? and How advisable is it that the public know about this lawmaking? It is possible, of course, that in a given system judicial creativity and judicial lawmaking have reached proportions that might shake the public's confidence in the judiciary, if the public knew about them. The proper way to deal with this situation is not to hide the reality from the public, but rather to change the reality. Therefore, whatever the extent of judicial creation and judicial lawmaking, the public deserves to know about it. Professor Stone wrote about this:

> Citizens left to believe that burdens flowing from a judgment inevitably flowed from pre-existing law, when in fact decision on the law might have been the other way, are in a sense being deceived. The right to know the architect of our obligations may be as much a part of liberty, as the right to know our accuser and our judge.[64]

In a democratic state, the public is entitled to know who creates the laws and within what borders. The truth should not be concealed. The public's confidence in the judiciary will be hurt when the public finds out that judges say one thing and do another. Judge Jerome Frank discussed this:

> Courts should not conceal from the public their delegated power of sub-legislation, but should make every effort to inform the citizenry of how that power is exercised. If judges speak always of "interpretation," if always they avoid and resent the use of the phrase "judicial legislation," they conduct

---

63. See Radcliffe, *supra* note 42, ch. 3, at 271: "We cannot run the risk of finding the archetypal image of the judge confused in men's minds with the very different image of the legislature." See also Lord Scarman in *Duport Steel Ltd. v. Sirs* [1980] 1 All E.R. 529, 551: "Great judges are in their different ways judicial activists. But the Constitution's separation of powers, or more accurately functions, must be observed if judicial dependence is not to be put at risk. For if people and Parliament come to think that the judicial power is to be confined by nothing other than the judge's sense of what is right (or, as Selden put it, by the length of the Chancellor's foot), confidence in the judicial system will be replaced by the fear of it becoming uncertain and arbitrary in its application. Society will then be ready for parliament to cut the power of the judges. Their power to do justice will become more restricted by law than it need be, or is today."

64. Stone, *supra* note 40, ch. 1, at 678.

themselves misleadingly, undemocratically. Correct advice to our citizens about the courts necessitates telling them the difference between "legislative legislation" and "judicial legislation."[65]

Thus, we must point out to the public the true borders of judicial discretion. We must explain that judicial discretion, judicial creativity, and judicial lawmaking all exist in practice; that they are done by virtue of the (explicit or implicit) approval of the legislature itself; that they are not unlimited; that the public, in ways established in the law for this purpose and through the bodies authorized to do so, is always entitled to intervene and to bring about a result it desires; and that such intervention does not harm judges or their status. When the public becomes aware of the truth, it will have more confidence in judges than if it is led astray. As Justice Douglas said,

> But the more blunt, open, and direct course is truer to democratic traditions. It reflects the candor of Cardozo. The principle of full disclosure has as much place in government as it does in the market place. A judiciary that discloses what it is doing and why it does it will breed understanding. And confidence based on understanding is more enduring than confidence based on awe.[66]

Awareness and Education

The main difficulty in enlightening the public lies in the public's ability to understand, for if judicial discretion is a difficult matter even for lawyers, it is all the more so for laymen. It contains fine and ultrafine distinctions. One suspects that the true picture will not be properly absorbed. There is a danger that once someone has lost his naivete, he will no longer know what to believe in.[67] Someone who has become convinced that the judge is not always the mouth of the legislature may believe that the law is always the mouth through which the judge speaks. There is an ever-present danger of a swing from one extreme to the other. But the solution to the difficulty lies not in ignoring it, but rather in attempting to solve it. When the public has trouble understanding, explanations should not be kept from it. It must be taught to understand.

---

65. Frank, "Words and Music: Some Remarks on Statutory Interpretation," 47 *Colum. L. Rev.* 1259, 1271 (1947).

66. Douglas, "Stare Decisis," 49 *Colum. L. Rev.* 735, 754 (1949).

67. See Holmes, *supra* note 122, ch. 1, at 292: "When the ignorant are taught to doubt they do not know what they safely may believe."

In an age in which youngsters do wonders with computers, it is possible to explain to them judicial discretion and its limitations. Just as the public is able to understand the secondary legislation of the executive branch, so too can it understand—if it is explained—the secondary legislation of the judicial branch. This educational function is placed, first and foremost, on the general educational system. It is placed in particular on the judges themselves. They must avoid repeating the old formulas, which do not reflect reality. They must explain the reality as it exists. This can sometimes be done in the judgment itself, sometimes outside the framework of the court. To be sure, the effort to educate must not be exaggerated. One must always come back to the basic principle that the judge's main function is to adjudicate, and all the rest is secondary. But within the framework of these secondary functions, I see an important place for education. The judge does not merely adjudicate. He also has an educational role.[68]

68. See Tucker, "The Judge's Role in Educating the Public about the Law," 31 *Cath. U.L. Rev.* 201 (1981); Rostow, *supra* note 3, at 208.

Chapter 8
Judicial Policy and Models of Adjudication

Judicial Policy Defined

Every judge should consciously formulate for himself a judicial policy for solving the hard cases. This policy involves the basic considerations—normative, institutional, and interinstitutional—that guide the judge in the exercise of his discretion. This policy is the sum of the judge's conceptions of how he will exercise his discretion in the hard cases. These are the basic standards for the use of judicial discretion within the range of reasonableness. Judicial policy, therefore, is an organized, conscious notion of how to handle the difficulties of the hard cases, or what Justice Witkon called " 'judicial planning,' a conscious, articulated process of planning for the future development of the law."[1]

Judicial Policy and Legal Policy

It is important to distinguish between judicial policy and legal policy.[2] Judicial policy is the conscious formulation of the considerations according to which the judge chooses among the different lawful alternatives open to him in the hard cases. Legal policy, on the other hand, refers to the goal of legal norms—the principles, social goals, and standards that the legislated or judge-made legal norm is intended to attain. The judge's

---

1. Witkon, *supra* note 17, ch. 1.
2. See Barak, *supra* note 2, ch. 3, at 46. Instead of legal policy one can talk about public policy.

judicial policy operates within the framework of the options that the legal policy leaves open in the hard cases.[3]

Every legal norm has a legal policy specific to it. In the easy cases and the intermediate cases, the formulation of this legal policy does not involve judicial discretion. In the hard cases, however, the judge must exercise judicial discretion in order to arrive at the legal policy. In the hard cases, every legal norm has a range of legal policy considerations that set it apart. Within the context of this range, judicial policy operates. While the legal policy changes from one norm to the next, judicial policy does not undergo these transformations. To the contrary: it is a comprehensive policy that guides the judge in the choice he must make in the hard cases, with respect to any given norm. Yet, it would be wrong to say that the legal policy is different for each norm while the judicial policy is the same. Thus, within the framework of judicial policy, the judge may formulate standards that take into account the nature of the particular legal norm in whose context the judicial discretion is then being exercised. Judicial policy changes with the move from one type of legal norm to another. However, this change in judicial policy is not the same thing as the change in legal policy. The change in judicial policy results from differences among norms when viewed against the backdrop of all the normative, institutional, and interinstitutional considerations. The change in legal policy reflects the different goals of different norms.

It is quite difficult to make this distinction between judicial policy and legal policy. Arguably, the judicial policy is simply the legal policy of the rule requiring the judge to act reasonably in the hard cases. Thus, the judicial policy is the legal policy of the norm of reasonableness.[4] However, this distinction between legal policy and judicial policy seems to be quite useful for it highlights different categories of considerations. Through the legal policy, the judge in the hard case discovers the various

---

3. Thus, judicial policy is meaningless in the easy cases and the intermediate cases. The judge must choose the one and only lawful possibility, and there is no room for judicial policy. The judicial policy in these cases can be said to be to choose the sole lawful solution. This usage eliminates the need for this special terminology in these cases. Judicial policy is important, therefore, only in the hard cases.

4. Sometimes judicial policy constitutes the legal policy of a given norm, beyond the norm of reasonableness itself. Thus, for example, when the norm being interpreted establishes the court's jurisdiction or the remedies that are in its power to grant, considerations of judicial policy may become part of the considerations of legal policy of that norm.

options that a given legal norm places before him. For example, when the legal norm is a statutory norm, the judge sets out to discover the legislative purposes, and in the hard cases, he formulates the various possibilities that follow from the goals behind the legislation. The legal policy, therefore, reveals the range of legitimacy of the various options in the hard cases. Judicial policy, on the other hand, involves the formulation of standards by the judge for choosing among the alternatives available to him in the hard cases. Quite naturally, these standards are external to the norm and to its purpose, though they are intended to determine the choice among the various options, all of which are consistent with the purpose of the norm. Thus, these standards are the normative, institutional, and interinstitutional considerations that I discussed earlier.

The Nonbinding Nature of Judicial Policy

By their very nature, the principles of judicial policy are not binding on the judge. If these principles were binding, judicial discretion would disappear. The case would no longer be a hard case and would instead become an easy case or an intermediate case. Judicial policy is not a policy anchored in legal rules. It consists of sets of considerations. Its significance lies in an awareness of the freedom of choice and the weighing of normative, institutional, and interinstitutional factors in the selection among the various alternatives. Of course, some of the factors may become so universally accepted over the years that case law or legislation will treat them as binding law. This means that judicial discretion will be further limited, and some cases will change from being hard to being easy or intermediate cases. Yet until this transformation occurs, judicial policy is an extralegal policy.

Judicial Policy—A Policy of the Individual Judge or of the Judicial Branch?

Judicial policy reflects the standards the judge consciously develops to solve the hard cases. Does each judge have his own policy? If judicial discretion in the hard cases were exercised purely subjectively, then the judicial policy would also change from one judge to the next. Yet as we have observed, one does not find this taking place. Judicial discretion contains a broad, objective swath that reflects what is accepted by the community of judges. Alongside this, of course, there is another area in which the objective standards are useless, and where the judge is left to his own devices. Within the context of the objective area, one can say that judicial policy, instead of being different for each judge, is common to all judges, that is, to the entire judicial branch. In this area, the judicial policy is the policy of the judicial branch. But as we have seen, next to the objective element in the exercise of judicial discretion there is also a subjective element, reflecting the judge's worldview and based on his personal experience and his conception of the judicial role. This subjective component—when purified of anything that is exceptional and extraordinary—differs, by its nature, from judge to judge.

Thus, judicial policy combines within it a variety of elements, some of which are common to all judges and some of which change from one judge to the next. The stronger the objective element in a given legal system, the greater the share of the judicial policy that is common to all judges. On the other hand, where the subjective element is stronger, the common aspect of the judicial policy narrows and the individual element gains. The greatness of the individual judge lies in his ability at times to conquer his impulse and to operate according to the general policy,[5] even if it differs from his own policy, and at other times to go against what is commonly accepted, giving free flight to his own policy. Of course, the central question becomes, In what circumstances should the judge conquer his impulses, and in what cases should he let them loose? Each judge must answer this for himself, basing his response on his experience and expertise.

The Policies of the Judicial, Legislative, and Executive Branches

We have seen that in certain contexts, one can speak of the policy of the judicial branch in its exercise of discretion. Is there similarly a policy of the legislative branch in the exercise of its discretion, and a policy of the executive branch in its exercise of discretion? In my view, these questions must be answered affirmatively.

I have said that judicial policy is the set of factors that guide the judicial branch when it chooses among a number of options that the law

5. See Mendelson, "Mr. Justice Frankfurter on the Construction of Statutes," 43 *Cal. L. Rev.* 652, 673 (1955): "The genius of a great judge in the reading of statutes lies not in a bias for this or that tactical value, however worthy, but in his respect for the limits of his own function—for that grand strategic division of labor between legislature and court, between Nation and State."

places before it. Judicial policy reflects the considerations—unique to the institution of judging[6]—that balance among normative, institutional, and interinstitutional factors. Alongside this policy, there are policies of the legislative and executive branches. These branches, too, are sometimes faced with situations in which they must chose one among a number of lawful possibilities. The legislative branch finds itself in this situation when it enacts a statute in a constitutional system. The executive branch faces this normative situation when it operates within the context of the constitution and the law. When these branches, each in its own sphere, face a situation of "discretion," they must formulate for themselves a policy for the exercise of the discretion. Indeed the normative, institutional, and interinstitutional considerations that I discussed also apply to the legislative and executive branches. These, too, must take into account the manner of the system's growth, its consistency and its natural development. So, too, do these branches have to consider their institutional limitations and their relationships with the other branches. Therefore, these branches also must articulate a conscious policy in the exercise of their discretion. For example, they must formulate a position as to when it is appropriate for a given legal norm—such as the rules of binding precedent or the rules of interpretation—to find expression in a piece of statutory legislation, and when this norm should develop by adjudication.

Of course, the policies of the legislative branch and the executive branch differ from that of the judicial branch. All three must formulate a policy that weighs the normative, institutional, and interinstitutional elements, yet the weight given to each of these elements as well as to their content differs from one branch to the other. For example, all the branches must take into account institutional limitations, yet these limitations change from one institution to the next. The limitations of the judicial branch are not the same as the limitations of the other branches. Thus the judicial branch must operate within the framework of society's shared values. On the other hand, the legislative branch—especially when it is not restricted by a constitution—can inject into the system new values that go against the social consensus. No doubt, it will be the rare case in which the legislative or executive branch will choose to act against the social consensus. Yet the nature of these branches' consider-

6. See Summers, *supra* note 21, ch. 2, at 723.

ations in making their choice differs from the decision-making of the judicial branch. Indeed, the nature of the branch dictates the nature of its considerations. Considerations of a different nature guide the legislative, executive, and judicial branch in the formulation of discretion.

The three branches of government all exercise discretion. But they do so in different ways and on the basis of different considerations. Consequently, they attain different results. The three branches all go down the route of legislation, but they travel in different vehicles. So their speed and the cost of their journey differ, as do the quality of the ride and the dangers and obstacles encountered along the way.[7]

Judicial Policy—The Politics of Judging?

Judicial policy might be said to be the politics of adjudication. Yet the term *politics,* as we have seen, has many meanings. To the extent one understands this term to mean lines of policy that determine how judicial discretion should be used, one can say that judicial policy is the politics of the judicial branch.[8] Similarly, to the extent one understands in the term *political* the exercise of governmental power that sets society's course,[9] the allocation of its resources,[10] and the policy it follows, judicial policy is indeed the politics of adjudication.[11]

If on the other hand *politics* is understood to refer to the issues upon which the nation's political parties disagree, and if one understands the politics of adjudication to mean the taking into account by judges of the views espoused by political parties in their contest for dominance, then judicial policy and politics obviously have nothing in common, and the less judicial discretion is identified with politics, the better.

The term *politics* is vague, much more obscure than it is clear. It immediately arouses opposition, and judges would therefore do well to

---

7. See Breitel, "The Lawmakers," *Cardozo Memorial Lectures,* vol. 2, 807, 822: "The two organs of government are traveling on the same road, only in different vehicles. The difference in vehicles makes for important differences in mode of operation, speed, and who can pass whom."

8. See MacCormick, *supra* note 20, ch. 1, at 238.

9. See Bell, *supra* note 38, ch. 1, at 247.

10. See Miller and Scheflin, "The Power of the Supreme Court in the Age of the Positive State: A Preliminary Excurse Part One: On Candor and the Court, or Why Bamboozle the Natives?" *Duke L.J.* 273, 274 (1967).

11. See Shapiro, "Judicial Modesty, Political Reality and Preferred Position," 47 *Cornell L.Q.* 175 (1962).

distance themselves from it. Nonetheless, its identification with judicial policy holds an important lesson for adjudication. It is essential for the judicial branch to understand the importance not only of how it perceives itself, but also of how the other branches view it, its actions, its role, and its functioning. It is inevitable that what the judge considers a normal adjudicative act deciding a dispute on the basis of a legal norm will sometimes be interpreted by the other branches, and by the general public, as a political act that threatens positions of power that those branches hold dear. The judge must recognize this reality. The deputy president, Justice Landau, discussed this in the following terms:

> There is still a great fear that the court will appear as though it has abandoned its appropriate place and stooped down into the arena of public debate, and that its decision will be received by part of the public with applause and by the other part with emotional and total rejection. In this sense, I see myself here, as one upon whom has been imposed this duty, to rule on the basis of law in every matter properly brought before the court, for I know in advance that the general public will not look to the legal reasoning but rather only to the final conclusion, and the rightful place of the court as an institution may be harmed, beyond the debates upon which the public is divided. Yet what can we do? This is our role and this is our duty as judges.[12]

''This is our role and this is our duty as judges.'' The judge must decide on the basis of his best judicial consciousness, which is founded upon the proper judicial policy. In so doing, he must recognize the charge concerning the ''politics'' of adjudication. Yet this claim must not control his actions. I spoke of this in a case:

> The entire issue is important, and stands at the center of our constitutional life. Questions of the rule of law and the authority of law combined in it with questions of the president's power to pardon, and the exercise of this power. We will deal with all of these from a legal perspective. The public is embroiled over this issue, but it is not this tumult that dictates our steps. We operate according to constitutional standards, and according to basic legal values that reflect the articles of faith of our national life. Our approach is guided not by fleeting moods, but by the basic national conceptions of our existence as a democratic state. . . . We know that the entire issue is the focus of public debate, and that from the viewpoint of political dynamics, our judgment may be used as a weapon in the struggle of political forces. We

12. H.C. 390/79 *Dweikat* v. *State of Israel*, 34 P.D. (1) 1, 4.

regret this, but we must carry out our judicial task. . . . We are one of the arms of government and our role is to make sure that the other arms operate within the framework of the law in order to ensure the rule of law over the government. The branches of government are lofty, but the law is higher than us all. We will not be fulfilling our judicial role unless we review, in the context of claims properly brought, the actions of the other branches, as are revealed in the claims now before us.[13]

Proper judicial policy—yes; politics of adjudication[14]—yes; politics by adjudication—by no means.

THE MODEL OF ADJUDICATION

The Various Models

The legal literature commonly distinguishes among different models of adjudication.[15] These distinctions mostly concern the activity of the system's supreme court, with the various models aimed at describing the nature of the activity of the state's supreme judicial institution. All the models assume judicial activity—in other words, decision in a dispute. They differ on the scope of judicial legislation, that is, the creation of a new norm. Some of the models reflect their creators' image of an ideal situation. Some of them are said to be models of a desired, but not hypothetical situation. Others believe that this hypothetical situation is dangerous and represents an undesirable state to which the existing model may deteriorate.

There are three basic, hypothetical models of adjudication by the supreme judicial tribunal: the declaratory model, the policy model, and the model of legislation as an incident to adjudication. At one end of the spectrum is the declaratory model and at the other end, the policy model. Between them one can locate the model of legislation as an incident to adjudication. Each of the three models has a solid core, which is surrounded by a penumbra. In this penumbral region there are many additional submodels, like planets that revolve around the sun. Of course, the

---

13. H.C. 428/86 *Barzilai* v. *State of Israel,* 40 P.D. (3) 505.

14. See J. A. G. Griffith, *The Politics of the Judiciary* (3d ed., 1986).

15. See Weiler, *supra* note 17, ch. 1; Winter, "The Growth of Judicial Power," in *The Judiciary in a Democratic Society* 29 (Theberge, ed., 1979); Atiyah, "Judges and Policy," 15 *Isr. L. Rev.* 346 (1980).

further one strays from the core, the weaker is the bond to it, and at a certain point one enters the domain of the gravitational pull of another model. Thus, the distinctions among the various models, especially at the margins, are imprecise, and in the penumbral areas they overlap.

The Declaratory Model

According to the declaratory model, the judge is involved in adjudication—in other words, in deciding disputes. Inasmuch as he establishes a rule necessary for the decision, he is simply declaring something that already exists. Even when he lays down a new rule, this is revelation, not creation. In his normative activity, the judge has no discretion. The law exists, and the judge must abide by it. There is a map, and the judge must follow its route.

This is the model that Montesquieu had in mind.[16] The judge is the mouthpiece of the legislature and repeats the language of the law.[17] One also finds this model in Blackstone's writings.[18] The judge expounds the rule hidden in the system.[19] Even when a subsequent judicial ruling overturns an earlier one, this does not mean that the old one was erroneous, but rather that it was not law at all. Case law is, therefore, retroactive by its very nature.

In the modern period, one finds this declaratory perspective at the core of the works of several writers, among them Professor Ronald Dworkin.[20] Although he does not accept all the features of the declaratory model, at the center of his approach lies the thesis that the judge has no discretion. The judge must operate according to the principles (where common law is concerned) or according to the principles and policies (where legislation is concerned) that exist in the system. He must effectuate that which is embedded within the system. He does not create

16. Montesquieu, *supra* note 13, ch. 1, at 209.

17. Professor Morris Cohen called it the Phonograph Theory: see M. Cohen, "The Process of Judicial Legislation," *Law and Social Order* 12, 113 (1933).

18. See Blackstone, *Commentaries of the Law of England* 88 (13th ed., 1978).

19. On the declaratory theory of law, see ch. 3. The declaratory theory is invoked and discussed within the framework of the question on prospective overruling of precedent: see Friedmann, "Limits of Judicial Law-Making and Prospective Overruling," 29 *Mod. L. Rev.* 593 (1966); Freeman, "Standards of Adjudication, Judicial Law Making and Prospective Overruling," 26 *C.L.P.* 166 (1973); Tedeschi, "Prospective Revision of Precedent," 8 *Isr. L. Rev.* 173 (1973).

20. Dworkin, "Natural Law Revisited," 34 *U. Fla. L. Rev.* 165 (1982).

rights; rather, he recognizes rights that exist independently of him. This view follows from a moral-liberal philosophical approach that acknowledges "natural rights." Rights are too important a matter to be left to judges.

The Policy Model

The policy model holds that the judge is involved not only with adjudication, but also with policy. Indeed, of the two, the adjudicative function is the more marginal. The judge's main task is to make policy. In this, the judge resembles the regular legislator. Like the legislator, the judge determines the society's values as he sees them and formulates the law accordingly.[21] The judge has absolute discretion. He is a lawmaker in his own right. When legislating, he takes into account considerations of societal consensus, much as the regular legislator must do. By ignoring these, he may damage the court's effectiveness. Thus, the judge has social goals. He plans strategy and tactics—within and without the four walls of the court—for attaining these goals.[22]

This model, which both lawyers and political scientists have sketched,[23] is based on the "realist" philosophy of the thirties.[24] It is a good reflection of the views of the adherents of the Critical Legal Studies school.[25]

The Model of Legislation as an Incident to Adjudication

This model places the decision in the specific conflict at the epicenter of the adjudicative process. Yet it also recognizes that incidentally to his decision in the conflict, the judge establishes law. Usually he repeats existing law. However, in a small but significant number of cases, he creates new law. In doing so, the judge exercises discretion, which is not absolute, but limited.

21. See M. Shapiro, *Law and Politics in the Supreme Court* (1964); M. Shapiro, *Courts* (1981).

22. Murphy, *Elements of Judicial Strategy* (1964).

23. See Miller, *supra* note 1, ch. 1; Schubert, *Judicial Decision Making* (1963); Dahl, "Decision Making in a Democracy: The Supreme Court as a National Policy-Maker," 6 *J. Pub. Law* 279 (1957); Glazer, "Towards an Imperial Judiciary," 41 *The Public Interest* 104 (1975); Goldman and Lamb (eds.), *Judicial Conflict and Consensus: Behavioral Studies of American Appellate Courts* (1986).

24. See *supra* note 104, ch. 1.

25. For bibliography see Kennedy and Klare, "A Bibliography of Critical Legal Studies," 94 *Yale L.J.* 461 (1984).

Within this model there are, of course, several submodels. Professor John Bell[26] distinguishes between the "consensus model" and the "model of legislation in the interstices": the former is based on the view that the boundaries of the judicial creation are delimited by the societal consensus;[27] the basis of the second model is that the judge acts as a legislator within the law's cracks.[28] The model of "legislation as an incident to adjudication" is accepted by the modern positivists (such as Hart and McCormick) and by the members of the Legal Process school (such as Hart, Sacks, and Fuller). This model is said to reflect the holdings of the British courts.[29]

The Proper Model: The Model of Limited Judicial Discretion

In this book I express reservations about the policy model, which, I maintain, does not accurately reflect the judicial process. It fails to describe correctly the judicial reality. It is also not the appropriate model; normative, institutional, and interinstitutional considerations compel its rejection. Taking this model to its extreme, one reaches the end of adjudication.

The declaratory model has some positive features. It preserves the ethos of adjudication. It has ensured public confidence in adjudication in the past and is probably equipped to continue to ensure this confidence, at least in the near future. It may protect fundamental rights that are recognized in the system. Yet as a model of judging, it does not reflect reality and is useless. It is based on a fiction and thus does more harm than good. In the final analysis, it boils down to the claim—which none dispute—that the judge must act within the range of formal legitimacy. The declaratory model cannot tell him how he should do so.

The only proper model, in my view, is the model of legislation as an incident to adjudication. This model recognizes the centrality of the decision in the dispute to the judicial process. However, it also acknowledges the existence of judicial legislation in the hard cases. In general, it correctly reflects reality. It represents an appropriate model to which one should aspire.

26. See *supra* note 38, ch. 1.
27. See Devlin, *supra* note 5, ch. 7; Wellington, *supra* note 20, ch. 1.
28. See *Southern Pacific Company v. Jensen,* 244 U.S. 205, 221 (1917) (Holmes J.): "I recognize without hesitation that judges do and must legislate, but they can do so only interstitially; they are confined from molar to molecular motions."
29. Bell, *supra* note 38, ch. 1.

I find fault with the consensus submodel because it focuses on only one aspect of the judicial process. To be sure, I agree that where a consensus exists, the judge should operate accordingly. Yet what if there is no consensus, or if it is unknown? The principle of consensus can and should constitute an important consideration in the framework of judicial discretion. But it cannot be a model that stands alone.

Neither do I find the submodel of legislation in the interstices to be appropriate, for it takes insufficient account of the normative, institutional, and interinstitutional factors. A judge neither thinks nor acts like a legislator and, even when he operates in the gaps of a statute, he does so in a judicial rather than a legislative manner. The judicial thought process controls all the judge's activity, whether this activity is directed at the law itself or at its interstices. A judge must think *about* the legislator; he must not think *like* a legislator. The normative, institutional, and interinstitutional considerations create a network of factors—at times supplementary and at other times contradictory—that the judge must weigh when he exercises discretion in the hard cases. On the basis of these considerations, he must formulate a judicial policy, which is the policy of the judicial branch.

The best model, in my view, is the model of limited discretion discussed by me. The judge creates law as an incident to the act of adjudication. He does so through the use of the limited judicial discretion that has been granted him.

Chapter 9
The Use of
Judicial Discretion:
The Case of
Overruling a Precedent

THE QUESTION

The legal problem of overruling precedent is a critical one, and it is faced by most supreme courts, both in civil law and common law traditions.[1] The authority to overrule exists in most countries, whether of civil law or common law tradition. Even the House of Lords in the United Kingdom is not bound any more by its precedents. The Supreme Court of the United States was never bound by its own decisions, and neither are those of Canada, Australia, and Israel. In all these countries, the question is the same: when should the highest court overrule its own decisions? Clearly, if a prior ruling is acceptable to the Court, the question does not arise. But what if the prior ruling is not acceptable? Here we must distinguish between two types of prior decisions. At times, the Court may view a prior decision as incorrect, unlawful, or premised upon a mistake (a wrong decision in an easy case). In such cases, the

1. See R. Cross, *Precedent in English Law* 12 (3d ed., 1977); Friedman, "Stare Decisis of Common Law and Under the Civil Code and Quebec," 31 *Can. Bar. Rev.* 723 (1953); Silving, "*Stare Decisis* in the Civil and in the Common Law," 35 *Revista Jurídica de la V. de Puerto Rico* 145 (1966); Cappelletti, "The Doctrine of *Stare Decisis* and the Civil Law: A Fundamental Difference or No Difference at All?" in *Festschrift für Konard Zweigert* 381 (Bernstein, Kotz, eds., 1981); Koopman, "*Stare Decisis* in European Law," in *Essays in European Law and Legislation* (O'Keefle and Schemars, eds., 1982); Bale, "Casting Off the Mooring Ropes of Binding Precedent," 58 *Can. Bar. Rev.* 255 (1980).

Court must deviate from the prior stand.[2] "It is both the moral and legal duty of the court to rectify the error and establish the correct rule."[3] But at other times, the prior decision is a possible one. It is lawful, but not an alternative the present Court would have chosen had it sat in judgment. These are the hard cases, which admit of more than one legal solution.[4] In such circumstances, it may be said that the present Court has discretion to overrule.[5] What considerations must guide the Court in making its decision?

THE TEST OF REASONABLENESS

The Supreme Court is faced with a hard case. The legal question in point can be answered in one of two ways. In a prior decision of the Supreme Court one answer was chosen, but now the Court considers the other one preferable. Shall the Court overrule its precedent? It is free to choose, being obliged neither to follow its precedent nor to deviate therefrom. In making the choice, however, *the judge* must act reasonably.[6] He may not toss a coin; rather, he must weigh reasonable considerations and balance opposing views. The judge must, on the one hand, consider the aggregate of considerations that support honoring the precedent and, on the other hand, appraise the full scope of those arguments that call for its overruling in favor of the alternative choice. The judge must grant appropriate weight to each set of considerations. Having done so, he must place them in the balance and choose the preponderate among them. In other words, he must select the view that gives rise to greater good than harm.[7] In carrying out all of this, the judge exercises discre-

2. See *Schick v. Minister of the Interior,* 26 P.D. (2) 33, at 42; Landau, *supra* note 17, ch. 1, at 296. C.A. 29/59 *Ein Harod HaKibbutz HaMe'uhad Ltd. v. Lugasi,* 13 P.D. 1883.

3. H.C. 547/84 *Ohf Ha'Emek Agricultural Society v. Ramat Yishai Municipal Council,* 40 P.D. (1) 113.

4. See ch. 1.

5. In several decisions it has been stated that when a case can be argued either way, there should be no departure from precedent. See, for example, *Shick, supra* note 2; also see *R. v. National Insurance Comp.,* [1972] A.C. 944 at 996. In my opinion, it is precisely in those cases that "can be argued either way" that the question of whether or not to overrule precedent arises.

6. See *Ohf Ha'Emek, supra* note 3, at 141.

7. See *United States v. Southern Underwriters Ass.,* 322 U.S. 533 (1944) (Jackson and Stone JJ.); also see *Florida Department of Health v. Florida Nursing Home Ass.,* 450 U.S. 147, 155 (1980) (Stevens J.).

tion. The contending views do not line themselves up before the judge
tagged with their appropriate weights. It is the judge who must make the
evaluation and, absent statutory direction, this act involves discretion.
Deciding among opposing considerations is a matter that concerns the
judicial policy[8] of the individual judge[9] and must be executed in conso-
nance with the judicial policy of the judiciary. The decision must fall in
accordance with a scheme of normative, institutional, and interinstitutional considerations, which I shall discuss. Of course, to the extent that
these considerations have been applied, the judge is on his own[10] and
must choose the solution that he considers preferable. In weighing
whether or not to overrule a precedent, a judge must act objectively. He
must realize not his personal views, but those that he sees as fitting the
demands of his society. Moreover, he must not show preference to his
own prior judgments as against those of others or promote previously
accepted or rejected ideas merely because they were once his own. All
are equal before the judge—including his own decisions.

Overruling a precedent of the Supreme Court is a serious, responsible
matter. Evaluating all the aspects fully and deciding whether or not to
overrule demands great sensitivity. This is part of the judge's craft—but
it is not craft alone. It is a process that must be confronted with unemo-
tional reason. Precedent is not holy and overruling it is not prophetic.
The judge faces a complex system of considerations of which he must be
aware. He must also be cognizant that overruling precedent is legislation
in its functional sense. Such legislation is part of the judge's duty; he may
not hide behind the claim that it is the exclusive realm of the legislature.
Developing the law and adjusting it to social realities are the role of the
judge. For the realization of this role, it is at times necessary that a court
overrule its own precedent.

NORMATIVE CONSIDERATIONS

Every judge acts within a given normative framework,[11] and his decision
must be consonant with that framework. This also applies to a decision

8. See Yadin, "True and Stable," 28 *HaPraklit* 152 (1979).
9. See *Yehoshua v. Appeals Committee Under the Invalids (Pension and Rehabilita-
tion) Law, 5709–1949*, 9 P.D. 617 (Witkon J.).
10. See Schaefer, *supra* note 94, ch. 2, at 22.
11. See ch. 5.

overruling an earlier precedent. Indeed, an important argument in favor of respecting precedent is that overruling it upsets and harms the normative framework.[12] The claim is that respect for precedent insures stability,[13] certainty, consistency, continuity, and reliance and thereby allows the public, the governmental agencies, and their attorneys to plan their conduct. Overruling precedent undermines the stability of the system and can introduce chaos. It upsets the certainty of the law. An existing, known rule is preferable to the uncertainty introduced by changes intended to improve it.[14] These changes seriously conflict with the reasonable expectations of the public who conducted their affairs in reliance upon the existing rule. Overruling precedent erodes consistency, a basic characteristic of every normative system, and one founded upon justice, fairness, and equality. Consistency implies that similar cases be similarly decided, but in the wake of deviation from precedent, similar cases receive disparate solutions. Last, deviation disrupts the continuity of the system and conflicts with the need that the present be integrated with the past in order to meet the future. The judge who deviates from existing precedent does not align himself with the existing legal fabric but rather breaks away to march to his own drummer. The resulting suspicion is that "in time the court will change from a 'house of judgment' to a 'house of judges' with as many opinions as members."[15] This undermines the entire system and its ability to contend with present needs.[16]

As against those considerations supporting the honoring of precedent, there are others that support deviation therefrom. These too are concerned with the normative system. At root stands the assumption that in order to survive, a normative system must develop and conform to changing needs.[17] Law governs the relations between persons, and when changes occur in those relations, it is only fitting that the law change as well. The history of law is the history of conforming the law to the

12. See Wasserstrom, *supra* note 89, ch. 2, at 60; Hart and Sacks, *supra* note 26, ch. 1, at 587.

13. See *Balan v. The Executors of the Estate of Litwinski,* 15 P.D. 71, 76 (Silberg J.).

14. See *Sheddon v. Goodrich,* 32 E.R. 441 (1803), 447 (Lord Elden): "It is better that the law should be certain than that every judge should speculate upon improvements of it."

15. Silberg J. in *Balan, supra* note 13, at 75.

16. See *supra* note 3, at 145.

17. See Barak, "Case Law and Social Reality," in *Sefer Sussmann (Festschrift in Memory of Justice Yoel Sussmann)* (Jerusalem, 1984, in Hebrew), 71.

changing needs of society. A normative system that does not allow for growth will ultimately stagnate. Stability, certainty, consistency, and continuity can therefore be insured only by insuring change. Standing still does not make for stability;[18] a widening gap between life and law leads to a state of instability that continues until the law changes. Just as an eagle maintains stability through motion, so the law is stable only when in motion.[19] Consistency and continuity can be attained only if case law develops, if society's new ideas are absorbed into the system, and if old, outdated ideas are discarded.[20]

Furthermore, occasionally a judicial decision may be adopted that, already when made, fails to reflect society's sense of justice. Maintaining such a precedent only aggravates that feeling of injustice.[21] Thus the stability and certainty achieved are the stability and certainty of injustice. Such a decision is ultimately injurious in this respect, for no decision can be stable or certain if it fails to reflect society's sense of justice. Indeed, overruling a precedent does upset the expectations of those members of the public who relied upon it. But this difficulty does not always exist. First, in many cases the parties act without knowledge of the rule or, if they are aware of it, without relying on it. Second, even when parties rely on a rule, often that reliance must take into account the possibility of change. Such is the case where a rule is controversial or where judicial opinion has raised the possibility of future change. Last, where there has been true reliance, the change can be made prospective rather than retroactive. Thus the problem of reliance and expectation need not ultimately burden the set of normative considerations.[22]

INSTITUTIONAL CONSIDERATIONS

Institutional considerations[23] support the honoring of precedent. The court is an institution intended to provide a service to the public. First and foremost, this service is the resolution of conflicts between parties on the basis of the existing law. The rule that arises from the resolution is but a by-product, not the essence, of the process. The providing of appropriate

18. See Levontin, "Thoughts on Precedent," 17 *Hok U'Mishpat* 1 (1955).
19. See Sprecher, *supra*, note 94, ch. 2, at 509; Douglas, *"Stare Decisis,"* 49 *Colum. L. Rev.* 735 (1949).
20. See *Kaufmann v. Margins*, 6 P.D. 1005, 1034.
21. See Levontin, *supra* note 18, at 1; also see *Yehoshua, supra* note 9, (Witkon J.).
22. See Cardozo, *supra* note 6, ch. 1, at 146.
23. See ch. 6.

and efficient service justifies the undeviating maintenance of precedent. The parties know what they face; the same law that guided them in conducting themselves before the conflict will serve to resolve it. They need not worry that the law might change, nor invest any effort in anticipation of that prospect. The court functions quickly and efficiently in accordance with tried and true rules. It need not constantly reexamine its assumptions. Indeed, the judicial task would be impossible, and the efforts of generations would be lost, were every decision open to reappraisal every time.[24] This would also encourage renewed recourse to the courts with every change in the bench. Additionally, while the results of an existing rule are known, those of a new rule are indeterminable; due to institutional limitations, the court is often unable to predict the ramifications of its new rule. Last, impartiality is fundamental to the judicial process and to the public's faith in its judges. This condition justifies respecting precedent;[25] deviation from a precedent that could well have been followed may create the impression of nonobjectivity and bias.[26]

But there are also institutional considerations that support overruling precedent. The court is not merely an institution that resolves individual conflicts; incidental to its decision it establishes a rule. When such a rule stems from the Supreme Court in a legal system that gives its decisions the authority of precedent, the rule is law (retroactively or prospectively) in the functional sense. Like the legislature, courts too must review their acts, adjust them to the present demands and correct mistakes—and the tools that serve the court in establishing the law are equally sound in changing it. Such conduct does not conflict with the need to guarantee judicial objectivity and impartiality, as every sensible person recognizes that it is the court's duty to change the law in order to bring it into line with social realities or in order to expunge earlier mistakes.

INTERINSTITUTIONAL CONSIDERATIONS

Interinstitutional considerations[27] also support respect for precedent and nondeviation therefrom. Judicial rule-making raises a problem insofar as its undemocratic nature is concerned. This problem becomes especially acute when the court deviates from its precedent, particularly where the

24. See Cardozo, *supra* note 67, ch. 1, at 149.
25. See Stevens, "The Life Span of a Judge-Made Rule," 58 *N.Y.U.L. Rev.* 1, 2 (1983); Cardozo, *supra* note 67, ch. 1, at 112.
26. See Lucke, *supra* note 70, ch. 1; see ch. 6.
27. See ch. 7.

overruling is prospective. Overruling precedent also infringes upon the principle of separation of powers, whose realization requires that changes in decided law be effected by the legislature rather than by the judiciary. Indeed, there is a sense that a judge transgresses the fine line between adjudicating and legislating when he overrules his precedents, particularly when the overruling is prospective.[28] Moreover, overruling precedent damages the public's conception of the judicial role and undermines the respect in which the public holds the courts and its faith in them. Precedent should not resemble a ticket valid only for the day of purchase.[29] The public has a certain conception regarding the legitimacy of the judicial function. Overruling precedent—particularly when it is prospective—harms that conception.

Countering these arguments, it may be said that overruling precedent does not change the judicial character from what it is absent overruling. The judge is involved in legislation when he creates a new rule that did not previously exist. It makes no difference in terms of democratic considerations or separation of powers if the judge is changing his own decisions. In fact, if we accept that in principle judges are involved in legislation, we must also accept that judges may change their legislation in accordance with the demands of the matter and the times. Furthermore, prospective overruling of precedent is no more legislative in nature than retroactive overruling,[30] but it does preserve the reasonable expectations of the public that relies on the old precedent. Moreover, the willingness of a judge to admit to his mistakes and the system's readiness to conform to changing circumstances by changing rules that appear incorrect increase the public's regard for—and trust in—judges and the judicial system.[31]

JUDICIAL DISCRETION IN WEIGHING CONFLICTING CONSIDERATIONS

I have discussed the various considerations that argue for and against honoring precedent.[32] It would seem that there is no clear-cut answer to

28. See Devlin, *supra,* note 5, ch. 7, at p. 1; Scarman, "Law Reform by Legislative Techniques," 32 *Sask. L. Rev.* 217 (1967).

29. As portrayed by Roberts J. in *Smith v. Alwright,* 321 U.S. 649, 669 (1944).

30. Kocourek and Kovan, "Renovation of the Common Law Through *Stare Decisis,*" 29 *Ill. L. Rev.* 971 (1935).

31. See Douglas, *supra* note 19, at 747.

32. Regarding the economic approach and the principle of precedent and deviation

the question of whether or not to overrule precedent; rather, the answer must be drawn from the balancing of the different considerations.[33] Our concern, therefore, is not with the victory of one or the other approach, but with compromise. It would appear that in arriving at that compromise, our point of departure must be respect for precedent. In my opinion, the various considerations require that the overruling of precedent be the exception rather than the rule and that it be practiced only in light of special circumstances. The burden of proof in this matter must properly rest upon him who seeks to overrule precedent, not upon him who intends to preserve it.[34] Therefore, where the scales are balanced, precedent should be upheld. Only where the scales clearly lean toward overruling should that path be chosen. The judge must ask himself whether the considerations supporting the new rule outweigh those supporting the old rule when taken together with the harm caused by the very act of change itself.[35]

When making this evaluation, weight must be given to the various considerations we have raised. In so doing, stability must not be weighed against change. Such an opposition is artificial, as it does not correctly reflect the nature of the law. The life of the law is one of renewal for the purpose of conforming the rules to social realities on the basis of experience and logic.[36] Thus the question we face is not that of stillness versus motion, rigidity versus flexibility, or stability versus change—rather, it is a question of the rate of motion, the degree of flexibility, and the amount of change. Similarly, in weighing the considerations of whether or not to deviate from a precedent, one should not place in opposition to each other the judicial functions of adjudication (which respects prece-

---

therefrom, see Landes and Posner, "Legal Precedent: A Theoretical and Empirical Analysis," 19 *J. Law and Economics* 249 (1976); for the approach from the political science perspective, see Shapiro, "Towards a Theory of Stare Decisis," 1 *J. Legal Studies* 125 (1972).

33. On the need for balance, see Cardozo, *supra* note 67, ch. 1, at 113; also see Jackson, "Decisional Law and Stare Decisis," 30 *A.B.A.J.* (1944).

34. O. W. Holmes, *Collected Legal Papers* (New York, 1921), 290; Witkon, *supra* note 17, ch. 1, at 480.

35. "Whether a precedent will be modified depends on whether the policies which underline the proposed rule are strong enough to outweigh both the policies which support the existing rule and the disadvantages of making a change." Schaefer, *supra* note 94, ch. 2, at 12.

36. See R. Pound, *Interpretation of Legal History* (Cambridge, 1923), 1.

dent) and of legislation (which favors overruling). Such an opposition does not reflect reality, for there is a measure of legislation in every judicial act. Thus the question concerns the extent of legislation. Indeed, within the framework of resolving disputes, the judge is obligated to advance the law and conform it to changing social reality.[37]

THE PROBLEM OF RELIANCE ON THE PRIOR RULE

One consideration that the judge must take into account in deciding whether or not to overrule a precedent is the extent of reliance on the existing rule. Where the public and administrative agencies extensively rely on the existing rule in conducting their affairs, only important opposing considerations—or prospective overruling—can justify deviating from the relied-upon precedent. The earlier decision created a web of expectations.[38] The public and the administrative agencies relied upon it and, as a result, decided on their conduct accordingly. Overruling it now would harm those legitimate expectations and could disrupt the orderly function of society and ultimately undermine the public's faith in the law and the courts. In such a situation it should be considered whether it would not be preferable that the alteration of the rule be left to the legislature. In that framework, a bill is promulgated and the various public interests are aired in the course of the legislative process. The legislative act is not retroactive and oftentimes permits the public to prepare for the new law's entry into force.

The above consideration is dominant in certain areas of property law. Certainty in proprietary interests is one of the most important foundations of orderly social function. A change in the law can damage that foundation where the public acquires proprietary rights on the basis of a decided rule.[39] Similar considerations apply to areas of contract law. There are several theories underlying contract law.[40] But whatever the theory, once a contract is created it brings about a system of expectations

37. See Pollock, "Judicial Caution and Valour," 45 *L.Q.R.* 239, 295 (1929).

38. See *Washington v. W. C. Dawson and Co.,* 264 U.S. 219, 238 (1934) (Brandeis J.).

39. See Landau, *supra* note 17, ch. 1, at 301; Weisman, "Some Fundamental Concepts of Property Law: A Critical Survey," 11 *Mishpatim* 41, 59 (1981).

40. For an examination of the various theories, see Barnett, "A Consent Theory of Contract," 86 *Colum. L. Rev.* 296 (1986).

for the realization of the obligations contained therein. This system of expectations is often based upon the existing law that gives force to the contract. A change in that law, such that certain contractual obligations are, for example, altered, shifted, or voided entirely, upsets the reasonable expectations of the parties and runs contrary to any theory of the law of contract. Similar considerations also hold for unilateral juristic acts. Thus, for example, where a testator makes a will on the basis of the rules of form of the inheritance law as interpreted by the courts, it would be an exceptional step for a court to modify its previous holdings and decide that wills made in accordance with the inheritance law are void because the law was improperly construed, by the same court, in the past.

Certain areas of tort law, as decided or construed by courts in the past, may also create reasonable reliance and expectations that should be weighed when the court alters the law by its decisions.[41] Such can be the case, for example, where the court considers changing the basis of liability from fault to absolute or strict liability. Such a change—assuming that it is legitimate within the system's framework—could harm the class of potential tort-feasers who based their affairs on the existing laws. For instance, a judicial change that founds their liability on a stricter basis would require a reworking of the insurance, of the premium, and of the policy of risk distribution. Thus were the new rule retroactive, this could have enormous damaging implications.[42] A court considering such a change should take this into account.

This consideration of public reliance on the existing rule is of limited scope. Often the parties and the public act without any awareness of the existence of the rule. Such is the case in broad areas of tort and contract law. It would appear, for example, that in the vast majority of cases, parties to a contract are not aware of contract law's rules of mistake and of frustration at the time they contract, and a change in these would not affect the reliance consideration. At times, even where the parties are aware of a rule, they do not rely upon it, and a change does not affect their reasonable expectations. Thus, though the inheritance law may empower the court to give effect to a will despite formal flaws, testators do not rely upon that rule in making wills. Rather, testators try to draft their wills in accordance with the legal requirements.[43] The provisions

41. See Keeton *supra* note 11, ch. 1, at 39.
42. See Schwartz, *supra* note 51, ch. 5.
43. See *Koenig v. Cohen,* 36 P.D. (3) 701, 718.

regarding the validity of a will notwithstanding flaws are a matter for the courts and do not create reliance. Therefore, in general, nothing impedes deviating from a precedent that concerns procedure (civil or criminal) or the law of evidence. The public does not, generally speaking, conduct itself on the basis of judicial rule-making in these fields. A party to proceedings has no ''vested interest'' in them and a change does not, therefore, affect the reliance principle.

From the reliance perspective, we may, in principle, distinguish those laws that create rights and obligations (primary laws) from those that grant relief for the infringement of those rights and obligations (secondary laws).[44] In general, the public relies more upon primary than upon secondary laws. Generally speaking, parties rely, if at all, upon laws related to the performance of a contract, without usually giving thought to those laws that govern relief in the event of breach. Similarly, parties usually do not consider the procedural relief that the court may grant them in the course of litigation. It would appear, therefore, that from this perspective, overruling a precedent that concerns secondary laws should raise fewer problems than overruling one that concerns primary laws.

At times, the parties in a case and the general public act with awareness of case law and in reliance thereon. Nevertheless, this does not preclude overruling precedent. Such is the case, for example, where the rule relied upon by the parties is controversial and there is support for its repeal. In such circumstances, the public must bear in mind, in arranging its affairs, that the rule may be subject to change. If parties do not act accordingly, they have only themselves to blame. This is particularly true in those instances where the old rule is premised upon outdated social perceptions and can be expected to change with changes in social outlook. Thus, for example, it was long held in Israel that occupiers of land did not bear a duty of care toward trespassers.[45] Over the years, it became clear that the rule—at least where the trespassers were minors[46]—was based on outmoded social concepts and that change was in the offing. Occupiers therefore had to expect change and direct their

44. See Hart and Sacks, *supra* note 26, ch. 1, at 135; also see Weiler, *supra* note 119, ch. 1.

45. See Cr. App. 35/52 *Rotenstreich v. A.G.*, 7 P.D. 58; C.A. 360/59 *A.G. v. Berkowitz*, 14 P.D. 266.

46. See C.A. 146/64 *Berstlinger v. Rubinstein*, 18 P.D. (3) 215; C.A. 63/64 *Gabbai v. State of Israel*, 18 P.D. (4) 582.

behavior accordingly.[47] Such is also the case in regard to the duty of care in tortious negligence,[48] liability for a "breach of statutory duty,"[49] the rules of "standing" in administrative law,[50] the laws concerning accessories to criminal offences,[51] offenses of strict liability,[52] and various other areas regarding which legal scholars have urged change and judges have indicated—*obiter dicta* and in dissenting opinions—that a change should be made in the case law.

Thus we find that the reliance principle does not hold in broad areas. Cardozo took notice of this in stating, "The picture of the bewildered litigant lured into a course of action by the false light of decision, only to meet ruin when the light is extinguished and the decision is overruled, is for the most part a figment of excited brains."[53] Even in those fields where the principle applies, it is neither the sole factor nor the deciding one. Alongside the principle stand others—which we shall consider— that can bring about the opposite results. In the end, the decision must fall on the basis of balancing the various considerations.

Courts will not infrequently change their holdings, despite the reliance of the parties, without addressing the issue of reliance at all. Such an approach is improper in my view. Even if the reliance principle is not in itself decisive, it should nevertheless be taken into account, with the judge explaining in his decision his reasons for deviating from the existing precedent in the face of such reliance.

THE EFFECT OF THE NATURE OF THE CONSIDERATIONS UNDERLYING THE EXISTENT RULE

An important factor that must be taken into account in the overruling of an existing rule concerns the legal policy underlying that rule.[54] We may distinguish in this regard between considerations of legal policy

47. See Barak, "Occupier's Liability Bill," 2 *Mishpatim* 129 (1970).

48. See, for example, *Jerusalem Municipality v. Gordon*, 39 P.D. (1) 113.

49. See F.H. 6/66 *Shehadev v. Hilu*, 20 P.D. (4) 617; C.A. 145/80 *Vaknin v. Beit Shemesh Municipal Council*, 37 P.D. (1) 113 (1983); *Sultan v. Sultan*, 38 P.D. (3) 169.

50. See Z. Segal, *Locus Standi in the High Court of Justice* (Tel Aviv, 1986, in Hebrew), 227.

51. See ch. 5.

52. See Cr. App. 696/81 *Azoulai v. State of Israel*, 37 P.D. (2) 565 (1983).

53. See Cardozo, *supra* note 6, ch. 1, at 122.

54. See Summers, *supra* note 21, ch. 2.

grounded upon principles (such as justice, fairness, and morality) or standards (such as reasonableness, negligence, and good faith), on the one hand, and those grounded upon policy objectives (such as the public good, state security, and the benefit of the child), on the other hand. Indeed, from the point of view of the normative considerations, a change or mistake in any of these three types of considerations may justify a change in the law, as long as the change is made in a natural, gradual, and coherent manner. The institutional and interinstitutional considerations might, however, distinguish between principles and standards on the one hand and social objectives on the other in terms of overruling precedent.

It would seem that the institutional considerations facilitate overruling a precedent that is based on principles and standards more than one based on social objectives; this is due to the institutional limitations of the court. It is easier for a judge to consider changes in principles and standards than changes in social objectives. The former requires less information and the information is less technical. Social objectives, by their very nature, are often based upon causal links between subject and object and it is often difficult for a judge to consider such relationships given the tools at his disposal. The implications of principles and standards for a given set of facts can be grasped more easily than the implications of social objectives. It is, therefore, easier for a judge to identify a mistake in the application of principles and standards than a mistake in the carrying out of social objectives.

It seems to me that interinstitutional considerations, too, more readily facilitate overruling a precedent based on principles and standards than one based on social objectives. Political agencies and the general public are generally more receptive to changes in rules arising from judicial decisions concerning principles and standards. Such decisions are usually viewed as inseparable from the judicial function. On the other hand, political agencies and the general public may feel that changes in a rule based on social objectives are more properly decided by political agencies, rather than by judges, who are neither elected nor answerable to the voter. Indeed, democratic considerations may more readily facilitate changes in law based upon principles and standards than in law based upon social objectives.

Naturally, such distinctions between the types of considerations are imprecise. Moreover, considerations of all three types are often inseparably intertwined within a single system. Last, the judge often fails to examine the nature of the considerations and the distinctions between them. Nevertheless, I believe that the distinction I have raised yields a concrete standard for evaluating the overruling of a precedent.[55] It seems to me that it can serve to explain the readiness of the courts to overrule precedents concerning duties of care in negligence.[56] Similarly, it may serve to explain the reluctance to overrule precedents treating of procedure[57] (primarily in civil and criminal procedure, less so in the rules of evidence). There are those who hold that the duty of care in tort is primarily founded upon principles and standards, and only to a lesser degree on social objectives.[58] Hence the greater willingness to bring about change in that area of tort. However, the rules of procedure are primarily based upon the social goals of procedural efficiency and stability, matters in which the inclination is toward less interference. But considerations of justice are also central to the rules of procedure. Civil procedure represents a certain balance between justice and efficiency;[59] indeed, to the extent that considerations of justice do play a role in civil procedure, they justify deviation from precedent in that field.

There are some[60] who distinguish between those fields of law "that concern the phenomena of life themselves" and those that are "the fruit of jurists' intellectual constructions." The courts should enjoy discretion in regard to the former, while the latter demand stability. One may, therefore, assume that overruling would be simpler in regard to the first type than in regard to the second. I find this distinction difficult. All fields of law treat of "the phenomena of life themselves," and all fields of law are based upon "jurists' intellectual constructions." In this I see no difference between administrative law and the law of negotiable instru-

55. This is also expressed in the rhetoric employed by judges when trying to justify overruling precedent. This rhetoric is generally based on claims of "justice" or "efficiency."

56. See *Berstlinger, supra* note 46, at 223.

57. See *Ein Harod, supra* note 2, at 1892; *Weismann v. Farzhi,* 17 P.D. 1527, 1531; *Davidson v. Davidson,* 27 P.D. (2) 20 (1973), 23; see *Port Authority, supra* note 28, ch. 6, at 536.

58. See *McLughlin v. Brain,* [1982] 2 W.L.R. 982, 998 (Lord Scarman).

59. See Sussmann, "When We Do Not Know What 'Justice' Is, We Should Prefer Order," in *The Importance of Procedure and the Protection of Justice* (Jerusalem, 1966, in Hebrew), 9.

60. See Landau, *supra* note 17, ch. 1, at 300; and see Pound, *supra* note 17, ch. 1.

ments; between the law of tort and property law. I believe that what underlies this distinction—in addition to the reliance principle discussed earlier—is the difference in the legal policy that lies at the foundation of the various rules.

I would reemphasize that this consideration regarding the nature of the legal policy underlying a rule is not in itself decisive. It is one of several considerations that must be weighed in deciding whether to overrule a precedent. At times it joins other considerations in leading to a particular solution. For example, when reliance joins with a rule that treats of social objectives, the considerations arguing against change are bolstered. As opposed to this, when there is no reliance factor and the rule is grounded upon principles, such as justice or morality, the arguments in favor of overruling are strengthened. The primary difficulty arises when the various considerations lead to opposing conclusions. Where, for example, the reliance consideration justifies respecting precedent and the principles grounding the precedent, based upon justice and morality, justify overruling, the judge must balance the various considerations.

THE EFFECT OF THE PASSAGE OF TIME

It is interesting to consider what effect time may have upon a judge's willingness to overrule a precedent laid down by the court on which he serves. For example, does a precedent's ''youth''—where the decision was but recently rendered—inhibit overruling or facilitate it? There would appear to be conflicting considerations in this matter. The normative consideration seems to favor an approach whereby the newer the precedent, the more easily it may be overruled, while the longer the precedent's ''tenure,'' the harder it is to deviate from it. The reason for this is found primarily in the reliance factor. A new decision, not yet firmly rooted, creates no reliance.[61] But this approach holds only up to a certain point within the normative framework. Beyond that point, the more time that passes, the more outdated the rule becomes and the easier it is to deviate from it. With the passage of time, the chances increase for

61. See *Southern Pacific Co.* v. *Jensen,* 263 U.S. 219, 238 (1924) (Brandeis J.): ''The doctrine of *stare decisis* should not deter us from overruling that case and those which follow it. The decisions are recent ones. They have not been acquiesced in. They have not created a rule of property around which vested interests have clustered.''

a change in the legal policy that grounded the precedent. Thus a growing schism develops between the precedent and other decisions, and the number of exceptions increases. Ultimately, a point is reached where explicit overruling is the best course. Indeed, judicial rules are like human beings. At the outset, they gain strength with years, but eventually they weaken with the passage of time.[62]

The institutional and interinstitutional considerations may operate in the opposite direction. It can be argued that once a question is brought before the court and a decision rendered, it is improper to reopen the question. In addition to wasting the court's time, the credibility of the court would be undermined.

Here, too, we face a question of balancing. I find the normative considerations more convincing. The court's time will be ''wasted'' in any event. The question is whether it will be wasted now, when the decision can be easily overruled without harming reasonable expectations, or in the future, with all the difficulties that will entail. Furthermore, I do not believe that the question of credibility is clear-cut. One can easily argue that a refusal to overrule a mistaken, harmful decision simply because it is new does greater harm to the court's credibility than an honest admission of a recent error. Indeed, my opinion is that the ''fresher'' the decision, the less we should feel inhibited from overruling it, while the more firmly rooted a decision, the more we should feel burdened by the responsibility of overruling it. This, of course, holds true only up to the nebulous point beyond which the sooner the precedent is overturned the better.

THE EFFECT OF THE IMPORTANCE OF THE QUESTION

Justice Alfred Witkon observed that one may distinguish between major problems and technical ones in deciding whether to overrule a precedent:

> When we are faced with one of the major problems disputed by jurists and subject to the effects of time, place and social outlook, I would not counsel rigidity. In such a case, it may be necessary to periodically subject the rule to judicial review. However, where, as in the case before us, we are concerned

62. See Salmond, *Jurisprudence* 218 (11th ed. 1957): "The statement that a precedent gains in authority with age must be read to an important qualification. Up to a certain point a human being grows in strength as he grows in age; but this is true only within narrow limits. So with the authority of judicial decisions."

with a technical provision of the law, and the rule established by precedent is merely an attempt to interpret the vague and hidden intent of the legislature (which, if we erred, did not raise a finger to point out our mistake) then the construction we gave has meshed with the law itself and they have become one, and it would be rash and dangerous to act freely with the rule and upend it with every change in the composition of the court or with the appearance of a new plaintiff.[63]

I do not agree with this approach. First, the fear of recklessly acting freely with the law and of reversing it "with every change in the composition of the court or with the appearance of a new plaintiff" holds equally true for both the major problems and the technical ones. The search for the "vague and hidden intent of the legislature" is common to both types of problems. And the enmeshing of the construction "with the law itself" and their becoming "one" is true both for major problems and technical ones. Second, the distinction between major problems and technical ones is very problematic. Is the requirement of a written instrument in land transactions a major problem or a technical one? Third, and most important for our concern, I do not believe that the distinction is of much assistance in addressing the issue of overruling precedent. There are major problems in which the normative, institutional, and interinstitutional considerations justify upholding precedent and there are technical questions where those considerations justify overruling.

DISTINCTIONS ACCORDING TO THE LEGAL FIELD OF THE RULE

It is customarily believed that the extent of overruling precedent is related to the legal field in which the problem arises.[64] For example, it is said that it is more desirable to uphold precedent in property, contract, and commercial (companies and negotiable instruments) law than in constitutional and administrative law. In my opinion, these field-related distinctions do not significantly aid us in solving the problems associated with overruling precedent. We cannot, for example, make a sweeping statement that precedent should be respected more in property law than in other fields. All depends upon the nature of the question before the

63. C.A. 346/63 *Tripman v. Victor,* 18 P.D. (1) 366, 368.
64. See Landau, *supra* note 17, ch. 1, at 298; J. Stone, *Social Dimensions of Law and Justice* (Sydney, 1966), 662.

court. If the question concerns the extent of a protected tenant's rights, I would generally counsel restraint, primarily for reasons of the reliance interest (and to the extent of that interest). However, where the question concerns the element of good faith in regard to the requirement of a written instrument for land transfer, I am of the opinion that considerations of justice support a readiness to deviate from precedent. Similarly, in contract law, where the fulfilling of contractual obligations and their extent are at issue, upholding precedent may be preferable due to the reliance factor. But where the question concerns fraud, mistake, or frustration, that consideration would seem to weaken. Thus it is not the field but rather the nature of the question that is decisive.

Should honoring a precedent be more desirable in civil procedure than in other fields? This approach holds that here stability and established order are of such importance that stability ensured by a mistaken decision is preferable to the correctness of a rule that would lead to instability. I have my doubts as to whether such a generalized approach is warranted. Civil procedure is based upon a balancing of justice and efficiency. But what is the point in preserving a rule that ensures neither? And why hold on to an efficient but unjust rule if it can be replaced by one that is both efficient and just? Why preserve a rule that guarantees rigidity where flexibility is required? I believe that the normative, institutional, and interinstitutional considerations show certain areas of civil procedure to be ripe for change where the precedent is not suitable. The reason for this is that there is no strong reliance interest in civil procedure. The judicial institution is well suited to deal with the problems of civil procedure, which are, after all, problems of "internal management" of the judicial process. Indeed, no one is better suited to the task than the courts. The other agencies have no claim in this field, and their own view is that the matter should be left for the judges themselves to decide. I believe that public faith would only increase if the courts would show themselves able to conform their procedures to standards of justice and efficiency that reflect modern sentiments rather than to entrench themselves behind rules that the passage of time has eroded beyond recognition. Of course, as in every case of intervention, a sense of proportion must be maintained. Normative considerations demand gradual development and controlled growth. One should not jump from one extreme to the other. An existing rule should not be changed unless it is certain that the alternative is better. But it would seem that in civil procedure, in particular, this can be achieved. The purpose of the changes must be to allow civil procedure to fully realize its purpose of efficiency and justice while preserving the legitimate interests of litigants and of the public. A rule that does not serve that end should not be retained simply by virtue of its stability.

In the United States it is said that in the field of constitutional law flexibility should be ensured. Thus the courts should not refrain from overruling a precedent if they believe it improperly decided. While some base this approach upon fidelity to the constitution rather than to its past interpretation by judges, others emphasize the difficulty of amending the constitution as justification for flexibility in changing its interpretation.[65] Still others point to the very nature of the constitution, which must reflect society's changing values.[66] Of course, this view is not unanimously held. There are those who hold that stability is necessary particularly in the constitutional field.[67] The reliance interest is especially strong in this area and change should come in but rare cases.[68] I would not advise a rigid rule in this matter. Here, too, I believe that each case must be considered on it own merits. For example, once it had been decided that the president of Israel is empowered to grant pardon even before conviction,[69] I believe the rule should stand even if it is thought that the matter should have been decided otherwise. The pardon process demands stability, and it would not be proper that pardons already granted should lose force. A change in this area should best be made by the legislature. As opposed to this, in matters that concern fundamental rights,[70] we should not bar greater protection of those rights in the future if social realities justify this.[71]

An important question is whether the criminal law is a category unto itself as regards overruling precedent in hard cases. On the one hand, it can be argued that a change in the criminal field implies a widening or

65. See *Burnet v. Coronado Oil and Gas Co.*, 285 U.S. 393, 409 (1932) (Brandeis J).

66. See, for example, Douglas, *supra* n. 19, at 739: "As constitutional law is concerned, *stare decisis* must give way before the dynamic component of history. Once it does, the cycle starts again." Also see Wright, "Precedent," 8 *Camb. L.J.* 118, at 135 (1943).

67. See *Pollack v. Farmers Loan and Trust Co.*, 157 U.S. 429, 632 (1894) (White J).

68. See Monaghan, "Taking the Supreme Court Seriously," 39 *Mod. L.R.* 1, 7 (1979).

69. H.C. 428/86 *Barzilay v. State of Israel*, 40 P.D. (3) 505.

70. *Disenchik v. A.G.*, 17 P.D. 169 (1963).

71. See A. Goldberg, *Equal Justice*, 85 (1971).

narrowing of criminal culpability. Such a change should—by reason of
the legality principle (*nullum crimen sine lege*)—more properly come
from the legislature. Moreover, it is every person's right to rely on the
accepted construction of the law to the extent that it serves him. A change
in construction is burdensome and harms a legitimate interest that he and
society hold. On the other hand, one may argue that there is no substantive difference between judicial lawmaking in criminal law and in any
other field. Though the change may affect the scope of culpability, it is
anchored in the law and is therefore consonant with the legality principle. The law exists, and the judge does not create culpability outside the
framework of the law, but rather interprets the law in a different manner.
Moreover, the reliance interest is often negligible and at times unreasonable. People often plan their conduct without knowledge of the law or
even on the assumption that their conduct is unlawful. As regards overruling, criminal law does not seem to me special in any way. As in other
fields, each matter must be considered separately. All accept that no
offense should be created without a basis in law, but I see no reason why
a construction given to the elements of an offense should remain un-
changed where a new construction more aptly reflects the legislative
purpose. I do not think that the question of whether the scope of culpability changes should be decisive. As long as the new construction is
lawful, I see no reason why it should not be arrived at judicially. The
normative, institutional, and interinstitutional considerations, too, support this approach. Criminal law, like any other field, must develop and
be framed in accordance with the demands of the times.

Once societal needs and perceptions change, a change may also
follow in the interpretation given to criminal provisions. Sometimes, of
course, the statutory provision is not sufficiently flexible to hold the new
content. At such times, the legality principle requires that the legislature
create a new vessel to receive the new social content. But where the
statutory provision is sufficiently flexible, the legality principle does not
require that the legislature be consulted. Rather, it allows the judge to
fulfill his classic role of adapting the law to changing social realities.
This adaptation must be gradual, natural, and organic, but if these
conditions are met—and there is no a priori reason that they should not
be—no normative reason prevents change of the criminal law via judicial reinterpretation. The institutional considerations also support this
approach. The courts generally possess the necessary tools for treating of

the criminal phenomenon. There is no institutional reason for them not to fulfill a creative role in this field. Neither is there any matter of principle among the interinstitutional considerations that would limit judicial activity in the criminal field.

PROSPECTIVE OVERRULING?

On occasion, after examining a previous decision and finding that he desires to change it, a judge finds that the reliance argument is so strong—whether alone or together with other arguments—that it prevents him from realizing his desire. In such circumstances there would appear to be but two choices: honoring the precedent or retroactively overruling, with the scales favoring the former. Here, however, a third possibility arises:[72] overruling the precedent (for the reasons that support this), while giving the new rule only prospective force (in order to avoid harm to the reliance interest). We thus find that prospective overruling offers itself as a solution to the reliance problem. It proposes to achieve the benefits of overruling precedent without having to pay the full price.

This technique raises two separate questions. First, a formal question concerning the court's power to give its decisions only prospective force absent specific statutory authority to do so. Second, a substantive question concerning whether or not it is proper and wise for the court to have recourse to this technique. The first is a question of power; the second, one of discretion.

There are two sides to the question of power. First, is the characteristic of retroactivity inherent to case law, so that a precedent—or the deviation therefrom—cannot be divorced from its retroactive effect? Second, are the courts, in the framework of any given legal system, empowered to give their decisions only prospective effect absent a specific legislative provision? The accepted opinion is that nothing inherent to case law requires retroactive effect. It is, therefore, for each legal system to establish its position in this matter.[73] Where the authority of precedent itself derives from the judiciary, the question of prospective force, too, resides with the judiciary. In such systems, the answer to the

72. See G. Tedeschi, "Prospective Revision of Precedent," 8 *Isr. L. Rev.* 173 (1973); Currier, "Time and Change in Judge-Made Law: Prospective Overruling," 51 *Va. L. Rev.* 201 (1965).

73. See *Great Northern Ry. v. Sunburst Oil and Ref. Co.*, 287 U.S. 358 (1932).

question of power is that judges *may* give their decisions prospective force. What remains is only the question of the wisdom of employing this technique.

We turn now to the second question, regarding the wisdom of adopting the juridical technique of prospective overruling. Opinions are divided in this matter.[74] On one side stands a long line of judges and jurists who hold that the technique is desirable.[75] Among them we may count Professor John Wigmore[76] and Justices Cardozo[77] and Frankfurter[78] and Judges Schaefer[79] and Traynor.[80] On the other side stands a broad front of judges and jurists who hold that prospective overruling is improper.[81] Among these we may mention Judges Reid[82] and Devlin[83] and Professors Rupert Cross,[84] Lon Fuller,[85] Wolfgang Freidmann,[86] Dennis Lloyd,[87] and Guido Tedeschi.[88] The question of prospective overruling

74. For the various views in this matter see Nicol, "Prospective Overruling: A New Device for English Courts?" 39 *Mod. L. Rev.* 542 (1976); Note, "Prospective Overruling and Retroactive Application in the Federal Courts," 71 *Yale L.J.* 907 (1962); Kaplan, "Prospective Overruling of the Supreme Court Precedents," 9 *Mishpatim* 221 (1979).

75. See Kocourek and Kovan, *supra* note 30; L. Jaffe, *English and American Judges as Lawmakers* (Oxford, 1969), 56; Traynor, "Transatlantic Reflections on Leeways and Limits of Appellate Courts," *Utah L. Rev.* 255 (1980).

76. See Wigmore, "The Judicial Function," in *Science of Legal Method* (1917), xxvii.

77. See B. N. Cardozo, *Selected Writings* (New York, 1947), 35.

78. See *Griffin v. Illinois,* 351 U.S. 12 (1956).

79. See Schaefer, "Precedent and Policy," 34 *U. Chi. L. Rev.* 3 (1966); Schaefer, "The Control of Sunbursts: Techniques of Prospective Overruling," 42 *N.Y.U.L. Rev.* 631 (1967); Schaefer, "New Ways of Precedent," 2 *Manitoba L. J.* 255 (1967); Schaefer, "Prospective Rulings: Two Perspectives," *Sup. Ct. L. Rev.* 1 (1982).

80. See Traynor, "Limits of Judicial Creativity," 63 *Iowa L. Rev.* 1 (1977); Traynor, "Quo Vadis, Prospective Overruling: A Question of Judicial Responsibility," 28 *Hastings L. J.* 533 (1977); Traynor, *supra* note 75, at 255.

81. See Mishkin, "The High Court, The Great Writ, and Due Process of Time and Law," 79 *Harv. L. Rev.* 56 (1965); Freeman, "Standards of Adjudication, Judicial Law Making and Prospective Overruling" *Current Legal Problems* 166 (1973).

82. See *Birmingham City Co. v. West Midland Baptist (Trust) Ass.,* [1969] 3 All. E.R. 172, 180.

83. See Devlin, *supra* note 5, ch. 7, at 12.

84. See R. Cross, *Precedent in English Law* (Oxford, 3d ed., 1977), 230.

85. See L. Fuller, *Anatomy of the Law* (New York, 1968), 99.

86. See Friedmann, "Limits of the Judicial Lawmaking and Prospective Overruling," 29 *Mod. L. Rev.* 593 (1966).

87. See D. Lloyd, *Introduction to Jurisprudence* (London, 5th ed., 1985).

88. See Tedeschi, *supra* note 72.

has expressly arisen but once before the Israeli Supreme Court,[89] but the issue was not addressed on its merits. In England, too, the question arose in one case, where it was stated that the technique required study.[90] Lord Diplock has also advised careful study of the technique[91] and Judge Freidmann took a similar stand in Canada.[92] The technique of prospective overruling is applied in limited form in India.[93] It is widely employed in the United States.[94]

Before evaluating the technique of prospective overruling, it would be proper to consider its substance. The term *prospective overruling* covers several different techniques.[95] The first may be called purely prospective. In this method the court overrules its precedent for the future only. Its decision does not apply to the case at bar, to the public at large, or to pending cases. Against this method one may argue that the overruling is but *obiter dictum*. It can also be mentioned that there is little logic in not applying the decision to the case at bar, as who would argue in favor of change where that change will not benefit him? To this one may reply that there should be no discrimination among litigants. "Institutional litigants" may have recourse to the courts due to an interest in the rule itself and not in the outcome of a specific case.

The second technique is prospective-prospective overruling. This is a form of the purely prospective technique that sets a future date for the entry into force of the new rule. The purpose of postponement is to allow the public time to reorganize its affairs in anticipation of the upcoming change. It also affords the legislature an opportunity to take a stand in the matter. It can be argued that this technique transgresses the boundary between adjudicating and legislating. It can also be contended that, in effect, the technique places a gun to the legislature's head with the threat of "act or we shall act in your stead."

89. *Ketashvilli v. State of Israel,* 35 P.D. (2) 457, 462.

90. See *Jones* v. *Secretary of State for Social Services,* [1972] 1 All. E.R. 145 (Lord Simon).

91. See Diplock, *The Courts as Legislators* 17 (1965).

92. See Freedman, "Continuity and Change—A Task of Reconciliation," 8 *U.B.C.L.R.* 203 (1973).

93. See Nicol, *supra* note 74.

94. See Shapiro, "Prospective or Retroactive Operations of Overruling Decisions," 10 *A.L.R.* (3d) 1371 (1968).

95. See G. Calabresi, *A Common Law for the Age of Statutes* (Cambridge, Ma., 1982), 280.

A third technique is prospective-retroactive overruling. This technique applies the new rule prospectively to all but the case at bar, to which it applies retroactively. This method answers the objection that a decision to prospectively overrule is *obiter dictum*. It also encourages potential litigants. As opposed to this, it can be argued that the approach discriminates among different litigants. Why should preference be shown to those whose case fortuitously comes to trial before those of claimants who raise similar arguments in their pending cases?

A fourth technique was developed to overcome the latter objection. This technique, which is also prospective-retroactive, applies the retroactive force to all claims pending before the courts. Should objection be raised to showing preference to those who have filed complaints as against those who have not, a fifth technique exists. By this technique the decision is prospective-prospective, in that it comes into force at a future date, but upon entry into force it applies retroactively to all. Thus we have before us a prospective-prospective-retroactive approach that is nothing more than a retroactive approach with a delaying fuse.

In favor of prospective overruling, it is emphasized that this allows the court to deviate from precedent without running afoul of the problem of reliance. The court achieves the desired result (overruling an unacceptable precedent) without harming the reliance interest. Thus certainty and stability are preserved while the law is adjusted to social changes. Indeed, it is a kind of "wonder drug" that allows for simultaneous stability and movement. Just as a law repealing a previous law generally applies prospectively, and not retroactively, so applies a new judicial rule overruling an earlier precedent.

Several arguments can be raised against prospective overruling. First, the technique is complicated.[96] There is no single system for prospective overruling—there are several systems. The parties can never know which system the court will choose. As a result, the entire proceeding is upset, as the parties do not know how to conduct their affairs. Second, the system liberates judges from those few bonds that restrict their discretion. The retroactivity of decisions acts as a barrier to excessive overruling. When this barrier is toppled, there is the fear that all restraint will be lost and the system will be flooded with deviating decisions.[97]

96. See Stone, *supra* note 64, at 663.
97. See Hart and Sacks, *supra* note 26, ch. 1, at 627; Stone, *supra* n. 64, at 664.

Third, it may be argued that prospective change is unbecoming to the nature of the judicial process. In that process, rule-making is incidental to adjudication, while in prospective change the two are severed.[98] The judge becomes a legislator for all intents and purposes. This not only upsets the judicial process but seriously harms the public's expectations of the judiciary and, consequently, erodes the public's trust.

Deciding among these various opposing arguments is difficult. The normative consideration supports the prospective approach to overruling precedent. This approach allows for gradual, natural development while safeguarding normative coherence. The institutional consideration appears to me to be neutral. The argument concerning possible disruption of the judicial process is not strong, in my view, as the court can always warn the parties at the outset and they can direct their pleadings accordingly. The argument concerning the severance of judging from legislating also does not appear to me to be serious. Prospective overruling comes about in the framework of a trial, and if it applies to the parties at bar—as I would recommend—then the necessary link between adjudicating and legislating is supplied. The interinstitutional consideration—primarily that concerning the public's trust in the judiciary—is the most problematic. Indeed, if the public's trust in the judiciary would be eroded by prospective overruling, I would view it as an important— and, to my mind, decisive—argument against recourse to the technique. If this interinstitutional consideration is indeed valid, then in weighing it against the normative consideration I would give it preference. The primary question is, in my view, What are the merits of the claim regarding loss of public trust?

The question of possible harm to the court system cannot be answered theoretically. All depends upon the particular society and its expectations of its judges. It would seem that in the United States the public has become accustomed to prospective overruling and sees it as an integral part of the judicial process. Apparently, in that society the public's trust is not eroded when the courts adopt the technique of prospective overruling. On the contrary, the claim is that it increases the public's trust in courts that root out their own mistakes and do so in a just manner that does not harm the public's reasonable expectations. Yet various au-

98. See Cross, *supra* note 84, at 223.

thors[99] are of the opinion that the English public—unlike the American—is not prepared to accept the technique of prospective overruling. Others dispute this contention.

The central factor, then, in contemplating the possibility of prospective deviation from precedent by a Supreme Court in a country that has not adopted that technique is the attitudes held by the public in that country. It is difficult to assess these, as we usually have no data, and such data would be hard to obtain. One must, therefore, ask whether it would be worthwhile trying a system of prospective overruling or whether the attempt itself might be too dangerous. Different judges may hold different views on this question. When all is said and done, discretion, at this stage, is guided by the judge's personality, experience, and juridical philosophy. I can only express my own opinion. I believe that a Supreme Court should try the system by adopting one of the techniques, at first in clearly defined areas—in my opinion the prospective-retroactive one. If the attempt does not succeed, the Supreme Court can abandon it. If it meets with success, it can be expanded over time to other areas. It seems to me that we cannot express our opinion of prospective overruling until we have some experience with it.

CONCLUSION: BETWEEN TRUTH AND TRUTH— STABILITY IS PREFERABLE

The question I have considered concerns the circumstances in which it is proper to overrule precedent when there is discretion to do so. When all of the considerations lead in one direction, the decision is not difficult. Though there is discretion, the considerations show one solution to be preferable to the others, and it may be assumed that the judge will choose accordingly. But at other times, the various considerations lead in divergent directions. Then the judge must weigh the different considerations and ask himself whether the advantage resulting from change outweighs the harm it causes. To do this, he must evaluate the measure of benefit and the extent of harm. He must, for example, ask himself whether the advantage of a more just rule outweighs the harm in frustrating expectations. In making this evaluation he must act objectively. His intuition

99. See Freeman, *supra* note 81, at 204; Devlin, *supra* note 5, ch. 7, at 12.

must be controlled. The choice must be rational. But ultimately it cannot be denied that the judge faces a question of judicial discretion. He must himself decide what weight to assign the various considerations. It is but natural that the judge's weltanschauung—based upon his personal experience and judicial philosophy—will ultimately tilt the scales. And where the scales are balanced, it is best to uphold precedent. "Between truth and truth—stability is preferable."[100]

100. As I stated in *Ohf Ha 'Emek, supra* note 3, at 145: "The prior case law is not binding. The binding [by the present decision to the prior one] is not a result of an external requirement or the imposition of an 'internal affinity.' The binding is the result of the existence of the prior case law, which gives weight to the alternative there selected and prefers it to the other alternative there rejected. Of course, various considerations may exist that serve to balance the picture and cause the latter alternative to be preferred nevertheless. It is possible that the alternative that was chosen is causing unforeseen difficulties. It is possible that there exist judicial policy considerations for preferring it. But in the absence of such considerations, my opinion is that between truth and truth—stability is preferable."

Postscript
Judicial Discretion
in a
Democratic Society

In a society of laws, law, not man, rules.[1] This truism may lead one to conclude that the rule of law is incompatible with discretion. But this approach has been discredited, as concerns the giving of discretion to the executive branch[2] as well as to the judicial branch. The rule of law is compatible with governmental discretion, provided that this discretion is within the framework of the law ("formal rule of law") and that it is exercised on the basis of limiting standards ("substantive rule of law"). There is no contradiction between discretion—of the legislative, executive, or judicial branch—and the rule of law. On the contrary: society cannot attain the rule of law without a measure of discretion. Law without discretion ultimately yields arbitrariness. It follows that the main question is not whether it is appropriate for there to be judicial discretion, but rather Where are the appropriate boundaries of this discretion to be marked in a democratic society that aspires to the rule of law?

Judicial discretion in the ascertainment of facts is accepted in every society. The question becomes whether one should limit this discretion with evidentiary rules regarding admissibility. The Israeli system requires judicial discretion in the determination of facts to conform to an intricate web of laws of evidence that divide evidence into the admissible

---

1. See Dicey, *The Law of the Constitution* 262 (1885); Turpin, *British Government and the Constitution* 46 (1985).

2. See Davis, *supra* note 3, ch. 1, at 17; Harlow and Rawlings, *Law and Administration* 130 (1984).

and the inadmissible. Only after the admissibility of a piece of evidence has been established can one determine its weight.

In my view, these *rules of admissibility* should gradually be replaced with *rules of weight*. A professional judge should evaluate every bit of evidence according to its probative value, and highly probative evidence should not be excluded because it fails one of the tests of admissibility. The goal of the judicial process is the revelation of truth, and this goal might be frustrated if credible evidence is barred. Here too, of course, one must not jump from one extreme to the other. An appropriate legal policy might well justify excluding certain probative evidence, such as a defendant's confession that was not the product of his free will. Indeed, while we seek truth in the judicial process, we are not prepared to reach the truth by sacrificing human dignity. Dealing a defendant mortal blows might produce a truthful confession, yet a democratic society might still opt for the acquittal of such a defendant so as not to encourage violence against him and others similarly situated. We are concerned, ultimately, with striking a balance between the need of the democratic society to find out the truth and the same society's insistence on preserving other values it deems worthy of protection. Further discussion of this dilemma is outside the scope of this book.

Modern society recognizes judicial discretion not only in the elucidation of facts, but also in the application of the law to the facts. What is the proper scope of judicial discretion when the judge applies the law? Everyone concurs that a normative system made up only of rules that contain no grant of judicial discretion in the application of the rules is inflexible and undesirable, for it is powerless to deal with the special difficulties posed by the individual case. The need for flexibility[3] in order to ensure individualization[4] demands the granting of judicial discretion. Yet all agree, too, that a normative system comprised entirely of principles, social goals, and standards that impart judicial discretion is not desirable, for such a normative system might harm certainty, unity, and stability and might thwart human nature's deep-seated need to plan ahead.

---

3. See Pattenden, *supra* note 23, ch. 1, at 35: "The chief advantage of discretion can be summed up in one word: flexibility." See also Pound, "Discretion, Dispensation and Mitigation: The Problem of the Individual Special Case," 35 *N.Y.U.L. Rev.* 925 (1960).

4. See Davis, *supra* note 3, ch. 1, at 17.

Thus, modern society is founded in essence on a mixture of rules and principles,[5] precedent and discretion.[6] The central question, of course, addresses the proper balance between the two. What is the appropriate level of discretion and of rules without discretion? Where is the equilibrium point in the perpetual tension between stringent rules and flexible principles?[7] The tendency of the modern legislator seems to be to increase judicial discretion, through the use of language that characterizes principles, social goals, and standards. The law's movement is a pendulum motion that fluctuates between rules and principles,[8] with latter-day law moving from rules toward principles.[9] As Professor Atiyah noted,[10] this transition is not the result of a social approach that accords decisive weight to principles. It stems, on the contrary, from a pragmatic approach that seeks justice for the individual and that prefers this search to the preservation of abstract rules. Sometimes it stems from the legislature's inability or unwillingness to make a generalization, and its choice of the easiest path of retreat—namely, leaving the issue for adjudication.

Judicial discretion is not limited to the ascertainment of the facts and the application of the law. Judicial discretion exists also in the determination of the law itself. The study of this type of judicial discretion was the main focus of this book. This discretion exists with respect to any rule, principle, standard, whether statutory or case law. The interpretation of a legal norm always leaves some room for judicial discretion. There will always be hard cases. While it is possible to develop rules of interpretation that minimize the need for discretion, judicial discretion cannot be avoided altogether. Where there is law, there will be judicial discretion. The history of law is also the history of the broadening or narrowing of judicial discretion at different times and in different circumstances, according to proper policy considerations. Thus, even the most vehement critics of judicial discretion do not seek to eliminate it completely. The real question is not whether there should or should not

5. See Salmond, *supra* note 62, ch. 9.
6. Landau, *supra* note 17, ch. 1.
7. See Fuller, "Reason and Fiat in Case Law," 59 *Harv. L. Rev.* 376 (1946).
8. See Cohen, *supra* note 17, ch. 8, at 261.
9. See Dickinson, *supra* note 14, ch. 2, at 1081; Pound, *supra* note 3; Pound, *supra* note 27, ch. 2, at 54.
10. Atiyah, *supra* note 47, ch. 1.

be discretion. The real question concerns the proper scope of judicial discretion.

Every legal system has a normative structure that provides a known and unambiguous solution to some disputes. These are the easy cases and the intermediate cases. This is the static foundation that ensures orderly social life, maintains security and stability, and allows individuals to plan their actions in advance. Yet this is not the only framework that exists. Alongside it is an additional structure for solving the hard cases. This is a dynamic complex that ensures renewal and change. Both of these structures are essential to every legal system.[11] Neither can survive without the other.[12] Stability without change is decline. Change without stability is anarchy. The question always concerns the proper relationship between the two.[13] It is a mistake to view the law from the perspective of only one of these structures. It is wrong to see in law only stability. It is incorrect to think that every problem has only one lawful solution. But it is equally wrong to see in law only change. It is incorrect to believe that every problem is open-ended and that none has only a single lawful outcome. Reality is far more complicated. Justice Holmes wrote[14] that the life of the law is not logic but experience. In fact, the life of the law seems to be logic and experience together. The life of the law is complex. Stability and change are inextricably linked. Between them there is—to use Justice Moshe Landau's phrase[15]—"perpetual tension and constant interchange." The goal is to achieve change through stability.[16] In Professor Pound's well-known saying, "Law must be stable and yet it cannot stand still."[17] The problem facing the legal system in general, and the judicial branch in particular, is how to reach this goal. How are we to solve the hard cases?

The proper use of judicial discretion is essential for society. The

11. See Pound, *supra* note 27, ch. 2, at 54.

12. See Hughes, *supra* note 41, ch. 1, at 414.

13. See Weiler, *supra* note 119, ch. 1, at 54.

14. O. W. Holmes, *The Common Law* 1 (1881): "The life of the law has not been logic: it has been experience."

15. Landau, *supra* note 17, ch. 1, at 292.

16. See Fuller, *supra* note 7; Pollock, "Judicial Caution and Valour," 45 *Law Q. Rev.* 293, 297 (1929).

17. R. Pound, *Interpretation of Legal History* 1 (1923): "Hence all thinking about law has struggled to reconcile the conflicting demands of the need of stability and of the need of change."

proper use of judicial discretion is also vital for the judicial branch. In the hard cases, both the law and the judge are on trial.[18] The public's faith in the judicial branch is determined by the way the judge employs his discretion. I have sought to outline a system of normative, institutional, and interinstitutional factors to aid the judge in the proper exercise of his discretion. I have attempted to raise to the realm of rational discourse a collection of thoughts to help the judicial branch formulate a judicial policy on the exercise of judicial discretion. At the core of my approach lies the assumption that the judge makes law. This is lawmaking writ small, legislation between the lines. The judge does not simply declare what the existing law is. Yet he also is not involved exclusively in policy-making. The judge's legislating is incidental to his judging, and when he makes law he does so not as a legislator but as a judge.

The fundamental problem with legislation as an incident to adjudication is the so-called democratic problem. How can one reconcile judicial lawmaking with social democracy? Judicial legislation means setting policy. It means choosing between one private right and another; it means taking a stand as to individual rights versus public needs; it means having a say in the societal issues preoccupying the public. How is judicial discretion to be exercised so that it remains consistent with the demands of a democratic society founded upon the separation of powers? The question is one of substance rather than form. Formally, judicial creation derives its legitimacy from the legislature itself. Legislation is a devolution to interpretation. But what is the substantive basis for judicial lawmaking? I have attempted to demonstrate that judicial creation derives its force from the basic principles of the democracy itself. These principles balance the rule of the majority with the rule of the basic values of the nation. A judge who, in the exercise of his discretion, gives expression to this balance operates within the framework of the democratic conception of the society.

As for myself, I believe that this judicial creativity will find expression on many occasions in the future. Impatience, extremism, social gaps, and greed—all these often bring challenges to the fundamental values, and efforts to find easy solutions in stop-gap measures. In all of these, the society needs a judge who is faithful to his judicial role. He

18. See Stone, "The Common Law in the United States," 50 *Harv. L. Rev.* 4, 10 (1936): "The law itself is on trial, quite as much as the cause which is to be decided."

should obey the legislation and follow its instructions, even if he disagrees with them. But where the law is unclear, ambiguous, or open-textured, the judge should interpret it according to fundamental principles, not according to the fleeting moods of society; according to the articles of faith of the nation, as these found expression in the Declaration of Independence, not according to the ever-changing balance of political forces. I sincerely hope that people in democratic societies will not find their judges to be naive, seeing in everything a problem of security. The security of the state lies in the rule of law. I hope that democratic societies will not find their judges to be simpleminded, always seeing in fundamental values the final word. A constitution is not a prescription for suicide. I hope the modern society will find its judges to be careful and reasonable, examining every question from all its angles; aware of their creative function; balancing objectively among the various interests; applying the fundamental principles neutrally; and seeking to attain a delicate balance between majority rule and the basic rights of the individual—a balance that represents the equation of the democratic regime.

How is this balance to be achieved? How is judicial discretion to be exercised? I can offer no definitive answer to these questions. All I have managed to do is to indicate a number of factors—some of them normative, some institutional, and some interinstitutional—that the judge should take into account. Yet not even these factors are able to provide in every case a single answer to the problem with which the judge is faced. The law's world is broad and large. It is full of beauty and wisdom. It is only natural that there is more than one path along which it can be traveled, more than one way to absorb its beauty and to bask in its wisdom. All that remains is for me to repeat the words of President Moshe Zmora—the first president of the Israeli Supreme Court—who counted on the "lawyer's sense of professionalism,"[19] and who noted that in the final analysis, "As judges, we must seek to cull the answer from our legal and judicial consciousness."[20]

---

19. H.C. 65/51 *Zabutinski v. Weizman*, 5 P.D. 801, 813, relying on Justice Frankfurter in *Joint Anti-Fascist Refugee Committee v. McGreth* 341 U.S. 123.
    20. Ibid., at 813.

Index

Activism, 147
Adjudication, models of, 229–33
Agranat, S., 19, 47, 48, 67, 122, 126,
    142, 158, 159
Analogy, 30, 87, 89, 106, 107, 140
Atiyah, P., 196, 263

Balancing, 68, 78, 122; and public pol-
    icy, 14; and separation of powers, 203–
    05; and values, 146, 150
Bell, J., 232
Bentham, J., 169
Bishin, W., 201
Brown v. Allen, 162

Camden, 15
Cardozo, B., 6, 8, 9, 21, 38, 41, 53, 68,
    102, 124, 126, 132, 133, 141, 255
Cohn, H., 65
Common Law, 76–83, 87, 105–07
Comparative Law, 88, 170, 234
Consensus, 67, 115, 123, 213–15, 226,
    231–32
Constitution, 100, 102, 106, 192–203,
    252
Corbin, A., 144
Courts: and controversy, 176; and reform,
    181; and public policy, 183; required
    solution, 184; as institutions, 172; in-
    formation at the disposal of, 177; lim-
    ited means, 179
Critical legal studies, 35, 231

Cross, R., 255
Cueto-Rua, J., 48

Davis, K., 9
Declaratory theory, 4, 28, 94, 105–10,
    135, 137, 168–70, 190, 230
Delegated legislation, 103
Democracy: and judicial activism, 149–
    50; and judicial discretion, 192, 261;
    separation of powers, 205
Devlin, P., 210, 255
Dickinson, J., 68
Dickson, B., 102, 114
Diplock, W., 91–92, 103, 170
Dixon, J., 166
Douglas, W., 20, 220
Dworkin, R., 6, 10, 28–34, 105, 147,
    169, 230

Easy cases, 35–43, 49, 54, 68, 94–97,
    113, 117, 121, 135–37, 142, 168, 190,
    193, 205, 224
Edwards, H., 3, 139
Elon, M., 66
Etzioni, M., 214
Evidence, 178, 181, 183, 215, 246, 247,
    251, 262

Facts, 12, 177–78, 261–62
Fairness, 22–23, 33, 50, 66, 185, 216,
    237
Frank, J., 214

Frankfurter, F., 4, 60, 63, 65, 69, 127, 178, 189, 255
Freeman, M., 206, 209
Friedmann, W., 144, 255
Friendly, H., 178–79
Foundation of Law Law, 89
Fuller, L., 153, 255

Gaps in the law, 83–89, 96, 102
Gov Ari Ltd. v. Local Council for Planning, 37
Greenawalt, K., 27, 176
Greene, M.R., 125

Hamilton, A., 180
Hard cases, 10, 28, 31–32, 35, 40–43, 49, 69, 94–95, 97, 113–14, 117, 121, 124, 135–37, 142, 168, 175, 190, 193–94, 200–07, 224, 232, 263
Hart, H., 6, 7, 174, 176
Hart, H. L. A., 6, 22, 57, 69, 71, 80, 86, 232
Heshin, S. Z., 66, 158
Holmes, O., 40, 69, 71, 93, 101, 132–33, 140, 145–46, 161, 264
House of Lords, 32, 140, 181, 188, 235
Human rights, 20, 66, 68, 78, 183, 195, 200

Intermediate cases, 35, 39–43, 49, 54, 68, 94–97, 113, 117, 121, 135–37, 142, 168, 190, 193, 205, 226
Interpretation, 36, 55, 72–75; absurdity, 39, 75; and law-making, 99, 108; balancing, 68; history of, 73, 74; judicial discretion in, 55–76; purposive, 60, 75, 142; values, 64
Intuition, 133
Israel: declaration of independence, 66, 157, 195, 286; human rights, 68; judicial review, 200–03; political question, 212; Supreme Court, 42, 74–75, 140, 258–60, 188; values, 66

Judge: accountability, 192; admitting law-making, 218; as educator, 220; behaviour, 22–24, confidence in, 215; conflict of interest, 22, 66; concept of his function, 122; conservative, 151; experience, 121, 124; independence, 128, 192, 216–18; impartial, 189; intuition, 133–35; liberal, 151; member of penal, 186, 208; personal views, 125–33; personality, 41
Judgment: continuity, 164–65; dissent, 245; distinguishing, 80; penal, 186; ratio decidendi, 16, 40, 78–80; reasons, 23, 129, 189
Judicial: activism and restraint, 147–51; function, 122; law-making, 90–110, 114, 174, 218, 263–66; objectivity, 124, 129; philosophy, 124; policy and politics, 222–29; responsibility, 138; review, 193–203; time, 187
Judicial discretion: activism and restraint, 147–51; and administrative law-making, 103; and facts, 12, 261; and law-making, 99–110; judicial review, 198; and other branches, 207; and society's concept of, 206; and the court as an institution, 172–91; and the best possibility, 123; application of norms, 14–262; awareness of, 135–47; creating or declaring law, 105–110, 114; definition, 7; difficulties in understanding, 3; does it exist, 27–33; formal sources of, 90–110; giving reasons, 23; impartiality, 114, 289; incidental to adjudication, 173; in how many cases, 34, 41; in interpretation, 55–76; in values, 64; interrelations with other systems, 192–221; limitations of, 18, 20, 22; mystery of, 3; models of, 229–33; narrow and broad, 8; need for, 261; normative system, 152–71; object of, 12; personal experience, 121; public confidence, 215; scope of, 18; sources of, 45–110; stability and change, 264; substantial limitations on, 24; the authority of, 96–101; uncertainty of language, 46; uncertainty of normative system, 54; zone of legitimacy, 12

Justice, 14, 24, 50, 53, 88, 115, 149, 163–64, 187, 237, 246

Kahan, Y., 182
Kahane v. The Chairman of the Knesset, 20
Kardosh v. The Registrar of Companies, 19
Kaufman, I., 131
Kelsen, H., 4
Klinghoffer, H., 90
Knesset, 75, 155, 200–03, 212
Kohler, J., 56
Kurland, P., 195

Lacuna, 83–89
Landau, M., 6, 23, 67, 101, 125, 160– 61, 163, 174, 200, 228, 261
Language, 46–53
Lawyers, 208
Law-making: by judges, 90–110
Legal community, 9–12, 37, 39, 42, 61– 62, 80, 137, 168, 171, 190, 224
Legal process school, 232
Legislation, 46–76, 90, 102, 105
Llewellyn, K., 73
Lloyd, D., 255

Mansfield, 21
Marbury v. Madison, 217
Marshall, J., 217
McCormick, N., 232
Models of adjudication, 229–33
Montesquieu, C., 5, 94–95, 230

Natural justice, 22, 66, 173
Neo-Realists, 4, 35
Normative system, 152–54, 160–66
Norms, 13–18, 36–39, 46, 49, 56–58, 61, 76–110, 122, 142–47, 158, 164, 171

Objectivity, 116, 124, 139
Olshan, Y., 65

Paterson, A., 32, 140

Political question, 212
Politics: of the judiciary, 227
Port Authority v. Ararat, 182
Positivism, 25, 232
Pound, R., 50, 54, 146, 162, 264
Powell v. McCormack, 100
Precedent, 29–30, 38, 78–83, 91–93, 99–101, 137, 140–47, 152, 156, 168– 71, 191, 209; distinguishing, 80; over- ruling, 209, 234–60; *ratio decidendi,* 16, 78, 90; *stare decisis,* 137
Principles, 50, 64
Public policy, 52, 143, 183, 223

Radcliffe, C., 109, 218
Raviv v. Beit Yules Ltd., 145
Raz, J., 26, 33, 51, 57, 70, 136, 152
Realist, 4, 35, 121, 231
Reasonable person, 11, 53, 130
Reasonableness, 24, 71, 77, 113–51, 138, 185, 235
Reid, Lord, 107, 114, 145, 162, 255
Retroactivity, 43, 83, 108, 167–71
Richardson v. Mellis, 144
Rights, 20, 64–72, 78, 157–58, 183, 195–96, 200
Robinson, J., 23
Rule of Law, 96, 99, 126, 168, 212, 216, 228–29, 261
Rules, 86–87, 108

Sacks, A., 6, 7, 176
Salmond, J., 174
Sarid v. The Speaker of the Knesset, 212
Schaefer, W., 123, 134, 255
Separation of powers, 99, 203
Shamgar, M., 70, 99, 206
Simon, Lord, 109
de Smith, S. A., 10
Standards, 53
Stone, J., 139, 219
Sussman, J., 5, 7, 14, 19, 65, 74, 95, 103, 144

Tedeschi, G., 33, 36, 93, 106, 174, 255
de Tocqueville, A., 198

Torts, 53, 84, 155, 182, 185, 215, 243, 246–47
Traynor, R., 60, 127, 161, 255

Values, 64–72, 154, 165

Wagnin v. The Military Appeals Court, 59
Wigmore, J., 255
Witkon, A., 38, 110, 204, 222, 249

Zmora, M., 66, 266